George Hay

Works of the Right Rev. Bishop Hay of Edinburgh

Vol 7

George Hay

Works of the Right Rev. Bishop Hay of Edinburgh
Vol 7

ISBN/EAN: 9783743369184

Manufactured in Europe, USA, Canada, Australia, Japa

Cover: Foto ©Lupo / pixelio.de

Manufactured and distributed by brebook publishing software (www.brebook.com)

George Hay

Works of the Right Rev. Bishop Hay of Edinburgh

WORKS

OF THE

RIGHT REV. BISHOP HAY

WORKS

OF THE

RIGHT REV. BISHOP HAY

OF EDINBURGH

VOL. VII.

ON MIRACLES: VOL. II.

A NEW EDITION

EDITED UNDER THE SUPERVISION OF

THE RIGHT REV. BISHOP STRAIN

WILLIAM BLACKWOOD AND SONS
EDINBURGH
1873

THE SCRIPTURE DOCTRINE

OF

MIRACLES DISPLAYED

BY

THE RIGHT REV. DR GEORGE HAY
BISHOP OF DAULIS, VICAR APOSTOLIC OF THE
LOWLAND DISTRICT IN SCOTLAND

A NEW EDITION—IN TWO VOLUMES

VOL. II.

WILLIAM BLACKWOOD AND SONS
EDINBURGH
1873

CONTENTS OF VOL. II.

	PAGE
CHAP. XI. WHETHER THE EXISTENCE OF MIRACLES IS CAPABLE OF PROOF, AND OF WHAT KIND,	1
" XII. THE CONTINUATION OF MIRACLES. THE QUESTION STATED: DR MIDDLETON AND HIS PROTESTANT ADVERSARIES EXAMINED,	28
" XIII. REASONS AGAINST THE CONTINUATION OF MIRACLES EXAMINED, ...	85
" XIV. PRESUMPTIVE EVIDENCE FOR THE CONTINUATION OF MIRACLES THROUGHOUT ALL AGES, ...	130
" XV. POSITIVE EVIDENCE FOR THE CONTINUATION OF MIRACLES THROUGHOUT ALL PRECEDING AGES, DOWN TO THE PRESENT TIMES,	183
APPENDIX,	229

THE SCRIPTURE DOCTRINE OF MIRACLES DISPLAYED.

CHAPTER XI.

WHETHER THE EXISTENCE OF MIRACLES IS CAPABLE OF PROOF, AND OF WHAT KIND THAT PROOF MUST BE.

I. WE have seen that miracles are possible; that they consist in certain sensible effects which fall under the cognisance of our senses; and that they are produced by the free-will and pleasure of Almighty God, who, being sovereign Master of all creatures, can dispose of them in whatever way He pleases—either by His own immediate act, or by the operation of His angels. If, therefore, it has ever pleased, or shall please, God to perform a miracle, we may naturally expect it to be as capable of proof as any other fact. It is surprising, then, to see men of ability and learning bewildering themselves in so plain a matter.

They waste their time and misapply their talents in seeking metaphysical sophisms, by which they pretend to show that the existence of a miracle never can be proved. But in the eyes of common-sense their arguments can have no more weight than the well-known argument of Zeno against the possibility of motion. If in this these gentlemen act against their conscience, and seek to impose upon their fellow-creatures, it is certainly an unpardonable insult to mankind; but if they really think as they speak, it is one of the most humiliating proofs of human weakness, and shows into what a depth of folly man is capable of falling, when, proudly trusting to his own powers, he plunges without a guide into the mazes of imagination.

In the task I have undertaken, I am become debtor to the wise and to the unwise, to the learned and to the unlearned, on this subject; and therefore, however unimportant the present question may appear, yet, as infidelity has made much of it by denying the possibility of proving the existence of miracles, it is necessary to put this point also in its proper light, and to show the weakness and insufficiency of every argument against it. For greater clearness and precision, we may examine first, "If eyewitnesses of a miracle can have sufficient proof of its existence?" Secondly, "If the existence of miracles can be sufficiently proved to those who themselves are not eyewitnesses?" We shall consider these points separately.

II. The first question is resolved into this, "How far can we trust our senses in matters of fact which fall entirely under their cognisance?" For if our senses, when applied to their proper objects, give us a full conviction of their existence; if our knowledge here is intuitive, and incapable of further proof; if by the very constitution of our nature, we believe that we feel the sensations which are excited in our mind, and that the external objects which excite them do actually exist without us,—then it follows that eyewitnesses of any miraculous operation have the fullest proof of its existence which the nature of things can possibly admit, and that this proof must carry complete conviction to the mind. Now, that this is actually the case—that our senses give us an absolute conviction of the existence and effects of material objects, a conviction which it is beyond the power of the most refined reasoning to invalidate—I appeal to experience itself. I appeal to the feelings of our own souls; nay, to the experience of the most determined adversaries of religion.

Let us suppose that any of those unbelievers saw a miracle performed before his own eyes: a dead man, for instance, raised to life; a blind man restored to sight; a man walking over a river upon the surface of the water, or the like,—I ask, could he doubt the reality of the facts? Could he persuade himself that the man whom he formerly saw dead, but now sees walking, speaking, eating, &c., is still dead? that the man whom he knew before to be absolutely blind, but whom he now sees to have as much the use of his sight as he has himself, is notwithstanding still blind? that the man whom he sees walking upon the surface of the water is in reality walking on dry land? Could he persuade himself that what he saw with his own eyes was absolutely false, and that the reverse of what he saw was true?

Let any one call in what he terms the aid of reason; let him summon up every argument against the existence of miracles; let him profess that he sees no end worthy of God for performing them; that the facts are improbable, inexpedient, unnecessary; that the doctrine attested by them seems absurd, unintelligible, and contradictory; that the instruments are weak, and unworthy of the majesty of God. Let even Mr Hume himself appear armed with his "invincible argument;" let him bring in his "uniform universal experience;" let him put this into the scale along with all the others, and let him say, if he can, that all these reasons put together would be able to raise in his mind the smallest doubt of the real existence of the above miracles, in opposition to the testimony of his own senses, if, as we suppose, he were an eyewitness of them. No, no; every man's experience, and the conviction of his own mind, will teach him that the evidence from the testimony of our senses, in those things which properly belong to them, is an invincible proof, supreme of its kind, which needs no reasoning or argument, but convinces by instinct, and the fixed laws of our nature, with as much certainty as could be derived from the strictest demonstration. Nay, when, from the disorder of the medium, or the unsoundness of the organ, or any other casual circumstance, we suspect that our senses deceive us in some particular instance, we have no other way to examine and correct the deception—we must rest at last on this truth, that our senses, when properly applied, give absolute certainty of their proper objects, and that concerning these we must trust our senses in preference to all reasoning whatsoever.— See Beattie's Essay on Truth, chap. ii. § 2.

The answer to our first question, then, is plain and satisfactory—that those who are eyewitnesses of miracles have, from the testimony of their senses, the most convincing, full, and satisfactory proof that the miracles which they see really do exist.

III. Against this I find two objections; the one hinted at by Rousseau, vol. iii. of his Emilius, p. 111, in these words: "If we would receive as true all the miracles which the common and ignorant people, through every country of the world, affirm to have seen, every sect would be in the right," &c. Here he would insinuate that the only eyewitnesses produced or producible for the existence of miracles, are common and ignorant persons, and that in such matters they are easily deceived.

In the first place, however, it is absolutely false that such persons are the only eyewitnesses producible for the existence of such miracles as Christianity appeals to. Men remarkable for their extraordinary genius and extensive learning, as well as their veracity and candour, have given the most distinct testimony to miracles of which they themselves were eyewitnesses. But permitting this to pass, the allegation that the common people are easily deceived and ready to be imposed upon, could not in the least degree weaken the evidence for the existence of miracles, even were the common people the only witnesses of them. Miracles are facts which fall under the comprehension of the most simple minds. Ignorant people have eyes and ears as well as the learned—they can know if a man be cripple, blind, sick, or dead, as well as the greatest physician or most learned philosopher; and if they see this man restored again to the use of his limbs, to sight, health, or life, they can discern that change with as great certainty as a Rousseau or a Hume themselves, and can have as perfect and complete conviction.

I acknowledge, indeed, that the multitude may be deceived; but how? A designing person may gain credit with the many by an outward show of sanctity, and pretend to secret communication with the Deity and His angels, as Mahomet did; or he may perform many things extraordinary in the eyes of the people, by his superior knowledge of the powers of nature, and persuade them that these are true miracles; or he may bewitch them with sorceries, as Simon did the people of Samaria: but to convince even ignorant persons that they actually saw before their eyes a fact which had no existence, is what scarcely ever was attempted; and doubtless, though attempted, never could succeed. "Though men," says Mr Douglas in his Criterion, p. 312, "may believe speculative opinions to be true which are false, yet it is scarcely to be conceived that they can ever so far deceive themselves as to believe they saw facts which they did not really see." This observation is true of all mankind, of the ignorant and simple as well as the learned and prudent.

IV. The second objection is made by Mr Hume, and seems so strong in his eyes that he thinks it will easily account for all Christian miracles: "A religionist," says he, "may be an enthusiast, and imagine he sees what has no reality," Ess. on Mir., p. 185. Here enthusiasm is brought in as able to invert men's senses, and to overturn the constitutional principles of the human frame. Enthusiasm, no doubt, has great power to persuade men to believe as true what is false, and to esteem the whims of their own fancy, or even the suggestions of the devil, as the inspirations of the Holy Ghost; but I doubt if a single instance can be shown where it persuaded any one in his senses that he saw done before him what had no existence. And even though this should happen to the enthusiast himself, who pretends to perform the miracle, or on whom it was performed, are all those enthusiasts too who behold such pretended miracles? Yet many miracles are on record which were performed in the presence of declared enemies, and who could by no means be suspected of enthusiasm. Dr Campbell, in his dissertation on miracles against Mr Hume, answers this objection very solidly from this principle of experience.

V. "That an enthusiast is very liable to be imposed on, in whatever favours the particular species of enthusiasm with which he is affected, none who knows anything of the human heart will deny. But still this frailty hath its limits. For my own part, I cannot find examples of any, even among enthusiasts (unless to the conviction of everybody they were distracted), who did not see and hear in the same manner as other people. Many of this tribe have mistaken the reveries of a heated imagination for the communications of the Divine Spirit, who never in one single instance mistook the operations of their external senses. Without marking this difference, we should make no distinction between the *enthusiastic* character and the *frantic*, which are in themselves evidently distinct."—Part II. § 1.

In another place, after observing that the whole class of reformers, however useful miracles might have been to their views, yet never attempted to prove their mission or doctrine by these means, he adds: "But how upon our author's (Mr Hume's) principles shall we account for this moderation in the reformers? Were they, in his judgment, calm inquirers after truth? Were they dispassionate reasoners in defence of it? Far otherwise. He tells us (Hist. Gr. Brit. Jas. I., chap. i.), ' They may safely be pronounced to have been universally inflamed with the highest enthusiasm.' May not we then, in our turn, safely pronounce, this writer himself being judge, that for a man to imagine he sees what has no reality—to impose in this manner, not only on his own understanding, but even on his external senses— is a pitch of delusion higher than the highest enthusiasm can produce, and is to be imputed only to downright frenzy? Since the world began, there hath not appeared a more general propensity to the wildest fanaticism than appeared in this island about the middle of the last century. 'Tis astonishing that when the minds of men were intoxicated with enthusiasm, none are to be found who advanced a claim to the power of working miracles—a claim which, in the author's opinion (Mr Hume's), though false, is easily supported and wonderfully successful, especially among enthusiasts.

"It is true, one or two frantic people among the Quakers did actually pretend to such a power; but this had no other consequence than to bring the pretenders into general contempt. In the beginning of this century, also, the French prophets revived this plea; but by no part of their conduct did they so effectually open the eyes of mankind, bring discredit on their inspirations, and ruin their cause, as by this no less foolish than presumptuous pretence; and though they were so deluded as to imagine that they could restore a dead man to life—nay, though they proceeded so far as to determine and announce beforehand the day and hour of his resurrection, yet none of them were so insane as to imagine they had seen him rise, and not one of them afterwards pretended that their prediction had been fulfilled. Thus even a frenzy which had disordered their intellects could not in this instance overpower their senses."—Part II. § 2.

From these judicious remarks it plainly follows that the evidence of the senses, with regard to the objects proper to them, is not to be overpowered even by enthusiasm itself; and therefore, that those who are eye-witnesses of any miracle have, from the testimony of their senses, the most absolute and convincing proof of its existence.

VI. This first question being thus disposed of, the answer to the second naturally follows. For if eyewitnesses of a miracle, from the evidence of their senses, can have a full and absolute conviction, they doubtless can give testimony of this to others who were not present, and thus impart to them also as full a conviction as the nature of the case can possibly admit.

A miracle is a fact which depends solely upon the good pleasure and free choice of God; and the proof of its existence must be taken either from the evidence of our senses, if we ourselves see it, or from the testimony of others who have been eyewitnesses. There is no other way by which such facts as depend upon the will of free agents can possibly be proved; nor can any rational objection be made against their existence, when properly supported by either of these proofs, without directly striking at the proofs themselves, by supposing in them some defect or flaw. If, therefore, they possess all those conditions which, by the very constitution of our nature, command our assent, no objection, solely drawn from arguments extrinsic to these proofs, can have any weight against the evidence of the fact so proved by them. Now, as all the usual arguments brought against the existence of miracles vanish when opposed to the evidence of the senses in eyewitnesses, it follows that if such eyewitnesses are persons of veracity and probity, and possess those other qualities which preclude all suspicion of deceit, their testimony regarding what they saw must afford the most satisfactory conviction that what they assert is true, notwithstanding every metaphysical sophism to the contrary.

We can acquire the knowledge of facts past or distant only by the testimony of others; and the certainty which it affords us is in many cases as full and absolute as we obtain from any other source of knowledge. Nay, when the testimony possesses the necessary conditions, it never fails to produce the most complete conviction.

These conditions are, first, certainty that the witnesses were not themselves deceived ; secondly, certainty that they speak exactly according to their knowledge. When these two conditions concur, or when we believe that they exist, it is impossible to withhold our credit from the testimony. We may doubt if the witnesses were not themselves deceived—we may call in question their veracity; but if we have no doubt upon these points, it is no longer in our power to question the truth of what they say ; we are forced to believe it, and to believe it with the utmost assurance, by the very constitution of our nature ; and hence Dr Beattie, after some judicious observations, justly concludes, that " to believe testimony is agreeable to nature, to reason, and to sound philosophy," Essay on Truth, chap. ii. § 8.

VII. Now there are rules to ascertain when testimony is attended with the two conditions above mentioned—rules founded on principles born with us, and which are the foundation of human society, and of the whole intercourse between man and man,—namely, " That men are not fools and devoid of sense. That there are certain rules from which they seldom or never depart in their conduct. That there cannot be a joint combination among them to deceive. That if they sometimes deceive, it is not without some motive, particularly interest. That the whole world never conspires to deceive any man. That no man can deceive the whole world." These principles are ascertained by the concurrent belief of mankind, whose general practice is directed by them in the most important affairs of life—in proving genealogy, in settling property, in administering justice, and the like; and from them this general maxim is deduced relative to our faith in testimony, " That we must believe the testimony of men when, the facts testified by them being possible, we cannot believe they are deceived, or intend to deceive, without supposing that they have lost their reason."

VIII. " Our faith in testimony," says Mr Beattie, "doth often, but not always, amount to absolute certainty. That there is such a city as Constantinople, such a country as Lapland, and such a mountain as the peak of Teneriff; that there were such men as Hannibal and Julius Cæsar; that England was conquered by William the Norman; and that Charles I. was beheaded,—of these and suchlike truths, every person acquainted with history and geography accounts himself absolutely certain. When a number of persons, not acting in concert, having no interest to disguise the truth, and who are sufficient judges of that to which they bear testimony, concur in making the same report, it would be accounted madness not to believe them. Nay, when a number of witnesses, separately examined, and having had no opportunity to concert a plan beforehand, do all agree in their declarations, we make no scruple of yielding full faith to their testimony, even though we have no evidence of their honesty and skill— nay, though they be notorious both for knavery and folly; because the fictions of the human mind being infinite, it is impossible that each of these witnesses should, by mere accident, devise the very same circumstances. If, therefore, their declarations concur, this is a certain proof that there is no fiction in the case, and that they all speak from real experience and knowledge."— Essay on Truth, Part I. chap. ii. § 8.

IX. To the same purpose Mr Douglas speaks in his 'Criterion, or Miracles Examined,' on the force of proper testimony: "Two qualifications," says he, "must concur to establish the credibility of witnesses; a sufficient knowledge of the matters of fact they attest, and a disposition not to falsify what they know: and when these two qualifications do concur, we think ourselves obliged to admit what is attested as true."—P. 199. Dr Church, also, in his Vindication, p. 62, says: "It must be granted that present facts, which are appeals to the senses, are more striking and satisfactory than any long intricate reasonings. And hence miracles may be pronounced to be the shortest and clearest means of conviction of the divine authority of any mission, and consequently of any doctrine to those who see them. And further, as we may have sufficient certainty of their having been worked in times past, they must, if well attested, be full proofs, even to us who do not see them."

But it is needless to multiply testimonies on this point, as every one's experience must teach him that when we are persuaded that a person is not deceived himself, and that he truly speaks according to his knowledge, it is no longer in our power to withhold our assent from what he says. Consequently, if any miracle be attested by those who were eyewitnesses of it, and in such circumstances that we cannot suspect their veracity, we have from their testimony a full and convincing proof of the existence of the miracle,—a proof which, as Dr Beattie observes, "it would be accounted madness not to yield to;" and which, according to Mr Douglas, would oblige us to receive what was so attested as true.

X. We may consider this subject in another point of view, which will illustrate it still further. It is doubtless a just and convincing inference which is made from the effect to the cause. We see an effect produced; we know the cause which naturally and constantly produces such an effect. We argue, therefore, with the greatest certainty, from the known existence of the effect, that the cause producing it existed also.

The testimony of men concerning any matter of fact is an effect produced of which we are sensible. We know this effect may arise from two different causes, and from no other: it may either arise from the real existence of the fact itself, of which those men were eyewitnesses; or it may arise from their mistake or imposture, as being either deceived themselves, or wishing to deceive others. If we have any reason to suspect either that the witnesses were themselves mistaken, or intended to deceive others by their testimony, then it goes for nothing—it gains no credit—because it is not looked upon as an effect of the real existence of the fact attested by it. But if, on the contrary, the circumstances be such that we see it impossible that the testimony could arise from mistake or imposture, then it could have no other cause than the real existence of the attested fact—the existence of which therefore, we are no longer at liberty to deny.

XI. Upon these grounds the adversaries of Christianity pay every due regard to human testimony in the ordinary concerns of life, and make no difficulty in regulating by it their belief and conduct with regard to all natural occurrences. But being sensible of the strength of testimony in favour of religion and against their tenets, when allowed its due weight with regard to miracles, they have been forced to make a distinction between natural and supernatural events; and whilst they allow testimony its full authority in proving the former, they pretend that no credit can be given to it when applied to the latter.

"A miracle," says Mr Hume, "supported by any human testimony, is more properly a subject of derision than of argument," Ess. on Mir., p. 194. And again, near the end of his essay, he says: "Upon the whole, it appears that no testimony for any kind of miracle can ever possibly amount to a probability, much less to a proof." A little after, indeed, he corrects his too general assertion, and restricts the impossibility of proving the existence of miracles by testimony to such only as are wrought in favour of religion. "We may establish it as a maxim that no human testimony can have such force as to prove a miracle, and make it a just foundation for any system of religion." And in a note upon this passage, he adds: "I beg the limitation here made may be remarked when I say that a miracle can never be proved so as to be the foundation of a system of religion; for I own that otherwise there may be miracles, or violations of the usual course of nature, of such a kind as to admit of proof from human testimony."

I am, indeed, somewhat at a loss to comprehend Mr Hume's object in these passages, and am inclined to think that he has here fallen into one of the self-contradictions so frequent in deistical philosophy; for first, he he tells us, in general, a "miracle supported by any human testimony is more properly a subject of derision than of argument." If so, how is it possible that any miracle can admit of proof from testimony? Must we suppose him to mean that only such miracles as are in favour of religion, and supported by human testimony, are subjects of derision? But how, then, will he reconcile the obvious difficulty, that human testimony is sufficient to prove the existence of a miracle when separated from religion, but becomes a subject of derision when used to prove the existence of the same miracle if performed in favour of religion? Secondly, the whole scope of Mr Hume's argument throughout this essay, is to show that the existence of a miracle *as such*, and independent of any connection with religion, can never be proved by human testimony.

"A miracle," says he, "is a violation of the laws of nature; and as a firm and unalterable experience has established these laws, the proof against a miracle, from the very nature of the fact, is as entire as any argument from experience can possibly be imagined; and if so, it is an undeniable consequence that it cannot be surmounted by any proof whatever from testimony. A miracle, therefore, however attested, can never be rendered credible, even in the lowest degree."—Ess. on Mir., p. 179, 180: Lond. edit. 1750, 12mo.

Here we see, according to this author, that the objection against a miracle, from the very nature of the fact, as being a violation of the laws of nature, can never be surmounted by any proof from testimony. How, then, can he reconcile with this undeniable consequence of his formidable argument what he says in the note above cited, that "there may possibly be miracles, or violations of the usual course of nature, of such a kind as to admit of proof from human testimony?" Let him extricate himself as he best may; but this shows his insuperable aversion to religious miracles provable by human testimony, since he is determined to run the risk of his judgment being suspected, and his common-sense itself called in question, rather than admit them.

XII. Dr Middleton, also, with his adherents, is so averse to human testimony in proof of miracles, that he rejects all credibility of miracles founded upon such evidence, and openly professes that he knows no miracles, no revealed truths, nothing which can possibly be discovered of the ways or will of the Creator, but by attending to the revelation which He has made of Himself from the beginning, in the wonderful works and beautiful fabric of this visible world.—Pref. to the Free Inquiry, p. 22. We shall see more of the Doctor afterwards.

XIII. We are surprised when we hear men of learning and ability talk in such a strain. If they really think as they write, it is a palpable proof of their extravagant vanity and presumption. With the utmost confidence they set up the idol of their own judgment in opposition to the dictates of nature and common-sense, and even in opposition to the declaration of God Himself. Whilst unable to produce one good proof for their opinion, they either contradict themselves, as we have seen above in Mr Hume, or are obliged to pass extravagant censure upon others, condemning the most pious, virtuous, and learned men in every age of Christianity, which Dr Middleton never hesitates to do in support of his untenable system. Nothing, therefore, will better display the folly of pretending that the existence of miracles, or supernatural facts, is incapable of being proved by human testimony, than to show how diametrically contrary this assertion is to the common sentiments of mankind.

XIV. To begin with the people of God in the old law, how many extraordinary miracles, which had happened in every age from the beginning of the world, were handed down among them from generation to generation by human testimony, and upon this evidence alone were believed with the utmost certainty? They therefore judged this testimony full and sufficient proof of the existence of these miracles, and in their minds it produced complete conviction.

Perhaps it may be said that these miracles were related in the sacred Scriptures, and received from them the sanction of divine testimony. But it is to be observed that few of the people could themselves make use of these Scriptures; and copies of them were far from being common. We read, in the reign of Josias, that Helcias, the high priest, accidentally found a copy of the law, and sent it to the king; and that he and all the people were amazed when they heard it read before them (which shows how rare copies of that sacred book must then have been), 4 Kings, xxii. Besides, as to the divinity of this book itself, and consequently the truth of all the wonders it contains, whence did that people receive it? Almighty God did not give to every generation a new revelation. This was done at first by means of the sacred penmen who wrote it, attesting that they did so by inspiration from God, and giving proof of this by the miracles which they performed. This was a convincing proof, to those who thus first received them, that these books were divine; but it was their testimony to their children, and the testimony of their children to those after them, which was the great means by which both the divinity of the books themselves, and the miracles they contained, were handed down, and upon which they were believed by all succeeding generations.

XV. The case is exactly similar with the whole body of Christians under the new law. These in every age to this day, have believed with the utmost certainty numerous miracles when they saw them sufficiently attested by human testimony. Heathen nations, when converted to Christianity, have given proof of the same. They have believed as undoubted truths all the miracles related in the Gospel. If they did so upon the testimony of those who converted them, without their working new miracles in proof of what they preached, then we have what we desire to prove, that these converted nations esteemed testimony a sufficient ground on which to believe miracles.

If those missionaries themselves wrought miracles to prove the divinity of their mission and their doctrine, still they could not possibly be done before the whole people; and those who did not witness them could believe them only upon the testimony of those who were present: yet whole nations were converted, and actually believed these miracles upon that testimony, which therefore they judged a sufficient ground for doing so. Nay, the obstinate heathens themselves, who opposed the Christian religion, and used every effort of their genius and learning to find, if possible, a flaw in it, never had the effrontery to deny its miracles. Convinced by the strength of testimony, they acknowledged them, and only sought to evade the consequence by ascribing them to the devil and not to God. But this very evasion shows how much they felt that testimony produces complete conviction in proof of the existence of miracles.

XVI. The greatest condemnation, however, of this opinion of our modern unbelievers, is the express declaration of Almighty God Himself, Who judges testimony so thorough and complete a proof to convince His reasonable creatures of the existence of miracles, that He appoints this, and this alone, as the proper means to propagate throughout all succeeding generations the knowledge of those glorious miracles which He wrought among His chosen people. Thus, when giving commission to Moses to threaten Pharaoh with the plague of locusts, He tells him that He had wrought so many signs and wonders in favour of His people for this very end, that they and their posterity might know that He was the only true God, and that succeeding generations must be informed of these things by the testimony of those before them. "That thou mayest tell in the ears of thy son, and of thy son's son, what things I have wrought in

Egypt, and my signs which I have done among them, that ye may know that I am the Lord," Exod. x. 2. Again, among the many other excellent rules that Moses gave the people before his death, he says on this subject: " Only take heed to thyself, and keep thy soul diligently, lest thou forget the things which thine eyes have seen, and lest they depart from thy heart all the days of thy life; but teach them to thy sons and thy sons' sons," Deut. iv. 9. Hence we find the royal prophet expressly acknowledging that it was by the testimony of their fathers that they knew all the wonderful things God had done among them: "We have heard with our ears, O God, and our fathers have told us, what works Thou didst in their days, and in the times of old," Ps. xliv. 1.

Here we see that the testimony of their fathers not only taught them what was done in their time, of which they were eyewitnesses, but also what had been done before their days in the times of old, which they had in like manner received from those before them. Again, Ps. lxxviii., he declares his readiness to communicate the knowledge of the law of God, and of all His wondrous works, to his posterity, in obedience to the command which God had given for that purpose: "Give ear, O my people, to my law; incline your ears to the words of my mouth; I will open my mouth in a parable; I will utter dark sayings of old, which we have heard and known, and our fathers have told us. We will not hide them from their children, showing to the generation to come the praises of the Lord, and His strength, and His wonderful works that He hath done."

Observe here the resolution which the holy prophet makes to transmit to posterity the law and wondrous works of God, by teaching them to the rising generation; and he immediately adds his reason: "For He established a testimony in Jacob, and appointed a law in Israel, which He commanded our fathers, that they should make them known to their children : that the generation to come might know them, even the children which should be born ; who should arise and declare them to their children," Ps. lxxviii. 1, &c.

In this beautiful passage we are assured that the testimony of each present generation to their children was the very means appointed by God for ascertaining in all succeeding ages, not only the law itself, but also the testimony by which it was established at the beginning—"those wonderful works that the Lord had done," in confirmation of the divine revelation of the law, when He first gave it to their fathers ; and that God Himself expressly commands that this should be the means of conveying these things to posterity. After this, what idea must every serious Christian form of the pitiful evasion of a Middleton or a Hume, pretending that the existence of a miracle cannot admit of sufficient proof from human testimony, when we see that God Himself appointed this to be the only means of proving to all posterity the existence of those miracles which He wrought among His people ?

XVII. To this subject also belong those other branches of human testimony—the institution of feasts, the sacred ceremonies of religion, the erecting of public monuments, and the like—as memorials of miracles wrought on different occasions, which Almighty God was also pleased to make use of, and commanded His people to preserve the memory of what these things signified by explaining them to their children after them : see Exod. xiii. 8, 14, for the institution of the feast of unleavened bread, and the sanctification of the first-born ; also Deut. vi. 20, &c., for the meaning of the ceremonies of the law ; Joshua,

iv. on their passing over Jordan: Numb. xvi. 38, &c., for establishing the priesthood,—and many other such.

These show again that human testimony and its concomitants were judged by God Himself sufficient to prove the reality of all the wonders which He had wrought in favour of His people, and to perpetuate the memory of them for ever; and the result proves the efficiency and fitness of human testimony for this end, since it is by it that the memory of these things has been transmitted from those early ages in which they were performed, even to these our days; and we may safely venture to say, that, by the same means, it will be continued to the end of time.

XVIII. This appears still further from the command which Almighty God gave to His people to beware of favour of their doctrine, Deut. xiii. For on what grounds false prophets, even though working signs and wonders in did God lay this order upon them? We have seen this above—namely, that the stupendous miracles which He had wrought in favour of His truth, when He first revealed it, ought so fully to prove Him to be its author, that any contrary doctrine afterwards proposed should, for that very reason, be condemned and rejected; and even though its teachers should work signs, yet the same reason should convince them that these were not from God, but from the devil, and therefore also to be rejected. For according to the rules laid down at the end of the preceding chapter, when the doctrine is evidently false, and the miracles doubtful, the known falsehood of the doctrine is the infallible criterion by which to discover the imposture of the pretended miracle.

Now this obligation of rejecting false teachers, even though working signs, was not for those only who had seen the miracles wrought by God at the first revelation of His law, but for all their posterity in future times, to whom the knowledge of the primitive miracles was to be transmitted, by God's appointment, by means of human testimony. It is evident, then, that Almighty God judged human testimony not only sufficient to convince future ages of the reality of these miracles, but even to impart such a conviction of them, and of the truth of the doctrine attested by them, as to protect the people against the delusion of any false signs or pretended miracles which might be brought by the agency of Satan in order to propagate false doctrine.

XIX. The same we find in the new law. The doctrine revealed by Jesus Christ, and preached by His apostles, was supported, confirmed, and proved to be divine by the miracles wrought in attestation of it. These give such a conviction of the truth of that doctrine, that whatever new doctrine is contrary thereto we are commanded to reject and condemn as false, precisely because contrary to the Gospel; and St Paul pronounces a curse upon any one, though he were an angel from heaven, who should dare to preach any other gospel than that which he had preached. To the end of time, there will be an obligation upon all Christians to reject as false and erroneous every doctrine which is contrary to the truth revealed by Jesus; but the miracles, by which the doctrine of Jesus was proved to be divine, are conveyed to all succeeding ages primarily by human testimony—for that is the first step by which we come to the knowledge of the Scriptures themselves, in which these miracles are recorded. Therefore, here again human testimony is judged sufficient by Almighty God to convey to us the knowledge of these miracles, and of the doctrines attested by them, with such conviction as to make us proof against the attempts even of an angel from heaven, should he endeavour to delude us by any false doctrine contrary to the Gospel.

XX. If we suppose that Almighty God should be pleased to reveal His will to man, and perform miracles to attest that the revelation was from Him, and should wish the knowledge of this revelation, and of the miracles attesting it, to be transmitted to future ages, how is it possible for this to be done but by human testimony? Can a Middleton or a Hume devise any other way? Will they pretend that a succession of miracles must be kept up in every generation, and in presence of every individual, in order to prove the original revelation? Will they blasphemously say that the omnipotent Being has it not in His power to transmit with certainty the knowledge of these things to future ages? How ridiculous, then, is it to assert that miracles cannot be proved by human testimony, since it is absolutely the only natural means by which such facts can be proved to those who are not themselves eyewitnesses of them.

XXI. The result of all this is, that no rational objection can be made against the existence of any miracle which does not strike at the testimony by which it is supported. But if this stand the test, no metaphysical argument *a priori*, and extrinsic to the testimony, can ever influence the mind, or weaken the conviction which the force of that testimony gives. And yet, upon examination we find that all the arguments brought by the above gentlemen and their party are entirely of this kind.

XXII. Here I shall say nothing of Mr Hume's vaunted argument against proving the existence of miracles by human testimony, the futility of which has been already demonstrated by several masterly hands. I shall only observe, with Dr Campbell, that one positive credible testimony for the existence of a fact, possible in itself, is of more weight to convince a man of common-sense of the existence of such a fact, than ten hundred thousand millions of negative experiences against it; and this single observation, which is founded upon positive experience, and the feelings of our own heart, at once saps the foundation of all that Mr Hume has advanced upon the subject.

XXIII. The other arguments brought by the adversaries of revelation against our thesis may be reduced to these following: Miracles are unnecessary; they are inexpedient; they are incredible; they are trifling, and unworthy of the Deity; there are no ends to be gained by them worthy of such extraordinary divine interposition; the doctrine pretended to be attested by them is absurd, from which they conclude that no human testimony can render them credible in any circumstance.

I know not if these gentlemen have ever seriously examined the force of these reasons, or applied them to any particular case, or even put them into proper form, that they might see wherein their strength or weakness lay. I can scarcely think that if they had ever done so they would have exposed themselves to the contempt which such objections must necessarily evoke; nor do I find, in their writings or conversation, any serious reasoning, but a witticism or a sneer, with the words "incredible, unnecessary, inexpedient," and the like, interspersed in order to give an appearance of reason to their declamation.

But let us reduce their objection to form, that common-sense may estimate its value. Let us suppose, then, a miracle—that, for example, of a blind man restored to sight—to be attested upon oath by three or four men of known probity, who declare that they were eyewitnesses of it. Every man of ordinary judgment would be satisfied of the fact by such testimony. It could not be imagined that the witnesses were mistaken, as it is supposed they knew the man to be blind, and saw him perfectly restored to sight; much less could it be thought that men of known probity would attest a thing upon oath as eyewitnesses, if they had no had as full a conviction as the testimony of their senses could possibly give them. And if they be not mistaken in what they saw, and attest the fact precisely as they beheld it, the existence of the miracle is an undoubted consequence.

Let us now see the force of the objection when put in its proper form. In the mouth of a deist, it runs thus: "Several men of probity have attested upon oath that they saw a man, whom they knew before to be blind, miraculously restored to sight; but this appears inexpedient, unnecessary, without any good end, intrinsically incredible—therefore it is a mistake; no such miracle was performed." The major proposition is the state of the case as attested, the minor is the very argument of the deists; for surely none of them will dare to affirm that miracles are "inexpedient, unnecessary," or the like, in themselves. All they can say is, that so they appear to them; and from this they conclude, as from an answerable argument, that the best-attested miracles are falsehoods and fiction! How ridiculous the conclusion!

In order that a well-attested miracle be regarded falsehood or fiction, one of two things must be clearly proved, either that the witnesses are deceived in the testimony of their senses, or that they knowingly perjure themselves in order to deceive others. Now what connection is there between the apparent non-necessity or inexpediency of the miracle in the eyes of a deist and either of these two points? Because the miracle seems unnecessary or inexpedient to a deist, does it follow that the witnesses were deceived in what they saw with their eyes, or that they voluntarily perjured themselves by swearing contrary to their conscience? How unworthy of a philosopher to argue in such a strain!

XXIV. Their arguments from the unworthiness of the ends of miracles, and from the pretended absurdity of the doctrine attested by them, I have considered more particularly above, and have pointed out whence all their sophistry arises. I shall conclude this subject, therefore, by a few observations on the incredibility of the miraculous facts attested.

One can scarcely think men serious when they object to the existence of miracles on this account; or at least it were to be wished they would explain their meaning of the intrinsic incredibility of a miracle. If they mean that every miraculous fact involves an absolute contradiction—or, in other words, that a miracle is in itself impossible—let them rest upon that in plain terms, and prove it if they can; but if they allow that miracles are possible, how ridiculous is it to object that any possible fact is intrinsically incredible, when omnipotence itself is supposed to be the agent! Is any possible thing too difficult for God to perform? is any possible change in His creatures above His strength? Even Dr Middleton, with reason, dismisses such an objection: "To say that where the facts themselves are incredible," says he, "such miracles are to be rejected, is to beg the question, and not to prove it; a too precarious way of reasoning, because what is incredible to me may seem credible to another."—*Remarks on the Observator*, p. 26 *et seq.*

Mr Locke, whose justness of thought and strength of genius will not readily be called in question, is so far from regarding the extraordinary character of the fact as an argument against its existence, that in certain circumstances he draws the very opposite conclusion : "Though the common experience," says he, "and the ordinary course of things, have justly a mighty influence on the minds of men, to make them give or refuse credit to anything proposed to their belief, yet there is one case wherein the strangeness of the fact lessens not the assent to a fair testimony given of it. For where such supernatural events are suitable to ends aimed at by Him Who has the power to change the course of nature, there, under such circumstances, they may be the fitter to procure belief, by how much the more they are beyond or contrary to ordinary observation."—Ess. on the Hum. Und., iv. 16, § 13. This is a just remark, with which we shall here conclude the subject; because afterwards, when treating on the continuation of miracles in the Church of Christ, this objection from the incredibility of the fact must be resumed, and more fully refuted.

CHAPTER XII.

ON THE CONTINUATION OF MIRACLES IN THE CHURCH OF CHRIST—THE STATE OF THE QUESTION, AND THE CONDUCT OF DR MIDDLETON AND HIS PROTESTANT ADVERSARIES, EXAMINED.

1. WE now come to a point involving the most important consequences. Of late years men of the greatest ability and learning in the country have been deeply engaged in examining it, and they have published many learned and elaborate treatises in defence of their various systems. Some, with Dr Middleton, have contended that all miracles ceased with the lives of the apostles; others have asserted that they continued frequent in the Church during the first three centuries, and till the Christian religion was established by law in the Roman empire. Some have extended their duration to the end of the fourth and fifth, and others have endeavoured to show their continuation even during the sixth century. All, however, assert their total cessation at the respective periods which they are pleased to assign.

The Catholic Church, on the other hand, reposing with entire confidence on the sacred promises of her divine Master, and convinced by daily experience that these promises will hold good to the end of time, ignores these opinions of her adversaries, and maintains, in opposition to all their conflicting systems, that the power of working miracles never has, and never will be withdrawn from her communion. She maintains that, from time to time, in all preceding ages, Almighty God has raised up great and holy men among her children, by whom He has wrought many miraculous signs and wonders, and that He will never fail to do the same in succeeding ages to the end of the world, in defence of His truth, and to the confusion of all who separate themselves from her.

This constant doctrine of the Catholic Church, if true, shows the folly of her adversaries in their disputes among themselves. Their systems are founded upon a false assumption; they take for granted the very thing which is denied. For if what the Catholic Church teaches be true, that the power of working miracles has never ceased in her communion, how ridiculous is it to pretend to fix a period at which miracles have actually ceased! Their conflicting opinions serve only to establish her claim; and the arguments by which they prove the continuation of miracles down to their respective assumed periods of cessation, afford the most convincing proof that they have never ceased at all.

It is not my intention to examine the comparative merits of the various systems. In reference to the main point, they all stand in the same predicament. I acknowledge the abilities of their respective authors in proving beyond reply the continuation of miracles during the several periods assigned by them, but must differ from them in the supposition on which they all proceed, that miracles have actually ceased after any one of these periods; and what I propose to prove is the truth of the belief of the Catholic Church, that miracles never have ceased, and never will cease, in her communion while the world remains. But before I enter upon this important matter, it will be proper to explain the state of the question, the nature of the miraculous powers, their different kinds, and the teaching of the Scripture concerning them.

II. The extreme opposition which the Christian religion must naturally have encountered at its first promulgation in the world is evident. The incomprehensibility of its sublime mysteries demanded the perfect humiliation of the pride of human intellect. The purity and severity of its morality required the mortification of self-love, and of all the lusts of the heart. Its first preachers were men of no position in life; they were destitute of all human means to assist them in their vast undertaking, and of every earthly qualification which could recommend them to the regard or esteem of the world. Against them were arrayed the deep attachment which mankind naturally have to the religion in which they have been bred, especially when it flatters their inclinations, and lays no restraint upon their passions; the pride and obstinacy of philosophers; the inveterate malice of the heathen priests, and of all whose interest was concerned in the support of heathenism; and, above all, the rage and malice of hell, the power of which was restrained in proportion as the truths of the Gospel gained ground. The power of kingdoms and empires was exerted against Christianity, and it was necessary that Almighty God, its divine Author, should stretch out His omnipotent hand in its defence, and, by miracles suited to the opposing difficulties, enable it to conquer them, and convince mankind that that religion was from Him.

For, considering all the circumstances, it never could have been adopted by mankind had they not been fully satisfied that God was its Author.

St Augustine justly observes, that had this been accomplished without miracles, this itself would have been the greatest of all miracles. But Almighty God, *qui disponit omnia suaviter et fortiter*, who disposes all things with strength and sweetness—who never fails to bring to pass by His almighty power whatever He is determined to accomplish, and who always brings about His designs with the greatest sweetness, by means congenial, the best adapted to the end proposed—effectually did establish the Christian religion in the world, notwithstanding all opposition, and gave mankind irrefragable proofs of its divine origin, by the profusion of supernatural gifts and graces which he bestowed upon those who professed it. Nothing could be better adapted to the end proposed than this; for by these supernatural graces Christians themselves had an internal experimental feeling of the truth of their religion; they felt its wonderful effects in their own hearts—the divine light which beamed forth in their understandings, the entire change of their affections, which became detached from all the perishable objects of this life, and fixed on God and those eternal goods which their holy religion proposed to them; the interior consolation and peaceful joy which the Holy Ghost communicated to their souls; the fortitude and strength which He gave them to overcome all difficulties—nay, which made them even love the very torments most dreaded by human nature when suffered for His sake.

These were proofs indeed—internal feelings, experimental proofs, which gave the fullest conviction to those happy souls who felt them, and made them at the same time the most proper instruments for convincing others that the religion which they professed was truly divine. In fact, their heroic fortitude under the severest trials; their amazing patience in the midst of torments; their profound humility; their admirable meekness and charity towards their inveterate enemies, joined to the stupendous miracles wrought by their means,—gave a force and efficacy to their words which made the deepest impression on the minds of the heathens, gradually overcame their obstinate prejudices, and at last converted them to the faith and law of Christ.

III. The nature and different kinds of these spiritual gifts and graces are described by St Paul in the following terms : " To one indeed by the Spirit is given the word of wisdom ; and to another the word of knowledge, according to the same Spirit ; to another faith by the same Spirit; to another the grace of healing by the same Spirit ; to another the working of miracles ; to another prophecy ; to another the discerning of Spirits ; to another diverse kinds of tongues; to another the interpretation of speeches: but all these things one and the same Spirit worketh, dividing to every one according as He wills," 1 Cor. xii. The following explanation of them is laid down by the learned author of the 'Miraculous Powers of the Church,' p. 3, as taken from the best commentators on this subject :—

IV. "By the word of wisdom is generally understood the gift of prudence or discretion, in the use of all other spiritual gifts, so that they be not exerted out of due time and place, &c.—a point wherein some of the faithful were deficient, as appears from the 14th chapter of the same Epistle. By the word of knowledge is meant a facility of expounding the doctrine of faith, so as to lay it open to the hearers in such a method as may be most suitable to their capacity. By faith, in this passage, is meant not that theological virtue by which we yield assent to every revealed truth on the testimony of God, but a certain strong confidence or reliance on God for the working of miracles.

"These three gifts are not miraculous, but the third has a particular relation to the miraculous powers. By the grace of healing, is understood the miraculous gift of healing bodily diseases, either by the laying on of hands, or prayer, or by anointing with oil, &c. See Mark vi. By the working of miracles, is understood the power of doing greater works than those last mentioned; as the raising of the dead to life; giving sight to the blind; casting out devils, &c. By prophecy is meant not only the foretelling of things to come, and the discovery of hidden secrets, but also the gift of expounding deep mysteries by the assistance of the Holy Ghost suggesting divers interpretations, which tend to instruction and edification. And if it be taken in this light, independently of the foreknowledge of things to come, it is not properly miraculous, though it belongs to the gifts which are called charismatic. The discerning of spirits is the gift of distinguishing the suggestions of the good spirit from those of the evil one.

"By the kinds of tongues, is signified the gift of speaking divers languages; which was conferred upon the apostles, and some of the principal disciples in a more eminent degree, to enable them to preach the Gospel, and to establish a regular ministry in different parts of the world. To others it was given in an inferior degree, insomuch that several of the faithful were inspired by the Holy Ghost to utter the praises of God in a language which they themselves did not understand, as appears from 1 Cor. xiv., the intent whereof seems to have been to foreshow that the Church of Christ should be spread through all nations, and speak all languages. By interpretation of speeches, is meant the gifts of interpreting what was spoken by another in an unknown tongue."

V. Now, two things are principally to be considered concerning these graces. 1. Their extension. And, 2. The manner and means of their transmission or communication. With regard to their extension, as they were the operations of the Holy Ghost in those in whom He dwelt, we find that, at the beginning, those who received that Divine Spirit by the laying on of the hands of the apostles in the sacrament of Confirmation, received more or less of those graces, according as it seemed meet to Him to bestow them. When He first descended upon the apostles, they and all the disciples received an ample communication of them, and spoke in different tongues the wonderful works of God. The Jews being amazed at so extraordinary an event, St Peter showed them, from the testimony of the prophet Joel, that this was nothing more than the accomplishment of what God had long ago foretold by that prophet; by whom He promised, that in the last days, when the Redeemer should come, He would pour out upon all flesh His Holy Spirit, Who would produce those admirable operations in His servants, as so many proofs, both to them and to the whole world, of the truth of His holy religion. The words of the prophet are these: " And it shall come to pass in the last days, I will pour out my Spirit on all flesh, and your sons and your daughters shall prophesy, and your young men shall see visions, and your old men shall dream dreams. And on my servants and on my handmaids, I will pour out in those days of my Spirit, and they shall prophesy," Acts ii.

It is clear that this promise was made not to a few individuals, but to all God's faithful servants on whom the Holy Spirit should descend. And a little after, St Peter assures us that it was made not to the Jews only, but also to those of all other nations who should be called to the faith of Christ; "For the promise," says he, "is to you and to your children, and to all that are afar off, even as many as the Lord our God shall call," verse 39. And, in fact, we find that this promise was generally fulfilled in all the faithful, Gentiles as well as Jews. Thus, when St Peter was preaching to Cornelius and his friends, the Holy Ghost came upon them, though Gentiles, in the same visible manner that He had descended upon the apostles, "and they all spake with tongues," Acts x.

When St Philip had converted the Samaritans, St Peter and St John went down from Jerusalem to confirm them, "and laid their hands upon them, and they received the Holy Ghost," Acts viii., Who immediately produced in them the usual signs of His presence. All were sensible of it, insomuch that Simon the magician, who wondered beholding the signs and miracles which were done by Philip, wondered much more to see the Holy Ghost, by whom these miracles were performed, and along with Him the power of miracles also communicated to all the people by the laying on of the hands of the apostles; and therefore offered them money to give to him the same power which they had, "that on whomsoever he should lay his hands the Holy Ghost also should come." In like manner, St Paul, finding certain disciples at Ephesus, who had not yet received, nor indeed heard of, the Holy Ghost, did no sooner baptise them, and lay his hands upon them, than the Holy Ghost came on them, and "they spake with tongues and prophesied," Acts xix. 6.

The above citation from 1 Cor. xii. shows that these graces were common among them; and they are also noticed in the first Epistle to the Thessalonians, and in that to the Galatians. From this it appears, first, that the extension of these graces at the beginning of Christianity was very great; and that they were generally bestowed upon all Christians, but in such order and degree as the Holy Ghost judged proper. Secondly, That this was done chiefly by means of the sacrament of Confirmation, or the imposition of the hands of the chief pastors of the Church after baptism: so that the apostles not only communicated these graces themselves to their converts together with the Holy Ghost, the Author of them, but also transmitted to their successors in office the power of communicating them to others successively, till the work of God should be accomplished.

From the repeated testimony of Christian writers during the first three ages of the Church, it is clear that these supernatural graces and miraculous powers continued to be bestowed on great numbers during all that period; and we find two reasons why they should have been so. First, Because the necessities of the Christian religion were much the same during all that time; for while the efforts of hell were united with the greatest powers upon earth, animated by the most violent passions of the human heart, to persecute, oppress, and destroy the Christians during the first three ages, it was necessary that Almighty God should never cease to stretch forth His hand in their defence, and to continue His supernatural and miraculous interposition both for their comfort and support, and for the confusion and conversion of their enemies. Secondly, Few or none embraced Christianity in those days of persecution who did not do so from their heart; they had no worldly motive to induce them, no temporal views to influence them; the conviction of its being the only way to save their souls was their sole motive for embracing it. Hence they were Christians in earnest, ready to sacrifice everything for their faith, and therefore well disposed for receiving the supernatural influences of the Divine Spirit.

But when the Roman emperors were converted to the faith of Christ, when Christianity was established by law, and it became even conducive to worldly interest to be a Christian, the face of things was changed. Christianity being then protected by the civil power, and every worldly motive concurring with the solid and convincing reasons on which it was founded, Religion no longer stood in need of the general continuation of those supernatural marks of the divine favour which had been necessary in the days of persecution. Besides, from the concurrence of worldly motives, numbers embraced the faith with views not purely spiritual, and carried a worldly spirit and a corrupted heart even into the sanctuary of God. Thus many became Christians who were altogether indisposed for receiving those divine communications of the Holy Ghost which had been so liberally bestowed upon the generality of the faithful in the three preceding ages.

About this time, then, a cessation of miracles is acknowledged to have taken place, and is attested by some of the greatest lights of the fourth century; but a cessation of what kind? A cessation of the above-named supernatural graces, both as to their extension, and the manner of their transmission. As to extension, they were no longer communicated as previously to the generality of Christians. They were now bestowed only upon the few, upon those chosen souls who, still preserving the primitive spirit of Christianity, lived in heart and affection, and frequently in person also, detached from the world, and who sought God in purity of spirit. "As to the manner of transmission," because the Holy Ghost, when communicated to souls by the imposition of hands in the sacrament of Confirmation, did not now give those external signs of His presence which He had done at the beginning, by the appearance of fiery tongues, or by bestowing the gift of languages. These were necessary while the Church continued under the pressure of persecution; but that necessity was now past, and therefore, though the communication of the Divine Spirit, and the confirming and strengthening those who receive Him, will continue to the end of time to be the never-failing effect of the sacrament of Confirmation in the worthy receiver, yet this is now done in an invisible manner, without the exterior signs which were given in the early ages.

VI. That this is the true nature of the cessation of miracles acknowledged by the holy fathers of the fourth age is evident from the express declaration of St Augustine. This great saint having, in different parts of his writings, mentioned this, and being well aware what use the enemies of the Church would make of such an acknowledgment, thought it necessary, in his book of Retractations, to explain his meaning more precisely, which he does as follows:—

"What I also said, that those miracles were not allowed to continue to our times, lest the soul should always seek after things visible, and mankind should wax cold by their frequency who had been inflamed by their novelty, is certainly true. For when hands are laid on the baptised, they do not receive the Holy Ghost now in such a manner as to speak with the tongues of all nations, nor are the sick now cured by the shadow of Christ's preachers as they pass by them, and others such as these, which it is manifest did afterwards cease: But what I said is not so to be understood, as if no miracles were believed to be performed now in the name of Christ: For I myself, when I wrote that very book, knew that a blind man had received his sight in the city of Milan, at the bodies of the Milanese martyrs, and several others besides; nay, such numbers are performed in these our days, that I neither can know them all, nor, though I knew them, could I enumerate them:" St. Aug. Retract., lib. 1. cap. 13. § 7.

From this passage it is evident, that the fact spoken of by the holy Fathers of the fourth century regards only the extension and visible signs of the communication of the charismatic graces, when the Holy Ghost was received by the imposition of hands after baptism, or some of those more extraordinary miracles which were performed in the days of the apostles, such as curing the sick by their shadow, and the like. But though in this sense they acknowledge a cessation, they no less strenuously assert the continuation of the gift of miracles, and its actual exercise in numberless instances in their own days, to many of which they themselves were eye-witnesses.

VII. Hence, then, the question concerning the continuance of miracles in the Church is only with regard to these latter. We do not inquire whether the Holy Ghost continues now to be communicated at Confirmation, with those visible signs of His presence, the appearance of fiery tongues, speaking languages, and the like, which He displayed at the beginning; nor whether these and the other graces above mentioned be now indiscriminately bestowed on all the faithful. It is plain that this is not the case; and it is acknowledged by all that a cessation of these took place before, or about the beginning of, the fourth century. But the question is, Whether or not Almighty God has in every age of the Church, down to these our days, raised up from time to time holy persons, whom He has replenished with His Divine Spirit, and by whom He has been pleased, on many occasions, to perform miracles for ends of the same nature, or similar to those, for which He performed miracles by His holy servants, in every period of the Jewish dispensation?

This is the precise state of the question; and that Almighty God has actually done so, is what I have now to prove. But it will throw light upon the question, and show still further its importance, if we first take a view of the manner in which it has been treated by Dr Middleton and his Protestant antagonists, according to the different systems which they have advocated.

VIII. The Doctor everywhere professes the highest veneration for the Protestant religion, and assures us, towards the close of his introductory discourse, that his design in his work against the continuation of miracles, is to fix the religion of Protestants on its proper basis; that is, on the sacred Scriptures. For these he professes the greatest regard, and on the credit of their testimony firmly believes all the miracles related in them, however great and amazing. He acknowledges, of course, that the power of working miracles was bestowed on the apostles, and on others during the lives of the apostles, but insists that it ceased entirely upon their death, and never more appeared in the Christian world; and the whole tendency of his inquiry is to prove as a consequence of this opinion, "that the pretended miracles of the primitive Church were all mere fictions." Introd. Disc., p. lxxviii. edit. Lond. 1755.

The motives which induced the Doctor to adopt this opinion were chiefly these: he found that many of the doctrines and practices which Protestants condemn as corruptions of Popery, were clearly taught by the Christian writers of the primitive ages, and he enumerates several manifest and striking examples in different parts of his Introductory Discourse. He saw that if true miracles were admitted to have been wrought in a Church which taught and practised these things, the things themselves could not be condemned; and therefore he concluded it was absolutely necessary for the support of the Protestant religion that no such miracles should be admitted. Besides, he was aware that if miracles in the first ages were admitted upon the credit of human testimony notwithstanding these doctrines and practices, it would be ridiculous to deny them in after ages, if equally well attested, merely because they were done in favour of the same or similar doctrines. Consequently, to allow their existence in one age of the Church upon human testimony laid him under an inevitable necessity of admitting them on the same ground even to the present time; and therefore he again concludes it to be impossible that the Protestant religion can stand or be defended if the existence of miracles be allowed even for one single age after the death of the apostles. This is evident throughout his Preface and Introductory Discourse, particularly from the following passages.

In the Preface, page v., he says, the general approbation which the Introductory Discourse met with "from those whose authority I chiefly value, has given me the utmost encouragement to persevere in the prosecution of my argument, as being of the greatest importance to the Protestant religion, and the sole expedient which can effectually secure it from being gradually undermined and finally subverted by the efforts of Rome." In his Introductory Discourse he begins by observing the advantage which the Roman Church takes of the belief of a continuation of miracles in her communion, and states that his system is the result of inquiry into the grounds of this belief. "This system," says he, " by the most impartial judgment that I am able to form, I take not only to be true, but useful also, and even necessary to the defence of Christianity, as it is generally received, and ought always to be defended, in Protestant Churches."

IX. A few pages after he gives an account of the motives which induced him to undertake this work. "I found myself particularly excited to this task by what I had occasionally observed and heard of the late growth of Popery in this kingdom, and the great number of Popish books which have been printed and dispersed among us within these few years; in which their writers make much use of that prejudice in favour of primitive antiquity, which prevails even in this Protestant country, towards drawing weak people into their cause, and showing their worship to be the best, because it is the most conformable to that ancient pattern. But the most powerful of all their arguments, and what gains them the most proselytes, is, their confident attestation of miracles, as subsisting still in their Church, and the clear succession of them, which they deduce through all history, from the apostolic times down to our own. This their apologists never fail to display with all the force of their rhetoric, and with good reason; since it is a proof, of all others the most striking to vulgar minds, and the most decisive indeed to all minds, as far as it is believed to be true." Introd. p. xxxvi.

This is very plain dealing; the continuation of miracles in the Church is the most decisive proof of the truth of her doctrine; but such continuation being incompatible with the existence of Protestantism, the only way to secure this is to adopt the Doctor's system, and absolutely to deny that any miracle ever was performed since the times of the apostles !

X. On the connection between miracles and Popery he observes as follows : " After the conversion of the Roman empire to Christianity, we shall find the greatest part of their boasted miracles to have been wrought either by monks, or relics, or the sign of the cross, or consecrated oil; wherefore, if we admit the miracles we must necessarily admit the rites for the sake of which they were wrought ; they both rest on the same bottom, and mutually establish each other. For it is a maxim which must be allowed by all Christians, that whenever any sacred rite or religious institution becomes the instrument of miracles, we ought to consider that rite as confirmed by divine approbation," Introd. p. lvii. A little after, reflecting on the imprudence of Dr Chapman and other Protestant divines, who, satisfied of the authority by which the existence of miracles is proved, have acknowledged and defended them for several ages after the apostles, he says : " Thus we see to what a state of things the miracles of the fourth and fifth centuries would reduce us ; they would call us back again to the old superstition of our ancestors, would fill us with monks, and relics, and masses, and all the other trinkets which the treasury of Rome can supply : for this is the necessary effect of that zeal which would engage us in the defence of them," p. lxi.

XI. To show the great advantage which his system gives for gaining the end proposed of disarming Catholics and securing the Protestant religion, he says: "Should the Romanists pretend to urge us with their miracles, and to show the succession of them from the earliest ages, we have no reason to be moved at it, but may tell them without scruple that we admit no miracles but those of the Scripture; and that all the rest are either justly suspected or certainly forged. By putting the controversy on this issue, we shall either disarm them at once; or, if they persist in the dispute, may be sure to convict them of fraud and imposture," p. lxxxii.

XII. So far the Doctor displays the necessity which he saw of establishing his system, from the impossibility of defending the Protestant religion, if any miracles are admitted among Catholics. What follows will show the necessity he felt of advocating his system, even from the end of the apostolic age, on account of the invincible force of human testimony proving the existence of miracles in all succeeding ages, if admitted in any one age after the apostles.

XIII. Speaking of the nature of the evidence by which the precise time of the duration of miracles should be determined, he observes, that the generality of writers appeal to the testimony of the earliest fathers, but without agreeing to what age this character of *earliest fathers* comes down; and then adds: " But to whatever age he (the observator) may restrain it, the difficulty at last will be, to assign a reason why we must needs stop there. In the mean time, by his appealing thus to the earliest fathers only, as unanimous on this article, a common reader will be apt to infer that the later fathers are more cold or diffident, or divided upon it; whereas the reverse of this is true; and the more we descend from those earliest fathers, the more strong and explicit we find their successors in attesting the perpetual succession and daily exertion of the same miraculous powers in their several ages: So that if the cause must be determined by the unanimous consent of fathers, we shall find as much reason to believe those powers were continued even to the latest ages as to any other, how early and primitive soever, after the days of the apostles," Pref., p. xiv.

A little after he adds: "As far as church historians can illustrate or throw light upon anything, there is not a single point in all history so constantly, explicitly, and unanimously affirmed by them all, as the continual succession of those powers through all ages, from the earliest father that first mentions them down to the time of the Reformation: which same succession is still further deduced by persons of the most eminent character for their probity, learning, and dignity in the Roman Church to this very day. So that the only doubt that can remain with us is, whether the church historians are to be trusted or not? For if any credit be due to them in the present case, it must reach either to all or to none; because the reason of believing them in any one age will be found to be of equal force in all, so far as it depends on the characters of the persons attesting, or the nature of the things attested," Pref., p. xvii.

XIV. This uniformity in ecclesiastical history, in attesting miracles in every age, is still further acknowledged as follows: "It must be confessed that this claim of a miraculous power, which is now peculiar to the Church of Rome, was universally asserted and believed in all Christian countries, and in all ages of the Church, till the time of the Reformation. For ecclesiastical history makes no difference between one age and another, but carries on the succession of its miracles, as of all other common events, through all of them indifferently, to that memorable period," Introd. p. xxxix.

XV. After relating the sentiments of Dodwell, Whiston, Waterland, and Chapman, who defend the continuation of miracles for some ages after the apostles, according to their respective periods, and Dr Chapman brings them even down to the end of the fifth century, he adds: "Thus these eminent divines pursuing their several systems, and ambitious of improving still upon each other's discoveries, seem unwarily to have betrayed the Protestant cause by transferring the miraculous powers of the Church, the pretended ensigns of truth and orthodoxy, into the hands of its enemies. For it was in these very primitive ages, and especially in the third, fourth, and fifth centuries, those flourishing times of miraculous powers, as Dr Chapman calls them, in which the chief corruptions of Popery were either actually introduced, or the seeds of them so effectually sown, that they could not fail of producing the fruits which we now see. By these corruptions I mean the institution of monkery; the worship of relics; invocation of saints; prayers for the dead; the superstitious use of images; of the sacraments; of the sign of the cross; and of consecrated oil; by the efficacy of all which rites, and as a proof of their divine origin, perpetual miracles are affirmed to have been wrought in these every centuries," Introd. p. xlv.

He then gives examples of all these in the earliest ages, ending with a rebuke to Dr Berriman, who defends the miracles of the sixth century, as far as St Gregory the Great, for which the Doctor says of him, p. lxix: "Thus the miraculous powers of the Church are expressly avowed by him to the end even of the sixth century, in which

Popery had gained a full establishment; yet this Protestant divine cannot conceive the least reason to dispute the miraculousness of those facts which established it; nay, he defies any man to prove that miracles had yet ceased in this Popish age. From all this he draws the just conclusion: "Since the zeal, then, of these Protestant guides has brought us within the very pale of the Romish Church, I see nothing which can stop their progress from the sixth age down to the present—for each succeeding age will furnish miracles, and witnesses too, of as good credit as those of the sixth," page lxxi. And afterwards resuming this point he declares: "That by granting them (the Romanists) but a single age of miracles after the times of the apostles, we shall be entangled in a series of difficulties whence we can never fairly extricate ourselves till we allow the same powers also to the present age," Introd., p. lxxxii.

XVI. It was necessary to give this extract of Dr Middleton's sentiments in his own words, because it is in this that we discover the real origin and rise of his extraordinary system, and the true motives which induced him to adopt and publish it to the world. Here we see evidently that it was not a rational and consequential result of facts and just reasoning, but a preconceived opinion which he was compelled to embrace from the impossibility of otherwise defending the Protestant religion. He was sensible of the insuperable power which the claim to miracles gives the Roman Catholics over their Protestant adversaries. He saw the weakness of everything that had been said against them by Protestants, if miracles are allowed to have been wrought among them. He saw, in fine, that what Protestants call the corruptions of Popery are to be found in the earliest ages of Christianity; and that it would be ridiculous to admit the miracles of those ages on human testimony, and deny those of after-ages, though equally attested; and from these clear truths he concluded, "That the only expedient which can effectually secure the Protestant religion from being undermined and subverted by the efforts of Rome, is at once to aim a bold stroke, and absolutely to deny all miracles whatsoever since the days of the apostles."

The resolution being once taken, which the necessities of the Reformation forced upon him, the next thing was to find such plausible arguments as might support it with at least a colour of reason; and here, indeed, it must be owned that he has done everything in defence of his bad cause which could possibly have been expected from a penetrating genius, extensive reading, and determined resolution. But as preconceived opinions are generally only flights of fancy, or the despairing necessities of falsehood, the Doctor's favourite system, when brought to the test of sound reasoning, is discovered to be without foundation, and calculated, if adopted, to produce results the most fatal.

This has been shown by the Doctor's learned adversaries of his own communion, who have fully vindicated the characters of the holy fathers of the primitive ages from the shocking representation which Doctor Middleton gives of them; for the Doctor grounds his whole proof upon this that these fathers, the most venerable Christian writers in every age, and all Church historians, are to be looked upon as "credulous and super'stitious fools, or a set of crafty knaves, possessed by strong prejudices, and an enthusiastic zeal for every doctrine of the Christian religion, scrupling at no art or means which might propagate the same; and, in short, were all of a character from which nothing could be expected that was candid and impartial," Preface, p. xxviii. In order to establish this point, which is vital to his system, the Doctor has exerted all his ingenuity and rhetoric, but to no purpose; his Protestant adversaries have examined him step by step, and have detected his false reasoning and sophistry. They have proved, beyond reply, that those venerable writers of the primitive ages were men of unspotted character, undoubted probity, unquestionable veracity, and most competent judges of the truth of the miracles which they related, having either themselves been eyewitnesses of them, or having heard them from such; or that the miracles were public and well known to the whole people among whom they spoke.

XVII. This alone is sufficient to destroy all that the Doctor has built on so sandy a foundation. But his Protestant opponents have gone further, and have shown that the system which he proposes is fraught with the following shocking consequences: First, that it destroys all faith in history. He acknowledges himself, that, as far as the church historians illustrate or throw light upon anything, there is not a single point in history so explicitly and unanimously affirmed as the continual succession of miraculous powers throughout all ages. If, therefore, notwithstanding this concurrent attestation, we are to look upon this succession as an absolute falsehood, how will it be possible to credit any historian whatever, or to believe any single fact attested by others, and of which we have not been eyewitnesses? Secondly, That it opens a door to universal scepticism. This is a natural consequence of the former. Thirdly, That it undermines the very foundation of the Christian religion itself. For if the immediate successors of the apostles, who had been their disciples and instructed by them, were knaves and impostors, as he pretends, is it not natural to suspect (to use his own argument on a similar occasion) that so bold a defiance of truth could not be acquired at once?

If this his argument be good, we must conclude that these early impostors had learned their knavery from their masters, and of course that the apostles themselves were as great impostors as their disciples. Besides, according to Protestant principles, the Bible is the sole ground of that religion, and it is a notorious fact that we at present have received the Bible as divinely inspired only upon the testimony of the primitive fathers and their successors, to our own days. If then these were all, as the Doctor represents them, crafty knaves or silly fools, and of such a character that nothing candid or impartial can be expected from them; nay, such impostors that we are unable to depend upon their word, even when relating facts which they declare they saw with their own eyes; how can we believe the Bible to be the Word of God, which comes to us through such a channel? What security have we that such a continued succession of villains, who, as he assures us, would stick at no art or means to propagate their principles, have not corrupted the Scriptures, and imposed their own forgeries on mankind instead of the Word of God? If so, there is an end at once of the Christian religion itself, upon Protestant principles!

XVIII. On this a Catholic must make another obvious reflection—namely, that the Doctor's system, with all its proofs, is founded upon the most childish supposition, a mere begging of the question; a supposition unworthy of a man of sense, much more of one who professes to be a teacher of mankind! He supposes that the respect which Catholics, after the example of the primitive ages, pay to the relics of saints, their prayers for the dead, belief in a purgatory, invocation of the saints, and the like, which he calls the corruptions of Popery, are really such in themselves; that such doctrines are impious, blasphemous, and superstitious; and upon this supposition alone he condemns all the miracles related by the fathers of the fourth age, "not only in general and for the greatest part, but entirely and universally as the effects of fraud and imposture," Introd., p. lxv.

"In this age," says he, "all its most illustrious fathers, now saints, of the Catholic Church, St Athanasius, St Epiphamius, St Basil, St Gregory of Nyssa, St Ambrose, St Jerom, St Austin, and St Chrysostom, have severally recorded and solemnly attested a number of miracles, said to be wrought in confirmation of some favourite institutions of those days, which, in the judgment of all the learned and candid Protestants, are manifestly fictitious and utterly incredible," Introd. p. lxv. Now, who does not see that this is merely begging the question, supposing and taking for granted what he ought to prove?

However incredible these institutions may seem to the Doctor and his Protestant brethren, they are far from appearing so to the great body of Catholics, who are endowed with as much common sense and sound judgment as the Doctor and his brethren. These receive them as divine, believe them to be truths revealed by God, and among many other proofs to show that they are so, they appeal to numberless miracles attested by the most credible eyewitnesses in every age, and recorded in the most authentic manner as performed by means of these very institutions, and consequently in approbation of them. How childish is it, then, in the Doctor, when, instead of attempting to prove that these institutions are fictitious or incredible, he takes it for granted that they are so, and upon this silly pretence alone would have the world adopt a system injurious in the highest degree to the characters of the most venerable personages that ever have appeared in the Christian world, and involving all the monstrous consequences, which, as his Protestant brethren have demonstrated, necessarily flow from it!

How glorious a triumph must it be to every thinking Catholic, to see one of the most learned and determined adversaries of his holy religion reduced to such despicable expedients in attacking it! Yet it is upon the above pitiful supposition that the Doctor's whole fabric is built; for assuming that the miracles related by the holy fathers of the fourth age are mere fiction and imposture, he takes up his position, and by a pretence of argument as weak as its foundation, he includes all the miracles, related by those of preceding and subsequent ages, in the same condemnation.

XIX. To show this line of conduct in its proper light, let us apply it to a similar case. It is certain that the mysteries of the Trinity, incarnation, original sin, and the other fundamental articles of Christianity, appear as incredible to deists and atheists as those which the Doctor calls the corruptions of Popery can possibly appear to him, or to any other learned and candid Protestant; put, then, his argument into the mouth of a deist against these great Christian truths; hear him haranguing against the books of the Gospel, against Christ and His apostles, and rejecting with disdain all the miracles recorded of them, because they were said to have been wrought in confirmation of some favourite opinions of theirs, the Trinity, the incarnation, and other such, which, in the judgment of all the learned and candid deists, are manifestly and utterly incredible.

What answer could the Doctor make to this argument? It is, in fact, the very one used by deists against the miracles of Christ and his apostles; and it is evidently the same as that which the Doctor uses against the miracles of their successors, and has exactly the same weight in the one case as in the other. If, then, he allows this argument, he must renounce his Christianity. If he condemns it, by the same breath he condemns his own system, and all the arguments on which he pretends to build it. What a comfort must not this be to every reflecting Catholic, to see that even a Doctor Middleton cannot attack his holy religion but by such means as would at the same time sap the very foundations of Christianity itself, so that Popery and Christianity must stand or fall together!

XX. I cannot leave this subject without further observing that the Doctor himself seems to have been aware of all the consequences which his opponents deduce from his system; for he calls it in his Preface, page i., "an experiment big with consequences;" but whatever these be, they give him no concern: "To speak my mind freely," says he, "on the subject of consequences: I am not so scrupulous, perhaps, in my regard to them as many of my profession are apt to be," Pref., p. viii. And when answering the objection made against his system, as rendering the Bible itself precarious and uncertain, he answers with the greatest coolness: "Though we allow the objection to be true, it cannot hurt my argument; for if it be natural and necessary that the craft and credulity of witnesses should always detract from the credit of their testimony, who can help it? Or, on what is the consequence to be charged but on the nature and constitution of the things from which it flows? Or, if the authority of any books be really weakened by the character I have given of the fathers, will it follow from thence that the character must necessarily be false, or that the fathers were neither crafty nor credulous? That surely can never be pretended."

This is plain speaking indeed, but strange language from one who calls himself a Christian. But what can he do? There is no other possible expedient for effectually securing the Protestant religion against the efforts of the Church of Rome: and therefore, right or wrong, be the consequences what they may, this plan must be pursued, and this system upheld.

XXI. Upon the whole, then, we may observe of the Doctor, 1. That in the outset he proceeds upon a mere "begging of the question," assuming the chief thing which he ought to prove. 2. That his system is founded upon a most unjust and uncharitable defamation, not of one or two particular persons, but of all the greatest lights of the Christian world; men revered in their day for their eminent sanctity and learning, and whose memories have been held in veneration in all succeeding ages; and these he defames not in one century or two, but in every age, from the days of the apostles to the present time. 3. That the arguments which he uses in support of his system are just the same that a deist or atheist employs against the miracles of Christ and His apostles, or that a heathen would have used against those of Moses and the prophets; and their strength is exactly the same in either case. 4. That the necessary consequences of his system manifestly tend to destroy the credit of all history, and to undermine the authority of the Bible itself. All this has been proved beyond reply even by the Doctor's Protestant antagonists.

Having thus examined Dr Middleton's system, and his manner of conducting his case, from which we have obtained important light, I now proceed to consider his Protestant antagonists, and see what discoveries can be made from them.

XXII. Those learned gentlemen of the Protestant religion who have appeared in the field against Doctor Middleton in this discussion, were all under the same necessity of proving these two points: " That the power of working miracles continued in the Church for a certain time after the apostolic age; and that this power was entirely withdrawn after that period."

As Christians, they were obliged to defend the first proposition; and, as Protestants, they were under the necessity of supporting the second. They saw the deadly blow which the Doctor's system aims at the Christian revelation, with the shocking consequences that follow from it, and therefore they deemed it incumbent on them, in defence of revelation, to prove that miracles did most certainly continue in the Church for some time after the apostles. But, at the same time, they saw that if this power be admitted to have continued in the Church without limitation to the present day, it would afford an unanswerable argument in favour of Popery, to the utter condemnation of the Reformation. They were under the necessity, therefore, of stopping in their career, and of confining the continuation of this power within such bounds as they thought most proper and convenient. In these two points these writers all agree, notwithstanding their great difference of opinion as to the duration of the power of working miracles. In this, indeed, they differ exceedingly; some, as we have seen above, assigning the end of the third century as the period of the cessation of miracles, some carrying them down to the end of the fourth, others admitting those of the fifth age, and others allowing many true and real miracles to be incontestably proved, even to the end of the sixth century.

From this dissension among themselves upon one of the two great points in debate, we must naturally infer that the arguments for the cessation of miracles at these respective periods cannot be conclusive; for, were the reasons at any one of these periods stronger than at another, there could be no dissension; but all would agree on that period which was proved by the most conclusive arguments. Seeing, therefore, that they do not agree, but that each one thinks his own arguments the best, this is an undeniable proof that they are all equally worthless and inconclusive.

But, however these writers differ in their conclusions, we find that they all proceed upon the same principle, their aversion to Popery, and only differ in their ideas of Popish doctrines, and about the date when those doctrines began. "No true miracles must be allowed after the corruptions of Popery were introduced into the Church!" This is the grand principle on which they all agree among themselves, and even with Doctor Middleton! But what are the corruptions of Popery? and when did they begin? In this they differ widely. To Dr Middleton nothing is more plain than that "the sign of the cross; praying for the dead; mixing the cup with water; sending the consecrated elements to the absent; keeping the consecrated bread at home in private houses and for private use; looking upon it as a defence against devils; styling the Eucharist the sacrifice of the body of Christ; offering it up in memory of the martyrs; calling it most tremendous mystery, dreadful solemnity, and the like." To the

Doctor nothing is more plain than that all this is rank Popery: "What is all this (says he) but a description of that sacrifice of the Mass which the Romanists offer at this day both for the living and the dead?" Introd., p. liii.

But the Doctor found these things manifestly taught and practised by the fathers and Christians of the second and third ages, by Justin Martyr, by Cyprian, by Tertullian, whose plain testimonies he cites for that purpose. Consequently, according to his idea of Popish corruptions, and in conformity with the above principle, which he lays down in common with his adversaries, he is forced to reject all miracles even in those early ages, and to maintain that the cessation took place just after the days of the apostles.

Others do not look upon the above articles as Popish corruptions, but think that "the sign of the cross," which the Church of England uses in baptism, may be practised without idolatry, and that mixing water in the cup, and even offering up the elements as an oblation or sacrifice, are consonant to primitive purity. They even believe that praying for the dead may be lawfully used, and with those Protestant bishops whom the Duchess of York, King James II. of England's first wife, consulted upon that head, they wish that this and some other points had not been done away by their reforming ancestors.

Persons of this turn of mind have generally an esteem for antiquity, and wish it to be thought that their religious principles were authorised and followed by the Christian world in the most primitive ages. They contend, that as Popery (that is, what they consider Popery) did not commence for some ages after the apostles, there is no reason for denying the existence and continuation of miracles during those pure ages; and therefore they uphold them against Dr Middleton, by the force of human testimony, by the authority of the Christian writers, of the holy fathers and church historians, who flourished during the period which they assign for their continuation.

Of these gentlemen it may be remarked that, although they have no other way of proving this continuation down to their respective assigned periods than this testimony, and declare it to be, in their opinion, a full and satisfactory proof, yet, the moment after these their respective eras, they deny it all weight, and treat it as utterly incapable of proving the existence of one single miracle. Why so? In the judgment even of their Protestant brethren the testimony is the same afterwards as before, nor can any rational cause be assigned why it should not be of equal value in both cases. But if it were allowed to proceed, it would favour Popery, and therefore, be the consequences what they may, it must be rejected. Is it not evident that this is mere trifling, and that all that they advance upon this subject is nothing but opinion and prejudice in favour of a preconceived hypothesis, which each one assumes as best suits his own fancy?

XXIII. It appears, then, that Dr Middleton and his Protestant opponents are in reality in the same predicament, all building upon the same foundation, "a mere begging of the question," and assuming as truth what they can never prove; nay, what is not only called in question, but absolutely denied, and looked upon as impiety and heresy by the great majority of Christendom. Whatever weight, therefore, this may have against Dr Middleton's system in the mouth of his opponents, it must militate with equal force against themselves. He and they must stand or fall together.

XXIV. This, however, will be more evident when we take a more minute view of their way of managing their cause. Between them and the Doctor there is the most perfect conformity. The same arguments by which they show the falsehood of the Doctor's system, and prove that the power of miracles continued in the Church after the apostolic age, show equally the falsehood of their own various systems, and prove that these powers most certainly continued in the Church after the different periods which they respectively assign. And the reasons by which they as Christians pretend to show that the miracles said to have been wrought after their supposed periods of cessation are falsehood and forgery, have the self-same force in the mouths of heathens and deists to prove that the miracles which they admit, and even the Scripture miracles themselves, are exactly of the same kind.

XXV. As it would be tedious, and indeed an endless repetition, to examine each of their systems apart, I shall confine myself to the one most commonly received by Protestants: That the power of miracles continued in the Church till about the end of the third, or the beginning of the fourth century, and was then totally withdrawn. This opinion is adopted, and strenuously defended by Mr Brook, in his "Examination of the Free Inquiry;" a work in which he has displayed, in a masterly manner, all that can be said in defence of this system, or indeed of any of the others; for in all the arguments are the same, and only arbitrarily applied to the different periods, without any reason for appropriating them to one more than to another. In examining, therefore, what Mr Brook advances upon this system, we, in fact, examine all the others at the same time.

XXVI. I have stated that Protestants who write against the Doctor's system have chiefly two points in view, and that their whole aim is to establish them: "That the power of working miracles continued in the Christian Church for some ages after the apostles; and that it was totally withdrawn from her at those particular periods which they respectively assign." The first of these propositions they maintain against Dr Middleton, the other against the Catholic Church. For the sake of perspicuity we shall treat them separately.

XXVII. In proving that miracles continued in the Church for some time after the apostles, two kinds of arguments are used; the first is drawn from presumptive evidence, the second from positive testimony. The first shows that it was reasonable to expect miracles after the apostolic age, removes such prejudices as might arise against them, and, of course, prepares the mind to believe them. The other shows that they actually were performed; and the two produce complete conviction. "The miracles of the earlier ages of the Christian Church (says Mr Brook) are probable in themselves; there is a strong presumptive evidence of their truth and reality. There is no sufficient reason to suspect that evidence; of consequence, when well attested, they are equally to be believed with any other common historical facts. They are not therefore to be set aside, where there is the unanimous testimony of credible witnesses, without destroying the faith of all history, without introducing an universal scepticism." Brook's Examin., p. 51.

A little after he adds: "If facts probable in themselves, the truth of which we have no reason to suspect from the nature of the thing, but, on the contrary, there appear manifest reasons why we should believe them, are nevertheless to be set aside as doubtful and incredible, though supported by the unanimous testimony of such persons who lived in those very times, and were eyewitnesses of them, all historic evidence must rest on so sandy a foundation as to be utterly insupportable by human testimony. There can remain no one rational and steady principle to direct us in judging of any past events represented to us in writing," p. 55. This, then, is the sum of the proof used by these writers for the continuation of miracles in the Church after the days of the apostles,— "presumptive evidence," which makes it reasonable to expect them in those times; and "positive testimony," which expressly asserts them.

XXVIII. This presumptive evidence, as displayed by Mr Brook, for the three first ages, consists of the following arguments: 1. "If the hand of God did continue to co-operate visibly with the saints of the apostolic age, throughout the whole ministry of all the apostles, it is not likely that this extraordinary providence should vanish instantaneously, and leave the Gospel to make the rest of its way by its own genuine strength. Such a supposition is utterly inconsistent with the natural notions we have of God's proceedings, as well as with what is revealed about them. Whenever the Supreme Being works any changes in nature, those changes are always made, not on a sudden, but in time, and by slow degrees; and in all the dispensations of His providence to the sons of men, as far as we know from reason only, the method of His proceedings is not hasty and violent, but ever gentle and gradual."

"The Jewish religion was established by an extraordinary providence. The divine interpositions in favour of that people were very frequent and notorious, till they had got quiet possession of the promised land, and till their whole polity, civil as well as religious, was effectually established; but even, though such extraordinary interpositions became less frequent, they were not totally withdrawn; God still continued to show among His peculiar people, at certain times, visible and supernatural tokens of His almighty power and overruling providence. And afterwards, in the days of Elijah and Elisha, when the frequency of these divine interpositions was renewed, it did not vanish instantaneously at the death of these two prophets; it was gradually withdrawn. Why, then, should it be thought an improbable thing that God should act in the same manner in defence and support of the Christian religion? What reason is there to suppose that He should be more favourable to the religious dispensation of Moses than to that of His own Son?"

2. "Had the miraculous powers been immediately withdrawn upon the death of the apostles, this must have been of the greatest prejudice to religion; for, by this means, the Gospel must have been left in a naked and defenceless state, to become a prey to the prejudices, to the malice, and to the outrage of men. The immediate successors of the apostles must have fallen into the utmost discouragement, discontent, and despondency of mind, seeing they had the same difficulties to struggle with as those before them, from a malicious and perverse world; and yet perceiving they had none of those powers and assistances to relieve and support them, which had been of late so liberally bestowed upon the disciples of Jesus in the preceding age. What an obstruction must this experience have occasioned to the furtherance of the Gospel? What an aversion to it must it have caused in some? What apostasy in others? What dejection, what murmuring, what despair in all?"

"Let a man seriously and impartially reflect on these things, and then judge whether it be not probable, that the same extraordinary providence which accompanied the apostles and other Christians upon the first preaching of the gospel, continued to exert itself in their favour during the whole ministry of the apostles ; and whether, upon the death of them, it is likely that it should cease at once, and not rather that it visibly resided in the Christian Church some time afterwards, and was at last gradually withdrawn, as the real exigencies of the Church were constantly and by degrees lessening, and the continuance of it made by that means less and less necessary."

3. "The necessity of divine interpositions in the administration of ecclesiastical affairs in those earlier ages of the Church, make it reasonable to believe that the same extraordinary providence by which these things were regulated during the lives of the apostles, did continue to direct and encourage the Christians some time afterwards. It was a thing of the greatest consequence in the infancy of the Gospel, that no person should be admitted to any high office in the Church but such only as were properly qualified. Nothing could have given greater offence to the Christian converts ; nothing could have brought a more just imputation upon the apostles themselves, or have been a more reasonable obstruction to the success of their labours, both among Jews and Gentiles, than to have observed such persons dignified with the most eminent parts of the ministry, who were either of bad principles or exceptionable conduct."

Now this could never have been avoided, except either " the apostles had been endowed with some extraordinary powers in making choice of pastors to succeed them, or some visible manifestations of the Spirit of God had appeared at their appointment ;" as was the case when Saul and Barnabas were separated by the Holy Ghost for the work to which He called them, or that the persons chosen had been eminent for their extraordinary graces, and endowed with power from above, as were Stephen and Philip, the deacons. As, therefore, the same necessity of holy pastors continued for the ages after the apostles which had been in their days, "May we not fairly conclude, from the great expediency and necessity of the thing, that the immediate successors of the apostles were assisted by the same extraordinary means, and possessed of the same extraordinary powers? Is it to be imagined that the providence of God, which was so profuse of its extraordinary gifts and miraculous powers during the lives of the apostles, as even to impart them to numbers of the laity and the lowest of the people, should immediately, after their deaths, become so sparing of them, as to refuse them even to the most eminently distinguished among the Christians for their superior piety and virtue, and to whom the whole management of the church discipline, and the defence and support of the Christian cause, were entirely committed?"

4. The circumstances of those times confirm all the above: "The Christians were surrounded on all sides with the most inveterate enemies, and situated in the midst of a people wholly devoted to the grossest and most determined bigotry and superstition, and totally abandoned to the greatest profligacy of manners. The doctrines of the Christians, which have so great a contrariety to the passions and prejudices of men, exposed them everywhere to the greatest ignominy and contempt, and brought on them a train of the severest calamities which the most virulent malice, inflamed and exasperated with the most outrageous zeal, as well civil

as religious, could contrive. Now, if ever God has visibly interposed in the affairs of men, is it to be supposed that, in such circumstances, this same almighty Being would suffer His most faithful servants to be exposed to such cruelty, merely on account of their fidelity to Him, without giving them any manifestations of His power and presence for their comfort and support?" Or how is it possible that His religion should have subsisted without them?

How much less possible that it should, in these circumstances, have made proselytes of its very enemies, and triumphed at last over all its adversaries, if it had not been supported by visible interpositions of the divine approbation? Human nature, left to itself, must have sunk under the pressure of such a complication of misery, and been at last absolutely overpowered by such heavy and weighty calamities. Under these circumstances, therefore, nothing appears sufficient to account for the uncommon progress of the Christian religion, but frequent and visible interpositions of the Deity. Doctor Middleton allows, in his preface, that, "in the first planting of the gospel, miraculous powers were wanted to enable the apostles the more easily to overrule the inveterate prejudices, both of Jews and Gentiles, and to bear up against the discouraging shocks of popular rage and persecution." May it not then reasonably be presumed that the same extraordinary powers were continued after the days of the apostles, while the same, and even greater prejudices existed, and while the popular rage and persecutions were even more violent?

5. The conduct of the primitive martyrs is another striking proof; their courage, constancy, and patience, accompanied with that astonishing spirit of meekness,

humility, charity, and joy in the midst of extreme sufferings, and the most exquisite torments, clearly show that there must have been a divine and supernatural power bestowed to support them in circumstances so trying, and to raise up human weakness to such amazing and heroic fortitude. Mr Brook dwells long upon this argument taken from the martyrs; but what is here quoted I consider to be the strength of what he says.

XXIX. After displaying these presumptive arguments, he concludes thus: " Dr Middleton, and every other man who professes himself a Christian, must allow that miracles were wrought in great abundance during the lives of the apostles; and that the Christian religion was at first published and propagated by an extraordinary providence. The question then will be, whether we have any probability of reason to conclude that the same extraordinary providence did continue after their decease? If the probability of an event is to be determined by the likelihood of its happening, and if that thing is allowed to be likely to happen which has frequently, and in a variety of instances, already come to pass: then it may reasonably be presumed that, if there were frequent interpositions of the Deity in the times of the apostles for manifest and important reasons, it is likely that, in the ages immediately succeeding to the apostolic, the same extraordinary interpositions should be continued, in similar cases, and where the same manifest and important reasons present themselves.

Probability, according to Mr Hume in his essay on miracles, "rises from a superiority of chances on any side; and according as this superiority increases and surpasses the opposite chances, the probability receiveth a proportionable increase, and begets a higher degree of belief or assent on that side in which we discover the superiority. Therefore, where an event has been frequently brought about, in particular circumstances, there is a probability of the same event being brought about again, in similar circumstances." In this manner Mr Brook displays the presumptive evidence for the continuation of miracles in the Church during the first three ages, the period which he assigns for their existence.

XXX. On examining these reasons, it appears that they may all be reduced to one ; the exigencies of the Christian Church, in the particular circumstances of those primitive ages, made it congruous that God should assist and protect her by supernatural and miraculous interpositions ; therefore it is reasonable to belive that He did so, especially as this is acknowledged to have been the case in the apostolic age, when the circumstances were similar.

XXXI. The same presumptive arguments are made use of by the other writers on this subject, only each one extends his energy to the particular period which he thinks fit to assign for the continuation of miracles, as Mr Brook here does to the first three ages. " It will be observed," says the Observator on the introductory discourse, page 25, " that this promise (viz., of working miracles) was not made to the apostles personally, but to them that should believe through their preaching, without any limitation of time for the continuance of these powers to their days. And when it is considered how great a part of the heathen world remained unconverted after their days, it is no unreasonable supposition that these powers did not expire with the apostles, but were continued to their successors in the work of propagating the Gospel."

To the same purpose, Le Moine, in the postscript to his work on miracles, says: "Our Saviour, before He left the world, promises these powers, not only to the apostles, but to private Christians. And as Christ's promise is without any limitation of time, we may reasonably suppose that they lasted as long as the Church had an immediate occasion for them, such as the farther conversion of the world. It is therefore highly probable, if not absolutely certain, that they did actually subsist in the Church for some considerable time after the days of the apostles." Thus these Protestant adversaries of Dr Middleton's system all agree in this principle, that the presumptive evidence for the continuation of miracles, drawn from the exigencies and necessities of the Church during the different periods they assign, is just and reasonable, and affords a very high probability that they actually did exist during these ages.

XXXII. But what is most surprising, even Dr Middleton himself agrees with them in this principle, and readily admits the force of this presumptive evidence for proof of the existence of miracles; only he craves the same liberty which they take of admitting its force during such a period of time as he thinks proper, and no farther; that is, he confines it to the apostolic age alone, instead of extending it to any succeeding period, as they do. Let us hear his own words: "My opinion," says he, "in short is this, that in those first efforts of planting the Gospel, after our Lord's ascension, the extraordinary gifts which He had promised were poured out in the fullest measure on the apostles, and those other disciples whom He had ordained to be the primary instruments of that great work, in order to enable them more easily to overrule the inveterate prejudices both of the Jews and Gentiles, and to bear up against the discouraging shocks of popular rage and persecution, which they were taught to expect in the novitiate of their ministry.

"But in process of time, when they had laid a foundation sufficient to sustain the great fabric designed to be erected upon it, and by an invincible courage had conquered the first and principal difficulties, and planted churches in all the chief cities of the Roman empire, and settled a regular ministry to succeed them in the government of the same; it may reasonably be presumed that, as the benefit of miraculous powers began to be less and less wanted, in proportion to the increase of those churches, so the use and exercise of them began gradually to decline; and as soon as Christianity had gained an establishment in every quarter of the known world, that they were finally withdrawn, and the Gospel left to make the rest of its way by its own genuine strength, and the natural force of those divine graces with which it was so richly stored, Faith, Hope, and Charity."

"All this, as far as I am able to judge from the nature of the gifts themselves, and from the instances or effects of them which I have any way observed, may probably be thought to have happened while some of the apostles were still living, who, even in the times of the Gospel, appear, on several occasions, to have been destitute of any extraordinary gifts; and of whose miracles, when we go beyond the limits of the Gospel, we meet with nothing in the later histories on which we can depend, or nothing rather but what is apparently fabulous." Pref. to the Inq., p. 26.

XXXIII. In these words the Doctor fairly acknowleges the three principal presumptive arguments used by Mr Brook. He grants that a sudden change from the plenitude of miracles, wrought at first by the apostles, to a total cessation of them, is not to be supposed; and therefore asserts that these powers were withdrawn gradually. He confesses that the necessities of the Gospel, at its first appearance, give a just presumption to believe that these powers continued till it was sufficiently established, and he allows that the circumstance of the times, at the first publication of the Gospel, made miracles necessary to overrule the prejudices and difficulties it had to encounter. The only difference is, that he confines these necessities of the Church within the narrow bounds of the apostolic age; whereas Mr Brook extends them to the first three centuries, as others do to the end of the fourth, fifth, or sixth. To act consistently, then, the Doctor must give some reasons why these presumptive arguments which he allows to have had so much weight in the first age, should have none at all after that period. He states his reasons, which we shall now examine, and see the replies made to them by his adversaries.

XXXIV. His first reason is against the argument drawn from the necessities of the Gospel, and consists in raillery, which is occasionally of very great service, especially in a bad cause: "They," says he, speaking of those who extend the promises of Christ of working miracles beyond the period he assigns,—"they appeal indeed to the text—where, though there is not the least hint of any particular time for which they (miracles) were to last, yet this they supply from their own imagination, and by the help of a postulatum, which all people will grant, that they continued as long as they were necessary to to the Church, they presently extend that necessity to what length they please, or as far as they find it agreeable to the several systems which they had previously entertained about them."—Pref. to Inq., p. 11 and 12.

To this ironical objection I find no direct reply made so far as I have seen by any of the Doctor's adversaries. I remark, however, that he here fairly grants that they are all guilty of what I have laid to their charge above, that is, of first adopting their particular systems, and then seeking reasons to support them. We have seen that this is the Doctor's own case, and that therefore he and they must stand or fall together. Hence we find that the very arguments which they use against one another are with equal force retorted against themselves.

In the promises which our Saviour made of miraculous powers to His disciples, as there is not the least hint as to the particular time of their extension, so neither is there of their limitation; it may therefore be justly retorted on the Doctor in his own words as follows: " This limitation he supplies from his own imagination, and by the help of a postulatum, which all people will grant, that miracles continued as long as they were necessary to the Church, and no longer, he presently limits that necessity to the apostolic age, as he found that most agreeable to the system he had previously entertained about them." And from this it is plain that the pretended necessity to which they all appeal is an argument turned to any side as these gentlemen please.

XXXV. His next argument is against the proof drawn from the heroic conduct of the martyrs, which he thinks may be easily accounted for from* motives of enthusiasm, a passion for glory and reputation; from the veneration paid to the sufferers if they survived the trial, the exalted happiness that awaited for them in heaven if they died under it, and the like. The improbability that such motives could produce the conduct which we see in the martyrs, is fully displayed by the writers against the Doctor; but the great argument against this objection

---

* Inquiry, 332 *et seq.*

is, that in the mouth of a heathen or of a deist, it has equal force against the argument drawn from the sufferings of Christ Himself, and the martyrdom of His apostles and others in the apostolic age, in proof of a supernatural dispensation manifested in them. "These considerations," says Mr Brook, "cannot be supposed to have had any more effect upon them (the martyrs after the apostles) than they had upon St Peter and St Paul, and some of the rest of the apostles, who met with the same affectionate treatment from their disciples."

A little after he adds, "It is no more an argument that no extraordinary assistances were granted to the primitive martyrs, because they had an assurance, not only of an immortality of glory, but of extraordinary and distinguished rewards, and of a degree of happiness proportionate to the degree of their suffering, than it is an argument that the Spirit of God did not rest upon Jesus, and in Him dwell the fulness of the Godhead bodily, because He endured the Cross, despising the shame for the glory that was set before Him: Or that no particular communications of God's Holy Spirit were vouchsafed to St Stephen, or no uncommon portions of divine grace were bestowed upon St Paul and the rest of the apostles, because in all their tribulations they had respect unto the recompense of reward, and esteemed those light afflictions, which were but for a moment, not worthy to be compared with the glory that was to be revealed," Brook's Exam., p. 42-44. Consequently, as the Doctor's objection proves too much against himself, and against the Christian religion, which he professes, it is justly rejected as proving nothing.

XXXVI. A third argument used by the Doctor is taken from the natural incredibility of miraculous facts, which in answering the objection against his system, as destructive to the credit of all history, he proposes as follows: "The history of miracles is of a kind totally different from that of common events; the one to be suspected always of course, without the strongest evidence to confirm it; the other to be admitted of course, without as strong reason to suspect it. Ordinary facts, related by a credible person, furnish no cause of doubting from the nature of the thing; but if they be strange and extraordinary, doubts naturally arise; and in proportion as they approach towards the marvellous, those doubts still increase and grow stronger; for mere honesty will not warrant them: we require other qualities in the historian," &c.—Free Inquiry, p. 350.

In answer to this argument, Mr Brook writes thus: "If the Free Inquiry had been the production of an infidel writer, it would be nothing strange to find frequent declarations in it that all miracles are to be suspected of course: that in all such extraordinary events doubts naturally arise, and in proportion as they approach towards the marvellous, those doubts still increase and grow stronger; the consequence of which declarations plainly appears to be, that an higher degree of evidence is required in such cases than any human testimony is able to afford. But in a writer of Dr Middleton's character, who must be supposed to believe all the miracles of the Gospel, and the wonderful propagation of the Christian religion, it is doubtless matter of great surprise to perceive that there have any expressions dropped from his pen which have the least tendency to such an opinion, or that can bear any such construction, or that may give any umbrage to a sincere believer: such a reflection upon the history and evidence of miracles will undermine the foundation of the Gospel history."—Examin., p. 52.

The force of this answer consists in this, that the miracles related in the ages immediately after the apostles are in themselves neither more extraordinary, nor more incredible, than those related in the Gospel. The presumptive evidence for them is as strong in the one case as in the other. If therefore those of the two succeeding ages are to be rejected on account of their supposed incredibility, those of the apostolic age must for a like reason share the same fate; for though the Doctor, as a Christian, may pretend to believe these last upon divine authority, yet a heathen or a deist will tell him that the divinity of the revelation depends upon the reality of the miracles, which are the chief proofs of that revelation, and therefore to be believed prior to the revelation; and that consequently the Doctor's argument against the miracles of these after-ages, from their natural incredibility when used by a heathen or a deist, has precisely the same force against those of the Gospel.

XXXVII. From all that we have said on the use made of the presumptive evidence for the continuation of miracles, I remark, 1. That as the Doctor and his adversaries all agree in allowing a just weight to this presumptive evidence during the periods in which they use it, if an equal, or far superior and better founded presumptive evidence, can be shown for the continuation of miracles after all their pretended periods, even down to the present times, or rather as long as the world shall endure, they cannot in reason reject it.

2. The Doctor's adversaries justly reject his reasons against their presumptive evidence for the continuation of miracles after the apostles, because they can be equally retorted against himself, and are plainly subversive of the very foundation of Christianity. But the

reasons which these gentlemen themselves bring against the continuation of miracles after the respective periods assigned by them, are either the very same, or of a similar nature to those brought by the Doctor; they can equally be retorted against themselves, and are equally subversive of Christianity. It follows, therefore, that all such reasoning can have no weight against the continuation of miracles beyond the periods assigned by them, and that notwithstanding all they have said, true miracles may have continued long enough after those assumed periods. This we shall afterwards clearly show; and in the mean time we proceed to consider what the Doctor and his opponents have said upon the positive testimony for the continuation of miracles.

XXXVIII. With regard to the Doctor, it is not easy to know what his opinion is concerning the nature of the testimony necessary to prove the existence of a miracle. He tells us, as we have just now seen, that the history of miracles is of a kind totally different from that of common events—that mere honesty in those who attest them will not warrant them; we require other qualities in the historian; a degree of knowledge, experience, and discernment sufficient to judge of the whole nature and circumstances of the case; and if any of these be wanting, we necessarily suspend our belief. —Inq., p. 351.

From this one might naturally imagine, that where all these qualities were found, there, at least, we should have a just and convincing attestation of the existence of a miracle. But by what follows he concludes that it is impossible we should rationally give credit to miracles, even where all these qualities appear in the one who attests them; for either this person who possesses these qualities, and attests the miracles, is a weak man, or a man of known abilities. "A weak man, indeed," says the Doctor, "if honest, may attest common events as credibly as the wisest; yet can hardly make any report that is credible of such as are miraculous; because a suspicion will always occur that his weakness and imperfect knowledge of the extent of human art had been imposed upon by the craft of cunning jugglers. On the other hand, should a man of known abilities and judgment relate to us things miraculous, or undertake to perform them himself, the very notion of his skill, without an assurance also of his integrity, would excite only the greater suspicion of him, especially if he had any interest to promote, or any favourite opinion to recommend by the authority of such works; because a pretension to miracles has, in all ages and nations, been found the most effectual instrument of impostors towards deluding the multitude and gaining their ends upon them."—Free Inq., ibid. From this whole passage it is evident that, in the Doctor's opinion, it is impossible that any human testimony should exist sufficient to convince us of the existence of miracles.

The folly of this opinion we have seen above; and, indeed, as Mr Brook justly observes, if the Doctor's reasoning in the above passage were true, it would "undermine the foundation of the Gospel history," because it would have the same strength in the mouth of a deist or a heathen against all the miracles related in the Scripture, as it has against miracles in general as used by the Doctor; for the heathen or deist would, with equal reason, say that either the sacred writers, who relate these miracles, were "weak men," or "men of known abilities," and in either case, according to the Doctor's mode of arguing, no credit could be given to their testimony, especially as they certainly had most "favourite opinions to recommend," and we can have no certain proof of their integrity but what is drawn from their own testimony.

However, that this is the Doctor's real opinion that no human testimony can form sufficient proof for the existence of miracles, not only appears from the above passage, but also from what he says in his preface concerning the concurrent testimony of church historians in all ages; "for there is not," says he, "a single point in all history so constantly, explicitly, and unanimously affirmed by them all, as the continual succession of miracles in every age down to the reformation; and it is farther deduced by persons of the most eminent character for their probity, learning, and dignity in the Roman Church to this very day." Here the Doctor fairly acknowledges the concurrence of these essential qualifications which he requires in those who attest miracles; men of the most eminent "probity and learning," or which is doubtless the same, "of the most eminent honesty, integrity and knowledge;" and yet he rejects their testimony, and would have us believe that all these men of characters so eminent in all ages, were only "crafty knaves and silly fools, from whom nothing candid or impartial can be expected" on this subject of miracles, whatever credit they deserve in other things which they relate.

Whether this be reasoning like a rational being I leave to the Doctor's admirers to decide. But as the argument used by him in the above quotation from this dilemma, that the persons attesting miracles are either "weak," or of "known abilities," may deceive by a show of reason, I refer to what I have said above, chap. xi. in examining the question, "Whether eyewitnesses themselves can have a convincing proof from their senses that the miracles they see really exist?" There it will appear that the Doctor's reasoning in the above passage is entirely founded on a false supposition that miracles are not plain facts, lying open to the testimony of the senses, of which the most simple and illiterate person is as able to judge as the most learned philosopher; whereas the contrary is undoubtedly the case with the generality of miracles, especially such as are principally referred to as proofs of doctrines.

XXXIX. The Doctor's Protestant adversaries, then, justly condemn this his opinion as subversive, not only of the faith and credit of all history, but of the Gospel itself, and therefore as altogether unworthy of a Christian, and utterly inexcusable in one who professes that name; and they lay down such qualifications and circumstances attending testimony, as render it a certain and unquestionable proof even of the existence of miracles, when it is accompanied by them. Some of their sentiments on this head we have seen above, chap. xi., when considering the nature of the proof for the existence of miracles; but as Mr Brook is particularly explicit upon it, I shall here relate the substance of his remarks.

"First," he justly observes, that "the validity of an evidence given to a matter of fact, either *viva voce*, or in writing, is not determined by the particular opinions which the witnesses may espouse in other matters, but by their knowledge of the things which they attest, and by their own integrity. In courts of civil judicature, where the nature of this evidence is best understood and most fairly examined, the character of a witness, and the competency of his knowledge as to the particular point under debate, is the only subject of inquiry, not his doctrines or persuasions. No distinction is made between a member of the Church of England

and a Sectarist; between a Romanist and a Protestant; between a Deist and a Christian. If their knowledge and veracity is unquestionable, the evidence of them all is admitted without exception. The same method is constantly pursued in all the dealings which men have with one another."

"The measures of credibility in historical facts are exactly of the same nature. The whimsical and extravagant doctrines of an historian, his strange and erroneous opinions in matters of speculation, do not at all affect the truth of his history, if his testimony as a witness, that is, if his knowledge and veracity be unexceptionable—and our want of belief in this case is not occasioned by want of evidence—but either by the force of some strong prejudices on the mind of the person to whom the thing is related, or by the improbability of the fact itself, which no human testimony is able to support. Whatever evidence is fair and reasonable in common historical facts will likewise be fair and reasonable in facts of an extraordinary and miraculous kind, if the nature and circumstances are such as not to render them liable to any material objection; for in such a case they are upon the same level with ordinary events, and therefore can require no higher degree of evidence."—Brook's Examin., chap. iv.

Secondly, he lays down the circumstances required in testimony, in order to render the evidence for miracles arising from it above all exception; which are, 1. When there is the concurrent testimony of various writers of different principles and persuasions, who lived in the very times when these facts happened, and were themselves eyewitnesses of them. Nothing, indeed, but the force of truth, and the reality of the things themselves, is able to create an agreement so unanimous and universal. 2. This becomes still stronger when it is confirmed by the testimony even of enemies themselves, and is contradicted by none. 3. When such testimony is given, and published to the world in the face of the most violent enemies, at a time when the truth of the facts attested might easily have been disproved, and a detection of the least fraud or fiction would most effectually have ruined the credit and authority of the witnesses, have heightened the malice of their adversaries, and have proved the lasting disgrace of their party. 4. All this is still more strongly corroborated when those who give the testimony profess it to be a firm tenet of their belief that every lie is criminal in the sight of God, and that he will not fail to punish those who speak untruths, even for the advancement of a good cause.

XL. From these principles, Mr Brook, with great reason, vindicates the miracles of the three first ages; because all the above circumstances concur in the testimony given by the fathers of those ages, for the existence of miracles in their days; whereas the exceptions made by Dr Middleton against their testimony are only taken from their particular opinions in speculative points, their mistakes in interpreting some parts of Scripture, their errors in the etymologies of language, their being misinformed regarding the authenticity of some books, and suchlike failings, of which the Doctor imagines he finds them guilty, and from which he concludes that they were all knaves or fools; and that their testimony for the existence of miracles which fell under the observation of their own senses, is absolutely unworthy of credit, even though attended with all the above circumstances.

This conclusion is justly set aside by Mr Brook, and the Doctor's other Protestant adversaries; and indeed we are surprised to see such an argument published to the world by a person of Dr Middleton's powers and penetration. But what could he do? The testimony for the continuation of miracles in each succeeding age, down to the present time, was equally strong, and equally attended by every corroborating circumstance, with those of the ages immediately succeeding the apostles; and therefore, if human testimony was admitted to be a sufficient proof of the miracles in the primitive ages, it could never be refused as an equal proof of those in all succeeding ages, which would be giving up the cause at once in favour of Popery. He was under a necessity, therefore, of producing some arguments for rejecting the testimony of all ages, and was forced to take the above, as his cause could furnish nothing better. These, indeed, he produces in the most specious form, and in the most persuasive manner, in order to conceal their weakness. But these were not the reasons by which he himself was persuaded. He had already taken up his opinion before he had invented the reasons. The true ground of his sentiments he himself expresses in these words: "If the cause must be determined by the unanimous consent of the fathers, we shall find as much reason to believe these miraculous powers were continued even to the latest ages as to any other, how early and primitive soever after the days of the apostles," Pref. p. xiv., and therefore, "by granting them (the Romanists) but a single age of miracles after the times of the apostles, we shall be entangled in a series of difficulties whence we can never fairly extricate ourselves, till we allow the same powers also to the present age."—Introd., p. lxxxii

XLI. We must now take a short review of the principles and proceedings of the Doctor and his adversaries. The principles in which they all agree, at least in appearance, and upon which they all proceed, are these: "Christianity must be defended; Popery must be condemned; whatever is necessary for the defence of Christianity must be admitted; whatever tends to establish Popery must be rejected." The Doctor thinks Christianity will be sufficiently defended if the apostolic miracles be admitted as founded on divine testimony; but that Popery must be established if miracles be admitted in any one age after the apostles on the credit of human testimony. He rejects, therefore, all the miracles recorded after the apostolic age, and declares in plain terms, as his reason for so doing, that miracles are of so peculiar a nature that no human testimony can render them credible; or, in other words, that their innate incredibility is such as cannot be overcome by human testimony.

Mr Brook is of opinion that Christianity cannot stand if the miracles of the first three centuries be rejected; they must therefore be defended. But if those of the succeeding ages were admitted, Popery would be established, and, therefore, they must be disproved. He of course rejects the Doctor's system with respect to the first three centuries; because it would destroy the credit of history and undermine the Gospel: and he rejects his argument from the incredibility of miracles, because, in the mouth of a heathen or a deist, it would with equal strength condemn the miracles of the Scripture itself. He holds, therefore, that miracles, as such, are as capable of proof from human testimony as any other natural event, except they be of such an incredible nature, either in themselves, or in their circumstances, as no human testimony can support. He asserts that the miracles of the first three centuries were by no means of this incredible nature, and therefore, that their existence is evident, from the testimony of the fathers, which is attended with every circumstance to render it undoubted.

But as he thinks that Popery would be established if miracles were allowed after the third age, he endeavours to show that the miracles of the after ages were all of this incredible nature, either in themselves or in their circumstances; and therefore not to be believed upon any human testimony whatever. Those who believe in the continuation of miracles to the end of the fourth century, act in the same manner. They see no such incredibility in the miracles of the fourth age, as appeared to Mr Brook, which could not with equal reason be urged against those of the former three. It is plain to them that the human testimony by which they are supported is, in every respect, equivalent to that on which Mr Brook admits those of the first three centuries, which, therefore, they affirm, cannot be rejected, without falling into the same shocking consequences which he so justly imputes to Dr Middleton's system, and thus they admit the miracles of the fourth age upon the very same principles, and for the same reason, that Mr Brook admits those of the preceding ages. But as it does not suit their purpose to allow miracles after the fourth century, they reject those of the fifth and succeeding ages, exactly as Mr Brook rejects those of the fourth.

Those who allow the continuation of miracles to the end of the fifth or sixth centuries, proceed in the same manner, both in admitting them to those periods, and in rejecting them entirely after. It now remains, therefore, to be shown, that the same arguments used to prove a continuation of miracles to the periods assigned by each of these systems, have equal strength to prove that continuation down to this present day; and that the pretended incredibility of the miracles in after ages is as groundless in itself, and as insufficient to invalidate the force of the testimony for them, as it is against those of any of the first ages, or even against those of the Scripture itself.

CHAPTER XIII.

REASONS AGAINST THE CONTINUATION OF MIRACLES EXAMINED.

I. SO convincing is human testimony, when the witnesses have a thorough knowledge of the facts, and are persons of known integrity, that no one would seriously call it in question; and if this testimony be attended with the corroborating circumstances mentioned by Mr Brook in the preceding chapter, it gives as full and invincible evidence of the facts attested as we have in the sciences from the strictest demonstration. This is acknowledged in the ordinary affairs of life, and is allowed even in proof of miracles by all the Protestant adversaries of Dr Middleton's system, to be as thorough evidence as a reasonable man can demand, or the nature of things will admit. But these gentlemen were well aware that in the Catholic Church perfect testimony can be produced for the continuation of miracles in every age even to the present time, and generally attended also with all or most of the corroborating circumstances abovementioned. They were obliged therefore to find some restrictive argument wherewith to diminish the force of such testimony when it told against them, and to show why the miracles said to have happened after their assumed periods should not be believed, even though attested by the most perfect human testimony.

The argument which they have chosen for this purpose has indeed a formidable appearance, and at first sight may seem to be unanswerable. It is no less than the natural incredibility of the facts attested; and what possible force of human testimony can persuade us of a thing which is in itself incredible? "The present question," says Dr Middleton, "concerning the miraculous powers of the primitive Church, depends on the joint credibility of the facts pretended to have been produced by these powers, and of the witnesses who attest them. If either part be infirm, their credit must sink in proportion; and, if the facts especially be incredible, must of course fall to the ground; because no force of testimony can alter the nature of things."—Pref., p. x.

Mr Brook readily agrees to this assertion, adopts it as a first principle in the present question, and, whilst he admits and defends the invincible force of testimony in commanding our assent even to miracles, he makes this the single exception: "Our belief," says he, "of past matters of fact, whether ordinary or extraordinary, against which there lies no reasonable exception from the nature of things, rests entirely upon testimony." And a little after, "Whatever evidence," says he, "is fair and reasonable in common historical facts, will likewise be fair and reasonable in facts of an extraordinary and miraculous kind, if the nature and circumstances of these facts are such as not to render them liable to any material objection."—Brook's Examin., chap. iv.

It is upon this ground, as we have seen above, that Dr Middleton rejects all miracles whatever that rest only upon human testimony, and admits none but those contained in the Word of God; and it is upon this ground precisely that the Doctor's adversaries reject all miracles recorded to have happened after the respective periods which they are pleased to assign for the duration of miracles in the Church. Their whole reasoning is reduced to these two points, that the miracles recorded before the time assigned by them for their cessation, were by no means incredible or improbable; and this they endeavour to show against Dr Middleton in defence of Christianity; but that all miracles said to have happened after the period which they fix, were absolutely incredible, and therefore not to be believed, however supported by human testimony; and this they maintain against Catholics.

Mr Brook is particularly earnest in displaying this argument, and has collected all that can be said in defence of it. It is necessary, therefore, to examine him attentively, in order to see the real worth of this boasted argument, upon which the issue of this important question in a great measure depends. For if it is found to be of sterling value, and the miracles of after ages are shown to be absolutely incredible, Catholics must give up the cause, and yield the victory to their adversaries; but if it can be proved absolutely inconsistent both with common sense and Christianity, then the perpetual duration of the miraculous powers in the Catholic Church will shine forth in full lustre, and the authority of the testimony on which it is supported must command our ready acquiescence.

II. The first thing to be remarked in this argument from the incredibility of the facts attested, is that it proceeds upon a supposition contradicted by common sense, and which is in itself a palpable absurdity. Here the precise point in question is this, "Whether or not a fact absolutely incredible in itself can possibly be believed, when attested by witnesses who are acknowledged to be competent judges of the truth, and people of known probity and integrity; and when their testimony is attended with those corroborating circumstances which carry with them the highest conviction?" Dr Middleton readily answers, that the credit of such a fact, however attested, must fall to the gronnd, for this plain reason, "Because no force of testimony can alter the nature of things;" in which he evidently shows, that by the incredibility of a fact he understands its impossibility; and indeed common sense shows that in the whole question "incredible" and "impossible" are synonymous terms; for if the fact fully attested, as above, be a possible fact, then it would be ridiculous to say it was incredible. You may call it "surprising, astonishing, extraordinary," or what you please, but you can never call it "incredible;" for no fact, possible in itself, can be incredible, when its existence is actually proved by the fullest evidence which the nature of the thing can bear, and is supposed to be the work of omnipotence. If the fact be possible, such evidence for its existence renders it fully credible, and commands our assent.

Let us then propose the question again, and substitute "impossible" for "incredible," and see how it appears. It will run thus: "Whether or not a fact absolutely impossible in itself can be believed, when attested by witnesses acknowledged to be competent judges of the truth, and persons of known probity and integrity, and when their testimony is attended with those corroborating circumstances which carry with them the highest conviction?" What answer would common sense give? Doubtless it would smile at such a question, and at once deny the supposition as a mere chimera, an absolute impossibility. For how could such a case ever possibly exist? How could an absolute falsehood ever procure such a testimony? How is it possible that men of known probity and integrity could ever combine to attest as a truth, and, consistent with their own knowledge, a fact which is absolutely "impossible in itself," and therefore absolutely false? How is it possible they could do so in the face of the world, and in the midst of their enemies, without having their folly exposed, and themselves rendered contemptible?

This would doubtless be the language of common sense; and with reason; for the testimony described is a certain and undoubted effect produced, and actually existing. This effect must have had an adequate cause producing it; and this cause could be no other than the actual existence of the fact so attested; for it is evidently impossible that such testimony should be given to a falsehood. If, therefore, the fact itself be supposed to be incredible, and therefore impossible, to suppose it supported by such a testimony is itself a mere chimera, an absurd supposition.

The consequence of all this is, that wherever any fact, however uncommon or miraculous it may appear, is in reality attested by such testimony as above described, it is unworthy of a philosopher to pretend to reject such testimony from any supposed incredibility in the fact so attested. A fact in itself impossible, and therefore no fact at all, can never be supported by such testimony; and a possible fact, when so attested, is by that very testimony rendered perfectly credible and worthy of belief. Hence, then, the only rational conduct in all such cases is diligently to examine the testimony, both as to the knowledge and veracity of the witnesses. If any flaw be found there, then indeed the credit of their attestation falls to the ground, whether the fact be supposed credible or incredible. But if the testimony stands its ground; if the witnesses are competent judges of what they narrate;

if they attest it as of their own knowledge, and in circumstances in which they must have been detected had what they said been false; and if they be persons of known integrity and worth; if the testimony upon the strictest scrutiny be found to be of this kind, then if we listen to the voice of reason, and our minds be not warped by passion or prejudice, it will be impossible to withhold our assent from the fact so attested.

III. But in order thoroughly to refute this unphilosophical argument, let us imagine the possibility of the case proposed. Let us suppose that a fact absolutely impossible in itself, and therefore absolutely false, should be attested by the evidence of human testimony, such as we have above described, and what would be the consequence? why, truly the very same as that on account of which Dr Middleton's Protestant adversaries cry out against his system, and so loudly condemn it; namely, that all faith in history would be destroyed, the credit of the Gospel undermined, and universal scepticism introduced. For upon what is our belief of past or distant facts grounded? Upon the credit of human testimony, and because such is the constitution of our nature, that when testimony is of the nature above described, and attended with the corroborating circumstances there mentioned, we are powerfully influenced to believe it from the interior conviction that such testimony in the circumstances cannot deceive us.

But if, for a moment, we suppose it possible—as in the above case—that testimony of this kind, attended with all its corroborating circumstances, may, in any one case, be given to an absolute falsehood, then it may be given to another also, and if so, to all. Consequently we cannot be certain of truth in any case, and the natural inclination which we feel to believe upon proper testimony is a false principle, upon which we can no longer depend with safety. What a multitude of false and fatal consequences would follow in particular cases if this were so? How false, then, the supposition which would produce them!

Let it not be said that human testimony may safely be trusted in ordinary events, and is to be rejected only on account of the incredibility of the facts attested. For, if we thus suppose it possible for a fact absolutely incredible, and therefore absolutely false, to be attended with such a testimony as above described, surely an ordinary event no way incredible in itself, may much more easily procure such testimony, even though it be a pure fiction. It is much more probable, for example, that men should invent and attest as a truth a thing ordinary or common, against which there lies no suspicion, than a thing naturally incredible, which is more likely to render their testimony suspected, and expose them to the shame of detection: consequently, if we suppose it possible that the fullest testimony should ever be given to a thing in itself impossible, and upon that account false, much more possible will it be for such testimony to be given to a falsehood regarding an ordinary event, which in itself contains no improbability; and such a possibility of falsehood attending the fullest testimony, must, of course, render precarious all such testimony, and prevent us from being thoroughly persuaded of anything whatsoever founded on it. And if so, what becomes of history? what becomes of the Gospel? what becomes of Christianity? And, in reality, will not this very argument against miracles, in any age, from their natural incredibility, or, in other words, impossibility, if it has any weight at all, militate equally in the mouth of a deist or heathen against those of the whole Scripture? Nay, is not this the very argument used by these gentlemen against Scripture miracles? and are not all the answers given to it by the defenders of the Scripture founded upon this very supposition, that it is impossible that full and perfect testimony, attended with all its corroborating circumstances, should ever be given to an absolute falsehood, much less to any fact in itself impossible?

Observe, then, how Mr Brook, and others who pretend to limit the duration of miracles in the Church of Christ to any of their assumed periods, are obliged to use such arguments as are evidently productive of all those fatal consequences for which they so loudly condemn Dr Middleton's argument, are subversive of history, of the Gospel itself, and in the mouth of a heathen would serve as strongly against all Scripture miracles as against any others. Happily, however, they are powerless, because, when duly considered, they are found to be destitute of common sense, and to proceed upon a supposition manifestly false and chimerical.

IV. Against what has been said, two objections will perhaps be offered with Dr Middleton from experience (see his 'Inquiry,' p. 351.), and the following: First, "There is not," says he, "a single historian of antiquity, whether Greek or Latin, who has not recorded oracles, prodigies, prophecies, and miracles; many of these are attested in the gravest manner, and by the gravest writers, and were firmly believed at the time by the populace; yet it is certain that there is not one of them which we can reasonably take to be genuine; not one that was not either wholly forged, or improved and exaggerated into something supernatural." Secondly, "The case of witchcraft," says he, "affords the most effectual proof of what I am advancing. There is not in all history any one miraculous fact so authentically attested as the existence of witches. All Christian nations whatsover have consented in the belief of them, and provided capital laws against them: now to deny the reality of facts so solemnly attested, and so universally believed, seems to give the lie to the sense and experience of all Christendom; yet the incredibility of the thing prevailed, and was found at last too strong for all this force of human testimony: so that the belief of witches is now utterly extinct and quietly buried." Here, it will perhaps be said, we have two examples from experience, where the fullest human testimony was given to facts utterly incredible, and which afterwards were found to be absolutely false. Therefore, as what has actually happened is certainly possible, and may happen again, it is far from being absurd or chimerical to suppose that facts absolutely incredible may yet be attended by the fullest human testimony; and when that is the case, the incredibility of the fact must invalidate all the force of the testimony, however strong in itself, and however well supported by circumstances.

V. The proper answer to this objection is to examine the two cases, to see if they really be to the point or not. With regard to the first, taken from the prodigies, oracles, and miracles among the heathens, to proceed with requisite clearness we must distinguish the fact related from the nature and causes of it. This distinction we have already made and shall again have occasion to make in reference to all miracles. The fact itself, properly speaking, is the only object of the senses, and consequently of human testimony. The nature and causes of it, —that is, whether it be natural or miraculous, whether from causes natural or supernatural,—this is properly a subject for the judgment to investigate. Sometimes this will appear even at first sight, at other times it will require attentive examination, in which the rules of the criterion serve to guide us.

Now as to the facts themselves referred to in the first case proposed, I ask, were any of them in reality attested by such human testimony as we are here speaking of? Are they related by authors of known integrity, who themselves were either eyewitnesses of these facts or had full opportunity of ascertaining the truth, and had used it? If they be indeed attended by such evidence, I believe every reasonable man will allow that they were undoubtedly true, and really had existence as attested. As to their nature and causes, whatever the witnesses of the facts may have said of these, is only their opinion, not their testimony. But if, on the other hand, these facts have never been attested in the manner above described; if they be only related as hearsays and popular reports, or, though gravely related, and even believed by the historian himself, yet if it be manifest that he believes them not from his own personal knowledge, nor even from a full examination of their truth, but has been carried away by the common current, then the case is beside the question, and not at all to the purpose; all the reasoning of the Doctor upon it is only vain beating the air. But, says he, "these facts, though fully believed, are now found to be false." True; but how is their falsehood discovered? not from their incredibility, whilst the testimony by which they are supported is allowed to be good. By no means; but solely by showing the insufficiency and weakness of the testimony.

VI. We come now to the other example taken from the belief in witches; and here it is amazing to see how far the Doctor, who professes himself a Christian, and expresses so high a veneration for the Bible, should forget himself. According to the manner in which he represents this case, the existence of witches is a thing absolutely incredible, and the belief in them is now utterly extinct; and yet we find their existence attested again and again by the very word of God itself. In it we find most severe laws enacted against them; and all recourse to them for help of any kind condemned and utterly forbidden. Nay, in the New Testament we find that the "portion of sorcerers" in the next world "shall be a lake of burning fire and brimstone, which is the second death."[*] Can it then be true, as the Doctor so confidently asserts, that the belief in witches, though thus attested by God Himself, is absolutely incredible, and that it is at present utterly exploded in the world? If so, what becomes of the Christian religion?—for if the testimony of God Himself proves false with regard to the existence of witches, it may be false also with regard to the incomprehensible mysteries and miracles of the Gospel: nay, this is what deists and heathens absolutely affirm. Did Dr Middleton reflect on the contents of his Bible when he made this objection? I scarcely think he did, or at least for his own honour, if he had no regard for the honour of God, he never would have made it.

VII. It is evident, then, that the boasted objection against the existence of miracles, from their supposed incredibiltiy, is a mere sophism, proceeding upon a supposition not only false, but impossible; for if the fact attested be possible, and the testimony unexceptionable, such attestation renders it perfectly credible. And if the fact be impossible, it is equally impossible that it should be attested by unexceptionable testimony; for it is impossible that a fact should be consistent with the knowledge of the witnesses, if it neither had, nor possibly

[*] See above, Chap. II. where this is treated at large.

could have any existence. Neither can it be supposed that men in their senses would combine to give out and attest, as consistent with their own knowledge, what they knew not only to be false, but an impossibility, as this very circumstance must immediately expose them to detection, and to the utmost shame and infamy.

VIII. Here then we might justly conclude this argument; for as the only reason brought against the existence of the fully attested miracles of after-ages, is their supposed incredibility, if this falls to the ground, as we have seen it does, no just exception can be taken against them. When sufficiently attested, they are undoubtedly to be admitted. But as great stress is laid upon this argument, and as several different kinds of incredibility are advanced in its support, I shall examine each of them in particular, as stated by Mr Brook.

First, however, it will be necessary to discover, if possible, what these gentlemen themselves mean by incredibility, and what is the precise idea which they attach to the word. I do not find that they give an exact definition of it; and from their writings it would seem that they are not agreed about its meaning; nay, there is reason to think that it is used by the same person in different senses, as best suits his purpose.

IX. To begin with Dr Middleton: In the quotation from the Free Inquiry given above, chap. xii. § 38, from the conditions of testimony which he there requires to prove the existence of any miraculous fact, it would appear to be his opinion that this incredibility is something real arising from just causes, and natural to every miracle whatever. But in his remarks on the Observator, p. 40, he entirely changes his opinion, and represents it as a mere ideal appearance, seated in our imagination; for the Observator having alleged that those miracles which are not incredible in themselves ought always to be admitted when sufficiently attested, and those only rejected which are in themselves incredible, the Doctor replies: "To say that, where the facts themselves are incredible, such miracles are to be rejected, is to beg the question and not to prove it; a too precarious way of reasoning! because what is incredible to me may seem credible to another." Here, then, according to the Doctor, the credibility or incredibility of a miracle is just as we fancy it to be; and is this a reasonable ground to overrule the utmost weight of human testimony?

X. Mr Brook, who treats this subject more at large in the first chapter of his Examination, speaking of the presumptive evidence for the miracles of the first three centuries, expresses himself thus: "What may with great plausibilility of reason be urged against the miracles of the fourth and fifth centuries, can here have no place. There is no ridiculousness or incredibility in the miracles themselves which are said to have been wrought: there is no impertinence, absurdity, or impiety in the ends for which they are supposed to have been performed, to shock the faith of a true Christian, or to raise any suspicion of the miraculousness of these facts: there is no apparent reason against our belief of miracles in those days: there is a strong presumption of their truth and reality: the miraculousness of those events which are recorded by the primitive writers of the Church is no objection to the credibility of them. We can discover manifestly the propriety and necessity of divine interpositions from the circumstances of those times; and where such a propriety and necessity appears, no Christian can have any reasonable objection to the belief of them; for every Christian, from the nature of his profession, must be supposed to think that the working of miracles is no way inconsistent with the idea of that God whom he serveth."

In these words, which are an abridgment of his sixth chapter, against the continuance of miracles after the third century, we find all that can well be said of the incredibility of any miracle. From this, then, I shall endeavour to put the true meaning of this term in its proper light, that we may form a distinct idea of it, and not bewilder our minds by any ambiguity. We shall thus be the better able to judge what weight it ought to have in the present argument.

XI. A miracle, then, is incredible when, for solid reasons, it cannot possibly obtain belief from a reasonable person. This incredibility may be conceived to arise from two causes, either from the fact itself, or from the circumstances in which it is said to have been performed. The uncommon nature of the fact, its amazing greatness, however stupendous, can never render it incredible in itself, unless it involve a contradiction, and be absolutely impossible; because, where Omnipotence is supposed to be the agent, nothing that is possible can be in itself incredible, as is plain to common sense. The incredibility, then, of the fact is in reality the same thing with its impossibility.

Again, the incredibility of any possible fact will arise from its circumstances, when they are such as to render it unworthy of Almighty God, or contrary to His divine perfections to perform it. This may be termed a moral, and the former a physical incredibility; and these two comprehend the whole idea attached by Mr Brook to this word, in all he states in the above quotation. The circumstances supposed by him to render a fact incredible which is in itself possible, are various and of different kinds. Some of the most remarkable we have already considered when treating on the "Ends and Instruments of Miracles." I shall here examine the others with the particular application made of them by Mr Brook, and shall expose their weakness and fatal consequences.

He observes that in the first three centuries there were manifest reasons of necessity and expediency for the good of the Church, which made it becoming that Almighty God should work many miracles, but that all those ceased at least from the days of Chrysostom. "Now, as the concurrence of Providence," says he, "is never wanting upon important and necessary occasions, so it is never exercised in a superfluous and impertinent manner;" and therefore this change of circumstances in the necessities of the Church gives every reason to believe that miracles were then withdrawn." In answer to this I observe, that all the reasons of necessity and expediency, produced by Mr Brook in his chapter on the presumptive evidence for the miracles of the first three ages, are reduced to this one: "The propagation of Christianity at the beginning required the help of miracles;" from which he argues thus: "When Christianity was propagated and established, it required them no longer; therefore they were then withdrawn." Here it is supposed, "that Christianity stood in need of miracles only for its propagation among the heathens;" and, "that this need of Christianity is the only reason worthy of God for which to work miracles."

The latter of these, when speaking of the ends of miracles, we have seen to be a manifest falsehood; the former we shall afterwards see is equally untrue, when we come to consider the presumptive reasons for the continuation of miracles; and, consequently, this reason for the incredibility of the miracles of after ages is of no value. Besides, this argument in the mouth of a heathen or deist would equally prove that no miracles were wrought among the people of God in the old law after their full establishment in the land of promise; for whatever reasons of necessity or expediency might be produced as presumptive proofs for the miracles wrought by God in establishing that religion, all these had entirely ceased; and, therefore, according to this argument, miracles after that period become utterly incredible, for " Providence never concurs in a superfluous and impertinent manner!"

XII. His second reason against the credibility of the miracles of the after-ages is from their number. "The number of the miracles," says he, "pretended to have been wrought in the fourth and fifth centuries is itself another just exception to the truth and credibility of them." This is a singular argument; however, he adds his reasons. "It may reasonably be presumed," says he, "that as the benefit of miraculous powers began to be less and less wanted in proportion to the increase and power of the Christians, so the use and exercise of them began gradually to decline; at least it cannot, I think, fairly be imagined, that as the real exigencies of the Church were continually lessening, miracles should become still more and more numerous; yet, in fact, we find, if the writers of these ages deserve any credit, that the power of working miracles was more extensive and universal in the time of Chrysostom and afterwards than in the days of the apostles themselves. Nor was the benefit of these miracles confined to societies of men only; it extended itself even to the caves and dens of beasts; the wonder-workers of those days, retired from the company and converse of their fellow-creatures, fixed their abodes in mountainous and desert places, and made the brute creation sensible of the extraordinary power and presence of the Almighty."—Brook's Examin., p. 302, &c.

XIII. If this were divested of its declamatory style, and reduced to a proper form of argument, it would be difficult to show any connection between its premises and the consequences drawn from them; but permitting that to pass, I observe on this passage: First, That it proceeds upon the same false supposition as the former argument, "That the propagation of the Christian religion is the only end worthy of God for which to work miracles;" for though the increase and power of the Christians made miracles less necessary in one respect, yet if, besides the propagation of religion, there be many other exigencies which require the help of miracles, then the above argument falls to the ground.

Secondly, Whether all the miracles related by the writers of these ages be true or false, is not to the point, and quite beside the question. Nobody pretends to maintain all and every one of them. Many of them may have been perfectly true, although full and unexceptionable testimony of their being so has not been handed down to us. All these, then, however numerous, are given up at once. We have to deal only with those for the truth and reality of which full and unexceptionable testimony can be produced. Now, how ridiculous is it to say, "There are great numbers of miracles related to have been performed in the fourth, fifth, and following ages, for the truth of which we have not at present full and proper evidence; therefore all those in these ages for which we have the most undoubted testimony of the gravest authors, and of eyewitnesses, are to be rejected as false and counterfeit!" and this is the full force of the argument, if it has any force at all.

Thirdly, It is false to assert that, according to the writers of these ages, "miracles became more extensive and more numerous after the days of Chrysostom than in the days of the apostles." In the days of the apostles, and during the first three ages, the chrismatic gifts of the Holy Ghost were poured out on all the faithful, and the visible effects of His divine presence and assistance were accomplished in speaking with tongues and prophesying, and in other miraculous operations in almost every Christian. This Mr Brook himself has proved at large in his chapter on the persons endowed with miraculous powers; and, to confirm what he says, he cities Mr Dodwell as follows: "Were we to run through all the testimonies above cited, from Justin Martyr, Irenæus, &c., we should find that they speak of the whole body of Christians, great and small, as endowed with these gifts on any signal occasion; but they insist particularly on the performance of them by those who had the least natural endowments, as the mighty hand of God was most visible when it displayed itself by the meanest instruments," &c.

Now it is certain that this universal communication of these gifts was withdrawn long before the days of Chrysostom, and that they were bestowed in a less conspicuous manner chiefly upon those holy persons who, secluding themselves from the corruptions of the world, studied only to render their souls acceptable to their Creator, and were thereby disposed for receiving these supernatural powers and graces. The real case is this, that after the conversion of the Roman emperors, learned Christian writers became more numerous than in the former ages, and greater portions of their writings have been transmitted to our days. In these writings many more miracles have been recorded than in those of the first three centuries; because both the number of authors, the quantity of their works, and the variety of their subjects, were much greater; but had all the several miracles of the first three centuries been committed to writing, there would certainly be no comparison as to their number; so our author here departs from truth in his representation of the case, and consequently his witticisms only serve to condemn himself.

Fourthly, The same mode of arguing, in the mouth of a deist and heathen, would equally serve to prove that the numerous miracles wrought by Elijah and Elisha, some of which were performed in the desert, were all fictitious. Put Jews instead of Christians, the exigencies of the synagogue for those of the Church, the times of Elijah and Elisha for the days of Chrysostom,—and the above-cited argument of Mr Brooks against the miracles of the fourth and fifth ages will equally serve the purpose of a heathen and a deist against those performed by these two great prophets. It will have exactly the same force, if displayed by the pen of a Middleton, against those of the three first centuries, for which Mr Brook so strenuously contends; and consequently, in proving too much it proves in fact nothing at all.

XIV. His third argument against the credibility of miracles related in the fourth and fifth ages, is singular, and composed of misrepresentation and sophistry. In the fourth century arose the Arian heresy,—one of the most dangerous that ever attacked the Christian religion. It consisted in denying the divinity of Jesus Christ, and in proclaiming Him to be a mere creature. The abettors of this doctrine were numerous, and many of them were persons of the highest authority and power, both in

Church and State. They spared no pains, shrunk from no crime to promote the interest of their party, and used every ungenerous and base art to calumniate and persecute the Catholics. The Catholics, on the other hand, opposed to the utmost of their power this torrent of impiety then pouring in upon the Church. Their zealous pastors, by word, writing, and their apostolic labours, endeavoured to confirm the faithful, to refute impiety, and to defend the honour of their Lord and Master. Many of the pastors, as well as of the people, suffered persecution, imprisonment, banishment, and even martyrdom itself, in testimony of the divinity of Jesus.

Certainly, if ever the exigencies of the Church required the protection of miracles for the attestation of the truth, the comfort of her children, and the confirmation of the faithful, it was at this time, when all the power of the Roman emperors was employed to undermine the very foundation of her faith, by an attack more dangerous perhaps than had ever been made against it by the heathens. Accordingly we find many remarkable miracles performed by orthodox pastors in defence of the Catholic faith. These are attested by men of the highest character for their integrity and sanctity, who were themselves eye-witnesses. They were performed not in secret, and afterwards related to the world, but in public, before multitudes, in the face of the world, in presence of the very Arians themselves, who lacked neither will nor ability to detect fraud or imposture, had there been any. Their effects were to confound the Arians, to stop their fury, and often even to convert them. More ample proof, both of presumptive evidence and positive testimony, cannot certainly be produced for miracles in any preceding age than for those performed upon this occasion; and yet, according to Mr Brook's logic, they were all frauds and impostures. To prove this, he represents the zeal and fervour of the orthodox pastors in defence of the divinity of Jesus Christ as merely the effect of pride and ambition, at least as much so as was the conduct of the Arians.

"During this long contest," says he, "which was managed with all the animosity and fury that the most bigoted and inflamed zeal could produce; when each party seemed more solicitous about their own power and authority than about the doctrines they espoused; when the whole struggle between them was more for conquest and dignity than for the sake of truth itself,—it is highly probable that, in many cases where private arguments and public decrees had not the desired success, appeals were made to a pretended divine power as openly exerted in confirmation of them."

In support of this assertion in regard of the Arians, he relates that Philostorgius the Arian has recorded numerous miracles as performed by the chiefs of that heresy; "all which" he tells us, in the judgment of that learned and accurate critic Photius, who has preserved a compendium of Philostorgius' history, "were mere forgeries, and inserted in his history only with the design to countenance and support the party in which he was engaged." Then to show that the Catholics were guilty of the like appeals to pretended miracles, he cites three or four miracles related in their favour, and, without finding the least flaw in the testimony regarding them, or even pointing out a single circumstance or reason to prove them forgeries, he only says in general that "their circumstances give us the strongest reason to suspect they were forged by the Homöousians in favour of their particular tenets,"—that is, by the orthodox Christians in favour of the divinity of Jesus Christ. From the above pretended probability, and the supposed reasons of suspicion, he draws this final conclusion: "Now it is not to be supposed but the same principles of zeal which induced either the Arians or Athanasians to commit the above-mentioned forgeries to propagate these and such-like fictitious stories, would extend itself to their other relations of the extraordinary kind that were made to serve the same purposes; and accordingly must render them all justly suspected."—Brook's Exam., chap. vi.

XV. It is certainly astonishing to see how industrious the mind of man is to blind and deceive itself when engaged in a bad cause. Of this the reasoning of Mr Brook is a striking instance; for charity will not allow me to suppose that he saw its disengenuousness and malice. He lays the foundation of his argument by strangely misrepresenting the conduct of the Catholic and orthodox party; and from this misrepresentation he supposes as highly probable that appeals would be made by both sides to miracles, to a pretended divine power exerted in favour of their respective tenets. The weakest judgment cannot fail to see the folly of such a supposition, and how contrary it is to common sense; for if the "contest was carried on with all the animosity and fury that the most bigoted and inflamed zeal could produce," how is it possible that either party should appeal to "pretended miracles" as openly exerted in their favour, without exposing themselves to inevitable detection and confusion? For would not the other party have immediately exposed such pretended miracles? Would they not have discovered the fraud, detected the forgery, and made a most powerful use of such pretences to confound their adversaries? Nay, is not this the very argument that

Mr Brook himself employs to prove the reality of the miracles of the preceding centuries, that they were performed in the presence of enemies who lacked neither will nor power to detect them, had they not been real? And is not this one of the very corroborating circumstances required by him to give human testimony its highest authority and value? But he proceeds to prove that this was actually the case, and tells us that Philostorgius, the Arian historian, has recorded many miracles said to have been performed by that party, which, according to the testimony of the great and learned Photius, were all forged and recorded by him only to serve a purpose. Then he mentions several said to have been done on the other hand, in favour of the Catholic doctrine, which, in his opinion, are no less fictitious than the former. Here is another gross misrepresentation. The Catholics did indeed appeal to miracles, real, not pretended ones; miracles performed in the presence of multitudes, and for the reality of which the fullest evidence of human testimony has been handed down to our days, and which were never contradicted nor called in question, even by the Arians themselves. Of these Mr Brook takes no notice.

The Arians seeing the advantage which the Catholics drew from these undeniable interpositions of Almighty God in their favour, had recourse to the same arms, and pretended that miracles had been wrought also by some of their party. But what was the consequence? Whilst the splendour of the miracles wrought in favour of the truth made the Catholic doctrine triumph over all its enemies, the pretensions of the Arians served only to confound them, and to bring disgrace and contempt upon their party; just as in our own days the same pretences to miracles in the Jansenists served more than anything else to open men's eyes, and to show to the world the folly and perfidy of that faction.

It was with reason, then, that Photius passed so severe a censure upon the miracles related by Philostorgius; but does he pass the same censure upon those related by St Ambrose, St Athanasius, St Augustine, and the other great lights of those times? By no means; he knew that these had all the evidence that could be desired to convince mankind of their reality, and that the Arians themselves had never dared to call them in question. As to those miracles which Mr Brook relates, as said to have been performed in favour of the Catholic doctrine, either there is full and sufficient testimony for them, or there is not. If not, then they are out of the question, it is not for them that we contend. If there be, then I defy Mr Brook, notwithstanding his bold and unproved assertions, to point out one single circumstance to render them incredible, one circumstance the parallel of which is not to be found in many of the miracles of the first three centuries, and even in those of the Scriptures themselves. It is clear, then, how ungenerous and unphilosophical it is in Mr Brook, from the above misrepresentations, and pretended improbability and suspicion, to conclude at once that all Catholic miracles were forgeries and fictions. For even allowing that the instances of Catholic miracles which he cites be not sufficiently attested to us, that does not prove them to be forgeries, because the proper testimony for them may have been lost. Much less does it follow that others are forgeries also, for which the most ample testimony, even with all corroborating circumstances, is preserved to this day. Yet this is the conclusion which he draws from his premises!

XVI. I cannot leave this argument without observing

that the same mode of reasoning, especially if the misrepresenting freedom also be allowed, will serve admirably for a heathen or deist to deny the miracles of Moses, because he and the Egyptian magicians both adduced miracles in defence of their respective tenets; or for Dr Middleton to deny all the miracles of the first three ages, because St Irenæus attests that the followers of Simon and Carprocrates pretended to work miracles as well as the true Christians. This shows how well calculated this mode of reasoning is to disprove the continuation of miracles in the Church after the first three centuries.

XVII. A fourth argument, though mentioned later by Mr Brook, must be noticed here, because it plainly contradicts the groundwork of the foregoing objection. Pointing out some of the differences between the miracles of the first ages and those after Constantine, he says: " Another circumstance is that public appeal which was made, that confident attestation which was given to the truth of them in both these periods, which may indeed be probably accounted for in the one case, but is utterly accountable in the other," page 325. He then explains this by observing, that " after the conversion of the Roman empire, the Christians must have been sensible that their forged relations could not easily be discovered; they were encompassed with persons well affected to their party, whose manner of education had infused into their hearts strong prepossessions in favour of such stories; that even a detection of false facts or false testimonies could be attended by no bad consequences; that the emperors themselves would connive at such proceedings; that the civil power would interfere and prevent insults," &c. What a shocking picture of the morality of those times! If this be true, what opinion must we have of all those great and holy men who flourished in them. Could Mr Brook say more to confirm the character given by Dr Middleton, that they were all extremely credulous and superstitious—scrupling at no arts nor means by which they might propagate their principles; and of a character from which nothing candid or impartial could be expected?

Now, if this be the case, how will Mr Brook defend the authenticity of the Bible which came to us through such hands? How will he support the credit of any history, or defend himself from those very arguments which he uses against Dr Middleton for the scandalous character which he gives of the ancient fathers? Above all, how will he reconcile what he here says with that which he laid down as the groundwork of his preceding argument? There he assured us that the fourth age after the conversion of the Roman empire was an age "in which a spirit of pride and ambition, a spirit of faction and contention, had spread itself through the world, and entirely possessed the hearts of by far the greatest part of Christians—that the contest between the Arians and Catholics was carried on with all the animosity and fury that the most bigoted and inflamed zeal could produce;" which made each party appeal to pretended miracles as openly performed in their favour.

From this one would naturally conclude that those appealing to false miracles could not fail to be detected by the vigilance of the other party; that it is most untrue to say they were encompassed with persons well affected towards them; that the detection of such false facts and false testimonies could not fail to injure those who alleged them, as their adversaries would certainly have exposed them to shame and infamy; that the emperors themselves, however they might connive at the doings of their own party, would yet most certainly have used all their authority to expose, discover, and punish, both in person and fortune, those who should so act in opposition to them. Besides, it is well known with what rancour and fury the Arian emperors on all occasions used their power in persecuting the Catholics and in taking every advantage over them. How, then, can Mr Brook so palpably contradict himself in giving us such opposite accounts of those times?

XVIII. His fifth argument, taken from the veneration paid to the relics of saints, he expresses thus: "The catalogue of miracles was not a little increased, it is probable, in the fourth and fifth centuries, by the superstitious regard to martyrs and their relics:" he then proceeds, to the great honour of Catholics, to show from the expressions of the most venerable fathers of the early ages how consonant on this point their doctrine is with what is taught in the Catholic Church to this day, and then concludes thus: "Now, in an age when such a kind of fanaticism universally prevailed, there is the greatest reason to believe that plain facts would be often exaggerated into extraordinary relations, and that any fictitious story, especially of the miraculous kind, which might do honour to saints or relics, would be eagerly embraced and diligently propagated."

In answer to this, I observe, 1st, That all he says here is a mere begging of the question, that the veneration paid to the relics of saints is superstition and idolatry. This is absolutely denied by the whole Catholic body, and therefore it is childish to assume as granted that which is the very point in dispute, and then to argue from it as from a certainty. 2dly, If he had consulted Dr Campbell, he would have proved to him, unanswerably, that no degree of fanaticism less than frenzy could ever possibly lead men to disbelieve their senses, or fancy that they saw what had no existence; and yet there are many miracles recorded to have been performed in these ages by relics, which are attested by men of the greatest integrity, who declare that they, as well as multitudes of others, were eyewitnesses. 3dly, Admitting all that he alleges, it amounts, by his own statement, only to a probability which, whatever weight it may have in relations not sufficiently attested, cannot have the smallest against such as are proved by the fullest evidence of human testimony, and attended with all its corroborating circumstances; and with these only are we concerned.

XIX. His sixth and seventh arguments against the credibility of the miracles related in the fourth and fifth centuries are taken from the supposed impropriety of the ends, and the unworthiness of the instruments, by which they are said to have been performed. But both these objections have been examined when we treated of the ends and instruments of miracles.

XX. His eighth argument is taken from the great esteem in which the monastic life was held during the two ages which he describes, and then he makes this application: "What has been written concerning monks, a few particulars only excepted, is only spoiled with fictitious stories; whilst the author, indulging his own zeal, relates not what the saint has really done, but what he wished he had done; this is the true cause and real spring of so many impertinent and ridiculous stories, so many absurd and incredible tales, with which the lives of Paulus, of Antony, of Hilarion, of Martin, of Macarius, and of various other monks, hermits, and anchorites, abound," p. 323.

Here is a bold assertion, but, like many others in Mr Brook's work, it is without the shadow of a proof.

Unluckily for him, the lives of the very saints whom he mentions were written and published to the world in such times and circumstances as must inevitably have led to detection if any falsehood had been inserted in them; and the miracles related were so public and notorious at the time that nothing can be better attested. Now, though it were admitted that the zeal of a writer might lead him to exaggerate, or even to invent any fact or circumstance in favour of the saint whose life he writes, this can reasonably be presumed to have happened only when the writer is justly suspected, and has not the qualifications necessary to render his testimony valid, and when the relation depends solely on himself. But when the writer is above suspicion both for his knowledge and integrity; when several persons concur in giving the same testimony; and when the circumstances are such as must have led to detection had it been false,—in this case it would be highly absurd to suppose the whole a fiction.

Besides, this argument, as well as the former, if admitted, would prove too much; for surely the regard paid to monks in the fourth and fifth ages could not exceed, nor perhaps equal, that paid by the people of God in the old law to Moses, to Elijah, to Elisha, and those other saints of God so remarkable in their days; much less could it equal that of the apostles to their Lord and Master, or that of St Luke to his great master St Paul. If, therefore, the affection and zeal which a writer has towards the person whose life he describes, is alone sufficient to invalidate his testimony, what an argument will not this give to heathens and deists against the Scripture miracles themselves?

XXI. As the origin and nature of the monastic life are but little known to many in this country, it will not be amiss here to give a brief account of it. We shall thus see the injustice of the many sneers and severe censures which Mr Brook and the generality of Protestants throw out against it, and also the weakness of the arguments they draw from it against the continuation of miracles.

During the first three ages, whilst the malice of hell and the greatest powers on earth were leagued against Christianity, and sought by the most cruel persecution to destroy it, the generality of those who embraced that sacred institution were saints. They made it the chief object of their lives to practise the sacred maxims of their religion, and to live in perfect obedience not only to its holy laws, but even to its evangelical counsels. As they had no earthly inducement to embrace that religion, but every worldly motive to the contrary, their only aim was their eternal welfare, of which they had conceived so just a value and esteem that they willingly renounced all the goods of this life, and sacrificed every worldly consideration, in order to secure it. Having taken off their affections from the things of this world, their whole study was to follow the maxims and example of Jesus Christ, and to become saints.

But when the Roman emperors were converted, and the Christian religion became the religion of the court, the face of things was sadly changed. It was now no longer necessary to renounce the things of this world in order to profess one's self a Christian. The example of the emperors induced even those to become Christians who loved the world more than the truth. A slight persuasion that it was reasonable led many others to profess it who had no idea of renouncing the pomps and vanity of the world, though this be so essential in order to live up to the laws and maxims of Jesus Christ; and those again who had neither honour nor religion, had less difficulty in feigning themselves Christians, when they saw that profession common, and considered it a means of promoting their worldly interest. Thus the holy society of the faithful, whose only aim was to renounce the world and follow Jesus Christ, found itself in a manner overwhelmed by multitudes who entered into it from human motives, without possessing in the least degree the spirit of the gospel. These strangers and disguised enemies outnumbered the true citizens of the holy city, and often became the most powerful in those things which depend upon external authority. The riches and worldly goods which were then consecrated to Jesus Christ by the piety of those who possessed them, and were committed to the management of the pastors of the Church, to be used according to the orders of the Prince of Pastors, corrupted the hearts of many who were not yet become strong, and the continuance of this temptation exceedingly augmented the number of those who fell. Their example corrupted others, and many followed the Christian religion, as mankind before had followed Paganism, and as numbers still follow false religions, without reflection or examination, for interest or by custom. Hence the deluge of iniquity which then appeared among Christians, and which has continued to the present time.

In the midst of these disorders, the love of Jesus Christ, a zeal for His holy law, a perfect contempt of the world, and the ardent desire of eternal good, were more eminently conspicuous in His most faithful followers, who detached themselves from the world, and became united to God with more fervour and perfection than even in the times of persecution. Not being able to exclude sinners from the society of the faithful, they withdrew themselves from the company of sinners, and even of those imperfect Christians who chose to remain among the sinful many. They renounced the world, which though now more favourable to the Christian religion, seemed to them for that very reason more dangerous to piety and virtue.

Vast numbers of both sexes not only left their possessions, as their predecessors had done under the heathen emperors, but also their country, their family, their friends, the very sight of men, and all the pleasures and innocent consolations of society, and retired to lonely deserts, passing there the remainder of their lives in the highest perfection, secluded from creatures, and wholly united with their Creator. This they did, not constrained by necessity to avoid the fury of persecution, but purely of their own free choice to fly from the contagion of a wicked world, and to avoid whatever might be an impediment to their advancement in Christian perfection. Those who made this happy choice were from their solitary life called monks* and anchorites;† and from the desert, the ordinary place of their retirement, they were sometimes called hermits.‡ Such was the origin, and such the nature and design of that mode of life.

This their separation from the world, however, did not in the least diminish that perfect union of benevolence and charity which the Christian religion requires among all its members. Their obedience to the laws of the Church was more perfect, their respect and submission to her pastors more sincere, their zeal for the purity of religion more ardent, and their love and charity for all Christians—indeed, for all mankind—was stronger and

---

* *Monachus*, one who lives alone.
† *Anachorita*, one who lives separated from the rest of the world.
‡ *Eremita*, an inhabitant of the desert.

more disinterested. They received and entertained strangers with more love and friendship than other men show to their nearest relatives, and they were never more pleased than when they had an opportunity of doing good in return for the greatest injuries. The more they avoided communication with the world in its false goods, so much the more feelingly were they sensible of the evils under which the Church in general, or any of the faithful in particular, laboured; and this was a reason for interrupting their course of solitude in order to converse with men, and even to leave their retirement in order to assist them. They received those who suffered for the truth under their protection, without fear of displeasing their persecutors. They opposed all errors and novelties without regard to the power or position of those who advanced them, and with the holy liberty of an Elijah, and a John the Baptist, whose example they followed in their sacred solitude, they reprehended even princes and their officers, when the cause of God and of justice required it. Many of them were instruments in the hand of God for converting infidels and reclaiming the greatest sinners ; and from among them the Church received numberless zealous pastors, who by word and example maintained the doctrine of Jesus Christ in its purity, and preserved the sanctity of Christian morality.

XXII. From this account of the monastic state, and of those who embraced it in its earliest period, we may justly infer that the high veneration and esteem paid to it by the Christian world was a natural consequence of its sanctity and perfection. The prophet Elijah, when he appeared among the people, was reverenced as an angel from heaven ; the sanctity and penitential life of St John the Baptist procured him such veneration from all ranks of men, that even the Pharisees themselves began to think that he might be the Messias whom they about that time expected. No wonder, then, that the holy solitaries who imitated these great saints in their seclusion from the world, in their purity of manners, and in the penitential austerity of their lives, should like them be esteemed as the chosen servants of the Most High God, and as such revered and venerated.

What Mr Brook, together with Dr Middleton, observes upon this, is extremely just: "That monkery in those days was an order of men so highly esteemed in the Church, and so much reverenced by the people, as to be reputed the perfection of a Christian life, and the very pattern of a heavenly one. The monastic state was thought an angelic institution, a blessed and evangelic life, leading to the mansions of the Lord; a way of life worthy of heaven, not at all inferior to that of angels; and the persons who engaged in this state were looked upon as the very flower and most valuable ornament of the Church, and were styled in a peculiar manner the servants of God. Accordingly, the principal fathers of the Church, both Greek and Latin, employed their whole authority and eloquence to extol the perfection and recommend the practice of the monkish order."—Brook's Examin., p. 319.

This is certainly true, and proved by Dr Middleton, in his Introd. Disc., from which Mr Brook takes it, from the express testimonies of the writers of those times. The obvious consequence that common-sense draws from this account is, that the monastic state must have been one of the highest perfection. Mankind must have been convinced by what they saw of the sanctity of those who professed it, otherwise it is impossible that so universal and so high an esteem could have been felt for it. Let us only judge from ourselves—let any body of men amongst us make ever so great a profession of virtue and sanctity—let the most eloquent tongues and pens of the age be employed in extolling their institute, and recommending it to others,—would this make any impression on the minds of mankind?—would it procure any regard or esteem for those men, if their lives gave the lie to their profession? No; this would only bring upon them the greater contempt, and expose their panegyrists to confusion. The praises then given by the holy fathers to the monastic order, the universal esteem and veneration paid to those who professed it, are the most convincing proof of their eminent sanctity, and of the high perfection in which they lived.

It is most unjust, then, in Dr Middleton, Mr Brook, and other Protestant writers, to pretend, from this very universal regard paid to these persons, to draw conclusions against them, and expose them on that account to contempt and ridicule, by attributing that regard to superstition and fanaticism. Common sense disavows such conclusions, and sees at once that the universal veneration which prevailed for ages, and continues to be paid through the whole Catholic Church, to monastic institutions to this day, could never have existed, had they not justly deserved it. No less unreasonable is it to pretend from this veneration that the miracles related of those holy personages were, on that very account, incredible.

It seems obvious that if Almighty God was pleased in those days to perform any miracles, these were the very persons by whom we might expect He would perform them; men detached from all worldly concerns, separated from the sinful world, living in the greatest innocence and purity of manners, sacrificing all for the love of God, and studying continually to please Him. If we may judge of the Divine conduct by what He had actually done in former times, these were surely the proper instruments in His hands for working miracles; and in this respect we have the strongest presumption in their favour. A positive testimony, then, that this actually was done; a testimony given by all the writers of those times, by men eminent for their intregrity and learning; a testimony given in public as of facts well known to their hearers, and which, if false, could not have failed to be detected, to the disgrace of those who attested them; if a testimony of this kind, joined to so just a presumption, does not amount to the fullest conviction, all faith whatever in human testimony must be discarded from the world. That such was in fact the case, we shall see in its proper place; and here we shall only conclude that nothing can be more unreasonable or more unphilosophical, than what has been said upon this subject by Dr Middleton and his Protestant antagonists.

XXIII. We come now to the ninth argument used by Mr Brook against the credibility of the miracles of the fourth and fifth ages. In this he seems to exult with particular confidence, and spends many pages in illustrating it. He proposes it as follows: "From the surprising likeness of the Popish and Pagan religion, &c., it has been rightly concluded" (by Dr Middleton, in his Letter from Rome), " and there is the greatest reason to believe, that the religious worship of the Catholics, in its principal and distinguishing parts, was originally derived from the Gentile ritual. In like manner, from the great similitude of the Pagan miracles, and those recorded in the fourth and fifth centuries; from the near resemblance of their several relations; from the likeness of the nature, the circumstances, and the occasions of them both,—it may reasonably be presumed that the histories of the miracles of monks, of saints, of martyrs of those ages, were taken, for the most part, from the extraordinary accounts which are given of ancient sages in the Gentile world." He then gives several examples of both; and in order to show the great resemblance between them, concludes with such an air of triumph and contemptuous disregard for all the miracles related in those times, that one would think he had really said something unanswerable. How far this is true these few observations will show.

XXIV. First, then, allowing that in many miracles related of saints there were a resemblance to some of the extraordinary things related among the Gentiles, which are certainly false, what conclusion could in right reason be drawn from it? Will it follow from this that the miracles related of the saints of God are as false as the others? Ridiculous conclusion! Where is the connection between the premises and the consequence? Is not the same resemblance to be found between heathen miracles and many of those recorded in the Scriptures? Does it therefore follow that the latter are false likewise? But allowing that this resemblance should justify some suspicion, on what miracles could that suspicion fall? Could it in the smallest degree affect such as are supported by the fullest human testimony that past matters of fact can have? Certainly not. And it is for such as these only that we contend.

The proper answer to this argument is to state the case plainly, which is as follows:—From the time that Satan—that haughty spirit—failed in his attempt to raise himself to an equality with his Maker, he has continually endeavoured to gratify his ambition by imitating the works of God among men. If the Almighty instituted priests, and oblations, and sacrifices, and temples among His chosen people, for His service, Satan endeavoured to obtain the same honours from his votaries. If Almighty God inspired His holy prophets to know things at a distance, or to foretell things to come, Satan, too, endeavoured to imitate this prerogative of the Divinity, in the delusive answers which he gave by his oracles, or by those who, like the young woman in the Acts, had familiar spirits. If Almighty God gave proof of His divinity by working miracles among mankind, Satan sought to procure homage to himself by similar means—either actually performing extraordinary things by enchantments, as in the magicians of Egypt and Simon Magus, or in deluding his blinded votaries by appearances, as were many of the prodigies related among the Gentiles, or by exciting false relations of such things among them, and causing them to pass for truth among the vulgar.

Now, how ridiculous would it be to say, that because there were priests, oblations, and temples among the heathens, to which those of the Church of England bear a great resemblance, therefore we may reasonably presume that these latter were taken from the former? Or to allege that because there were oracles and persons that had familiar spirits among the heathens, who foretold things to come, or discovered things secret, to which the prophets related to have existed in the first three ages of the Church have a striking likenesss; therefore it may reasonably be presumed that these latter were no less diabolical than the former, and were only adduced in imitation of them? No less ridiculous is it to argue, that because there is a likeness between certain miracles related of the saints of God, and some false prodigies among the Gentiles, therefore the former are no more to be regarded than they. It is not called in question that the miracles of Moses and the prophets are much more ancient than any of those related among the heathens. The natural presumption then is, that those of the Gentiles were taken from those related in the sacred Scripture, as it is certain that many of the articles of the heathen mythology are nothing but corrupt imitations of the truths contained in these divine oracles.

If, then, Almighty God, following the same dispensation of providence in the Church of His Son as He did in the old law, shall be pleased to work miracles by His saints, of the same nature and in similar circumstances with those performed of old by Moses and the prophets, can anything be more unworthy of a man of sense, or of a Christian, than to pretend that because there is a likeness in some of those miracles to the faint and imperfect imitations of the miracles of Moses and the prophets, that therefore they are to be rejected as fictitious, and as copied from heathen originals? Is it not more natural to conclude that as they are of the same nature with those of the Old Testament, performed for similar ends, and in similar circumstances, therefore they undoubtedly come from the same divine original? and that whatever is said against those of the saints, on account of their resemblance to those of the heathens, will equally affect those of the Scripture where the same resemblance is found? This reasoning will appear in the strongest light if we consider some of those very examples which Mr Brook makes use of to prove the likeness for which he contends.

XXV. "Pythagoras," says he, "and Apollonius, if

we may believe the writers of their lives, had an admirable gift of conversing with the brute creation." And then he adds some instances related of the authority they had over irrational creatures, and the obedience which these paid to their commands; but St Jerom relates examples of such a power in St Hilarion and St Anthony, as Ruffinus does of Macarius; and thence he concludes that these are no less fictitious than the former. But had he remembered his Bible, he would have found that Moses had a much greater power over both the irrational and inanimate creation than anything related of the two heathen philosophers; witness his conduct in the plagues of Egypt, where locusts, frogs, and other vermin came up in innumerable multitudes to punish the Egyptians at his desire, and at his desire disappeared. It is true that in the Scripture account of these things Moses is represented only as the instrument in the hand of God in working these wonders; but is it pretended that St Hilarion, St Anthony, and St Macarius were anything else in the wonderful power which they exhibited over the brute creation? Was it not in the name of God, and for His glory, that they performed these wonders? Why, then, refer their miracles to the fictitious stories of the heathens, and not rather to the miracles of the Holy Scripture, to which they bear a much greater likeness, both in themselves, and in the manner and ends for which they were performed?

XXVI. Again, says Mr Brook, it is related of Apollonius that he could render himself invisible. The same thing is related of certain saints, who being in imminent danger of falling into the hands of enemies, and having recourse to prayer, were rendered invisible, and by that means escaped. But is it not also related in Holy Writ that the people of Sodom and Gomorrah were struck with blindness with regard to the door of Lot's house, so that they groped about and could not find it? and that the Syrian army sent to take the prophet Elisha prisoner was treated in the same manner? And did not Christ Himself become invisible when they wished to make Him king? And did He not instantly render Himself invisible to the two disciples at Emmaus after He had made Himself known to them?

XXVII. "There was a certain family," he proceeds to say, "among the ancient inhabitants of Italy, called the Hirpi, who once a year, when they sacrificed to Apollo upon Mount Soracte, used to walk through the fire unhurt. But the Christian monks far surpassed these heathen priests in subduing the destructive power of fire," of which he relates some examples; and from the similarity he finds between them, concludes that these were no less fictitious than those of the Hirpi. But is it not also related in the Word of God that the three holy children walked in the midst of the fiery furnace unhurt, even without so much as the smell of fire upon their clothes? And does not Mr Brook strenuously defend the miracle that is related at the martyrdom of St Polycarp, when being laid on a pile of wood, to which fire was set, the flames refused to touch the saint, but formed themselves into an arch around him, without coming near him? How childish, then, is it to reject instances of this kind in the fourth century, merely because of their resemblance to what is related among the heathens, and yet so earnestly defend a much more uncommon effect of the same kind in the second? How unjust are men in their balances, especially when engaged in a bad cause!

XXVIII. "If Pythagoras and Empedocles," says he, "had the power of suppressing winds and stopping hail, of calming storms, of making rivers and the sea itself afford them and their companions an easy and safe passage, Martin and Gregory have not suffered this power to go unrivalled. True; but does not the word of God afford us several examples of the same kind? The Red Sea was obedient to Moses, the river Jordan to Joshua, and they afforded them and all their armies an easy and safe passage. Moses and Samuel commanded the storms and hail, and they obeyed them. Our blessed Saviour and St Peter walked upon the waters; and Christ rebuked the stormy winds and the raging sea, and there came a great calm. Is it, therefore, any thing incredible that Almighty God should do by a Martin or a Gregory, His holy and faithful servants, what He had so often done to others from the earliest times?

XXIX. Let us now stand still a while—to use the words of Mr Brook himself upon this occasion—and take a short review of this mighty argument, in which he so loudly exults, and see what important purposes it may serve. Can anything be more unchristian and uncharitable than to put miracles done by holy men, and in the name of the living God, in the same class and upon the same footing with the fictitious stories of the heathens, to which they have but a distant and unimportant likeness in the facts related; and not rather class them with those of the Holy Scriptures, to which they bear the greatest resemblance, both in the facts themselves, and in all their circumstances? Is it not ridiculous to pretend that, on account of this faint likeness to heathen miracles, they are to be rejected as fictitious, though ever so fully attested by the strongest evidence? Let common sense judge and decide the weight and importance of this argument.

XXX. After Mr Brook has collected all the various

arguments used against the credibility of miracles in the later ages, he concludes by attacking the testimony of the holy fathers themselves who relate them; and here he is guilty of so much unfair dealing and misrepresentation, that even his admirers, if they reflect, will be ashamed of it. It is not my intention to follow all that he says on this head. I shall only observe two things: first, his chief argument against the testimony of the holy fathers, Saints Chrysostom, Augustine, Jerom, Ambrose, and the others, is, that they contradict themselves and one another in the testimony they give of miracles in their days; sometimes affirming that miracles have entirely ceased, and even inquiring into the cause of this cessation; at other times relating miracles as performed in different places even in their own times and presence. On this Mr Brook expatiates with all his eloquence, and, by those small arts which are well known in the schools of logic, endeavours to display this argument as unanswerable. But how unworthy and ungenerous is this!

We have seen above, from the clearest testimony of St Augustine in his retractations, the distinction between the extension and universality of the chrismatic graces, with the visible signs of the communication of the Holy Ghost, and the performance of particular and occasional miracles independent of these graces: the former is acknowledged to have ceased before the days of St Augustine; the latter, we contend, has continued in every age of the Church till this day. Now St Augustine expressly declares, that wherever he speaks of the cessation of miracles, he means only those of the former kind, but by no means of the latter, many remarkable instances of which, he assures us, were consistent with his own personal knowledge. Mr Brook had read this passage of St Augustine, which is a key to all that the other holy fathers have said upon this subject, and entirely dissipates Mr Brook's objection. This he had read in St Augustine, because he refers to it. How, then, could he conceal the truth, and so grossly misrepresent the sense and meaning of these holy men?

XXXI. I observe, secondly, that Mr Brook, on this head, uses many pitiful reflections, to throw suspicion on the testimony of the fathers of the fourth and fifth ages, similar to those used by Dr Middleton against all the fathers in general, and which, if allowed, would stamp them as so many fools and knaves. Now Mr Brook having justly condemned all that the Doctor had said against those of the first three ages, how can he give the same ungenerous treatment to those of the fourth and fifth, especially as the self-same arguments by which he condemns the Doctor equally condemn himself? For if the fathers of the fourth and following ages were fools and knaves, from whom nothing candid or impartial can be expected, what becomes of the faith of history? what becomes of the Bible, which reaches us only through their hands? what becomes of Christianity? Let Mr Brook or his admirers answer these questions if they can, and Dr Middleton's party will learn what answer to give when they are urged by Mr Brook against them.

XXXII. I have now examined all the arguments of any note used against the credibility of the miracles related after the first three ages, and I have shown that they all proceed either upon false suppositions or misrepresentations; that the conclusions drawn from them, when the case is properly stated, have not the least connection with the premises; that they may all be used by deists and heathens against the miracles related in the Scriptures, with as great show of reason as they are used against those of the fourth and following ages; in a word, that they are mere sophistry, clothed in pompous language, sallies of wit and bold assertions, which may indeed impose upon superficial readers, but can never bear the test of strict examination.

Mr Brook has said all that can be said upon the subject; neither his ability nor inclination can be doubted. Since, therefore, all that he has said is so little to the purpose, we may infer that no reason can be brought against the credibility of the miracles of the fourth and following ages, either from the facts themselves, or from their circumstances; and, consequently, that such miracles in these ages as are properly vouched for by sufficient testimony, cannot in justice be rejected. This is further confirmed by what we have seen in the preceding chapter on the manner in which this question is treated by Dr Middleton and his Protestant adversaries. Their setting out by begging the question, and proceeding upon the same principles; their extending or limiting the necessities of the Church as best suits their system; their allowing the self-same reason to have the greatest weight in one age, and none in another,—evidently shows their utter want of all solid arguments against the continuation of miracles in any one age of the Church from her commencement to the present time.

CHAPTER XIV.

PRESUMPTIVE EVIDENCE FOR THE CONTINUATION OF MIRACLES THROUGHOUT ALL AGES.

I. WHOEVER seriously considers what we have stated in the two preceding chapters, will, I presume, readily admit that no solid argument can be produced against the credibility of miracles in whatever age they are said to be performed, provided their existence be sufficiently attested by unexceptionable witnesses. We have carefully examined all the pretended arguments usually employed to disprove the credibility of miracles; and we have shown them to be in every respect defective, frivolous, and utterly incapable of even weakening the credibility of any one well attested miracle. We are thus brought back to what I showed in another place, that as testimony is the only way by which the existence of miracles can be proved to persons not eyewitnesses, so it is a full, perfect, and sufficient means for this purpose; that all the metaphysical arguments brought against any miracle *a priori*, and extrinsic to the testimony, are mere sophisms, and can never have the least weight or weaken the conviction which the force of testimony gives; and therefore, that the only rational objection against a miracle must be such as strikes directly at the testimony by which it is supported. We might therefore supersede the consideration of all presumptive evidence for the perpetual continuation of miracles in the Christian Church, and proceed to prove it by positive testimony. But as we possess abundance of such evidence, and that of a more satisfactory nature than Protestant writers against Dr Middleton have used to prove the continuation of miracles down to the various periods assumed by them; and as the production of this will add strength and clearness to the positive proofs which we shall afterwards consider,—I propose at present to take a view of this presumptive evidence, and to show the ground on which it stands.

II. Though Mr Brook proposes the presumptive evidence for the miracles of the first three ages under several heads, yet these are all reducible to this one proposition and its consequence. "The exigencies of the Church, for the support and propagation of religion, made it highly becoming Almighty God to work miracles in these ages, therefore it was to be expected, and we may reasonably presume that He did so." This is the proposition upon which all the different systems of the duration of miracles proceed.

Dr Middleton adopts this as his reason for the continuation of miracles during the apostolic age, yet smiles at his adversaries for extending it beyond that age. He pronounces it highly "rash and presumptuous to form arguments upon the supposed necessity or propriety of a divine interposition in this or that particular case, and to decide upon the motives and views of the Deity by the narrow conceptions of human reason."—Pref., p. 20. This is certainly a just remark, in which we cordially agree with the Doctor, especially under the authority of St Paul, who, sensible of this great truth, exclaims, in a rapture of admiration, "O the depth of the riches both of the wisdom and knowledge of God! how unsearchable are His judgments, and His ways past finding out! for who hath known the mind of the Lord, or who hath been His counsellor?" Rom. xi. 33. And indeed there is nothing wherein our modern Christian infidels more manifestly expose their impious presumption, than in measuring the ways of God by their own narrow conceptions; reducing the works of the Omnipotent to the examination of their judgment, and boldly deciding by the feeble light of their blind understandings what it becomes or does not become the Deity to do.

Instead of this, the Doctor assures us, with no less reason, that "the whole which the wit of man can possibly discover, either of the ways or will of the Creator, must be acquired by a contrary method; not by imagining vainly within ourselves what may be proper or improper for Him to do, but by looking abroad, and contemplating what He has actually done." This rule is most judicious, and contains safe ground on which to proceed; for though there must be innumerable cases in which it will become the Almighty to act, though we can by no means judge of the propriety of these *a priori*, yet certain it is that God will never act either in the ordinary course of His providence, or by an extraordinary interposition, but when this is highly proper and becoming. If we contemplate, then, what Almighty God has actually done, in certain circumstances and for certain ends, we may safely conclude that it highly becomes Him to act in the same manner in similar circumstances, and where the same ends are to be obtained; and from this we draw as an undoubted consequence, that it is then to be expected, and we may reasonably presume He will do so.

However just and reasonable the above rule is, yet the Doctor is far from being as reasonable in the application of it; for he proceeds to tell us, that the only way by which we are to know what God actually has done, is "by attending seriously to that revelation which He made of Himself from the beginning, and placed continually before our eyes in the wonderful works and beautiful fabric of this visible world."—Pref., p. 21. Here the Doctor is doubtless to be blamed; for though this might suit a deist, who acknowledges no revelation but in the works of the creation, to admit no other way of knowing what God has done but by contemplating these works, yet it is ridiculous in a Christian who believes the sacred Scriptures to be the Word of God. These sacred writings contain an ample account of the conduct of the Almighty in a great variety of cases concerning the affairs of men, and of the dispositions of His providence in the government of this universe. Not only, then, in the works of the creation, but also in these divine oracles of the Scriptures, we have an ample field wherein to contemplate what God has actually done in many instances, and from them we may conclude with the greatest certainty what is at all times becoming Him to do in similar cases.

III. It is upon this ground that our presumptive evidence for the perpetual continuation of miracles is founded; and from this will be seen at once the wide difference between the nature of the evidence brought by us, and that used by Dr Middleton and his Protestant adversaries for their systems. Theirs is founded upon this general position, the exigencies of the Church, which each one interprets and applies according to his fancy, judging of the views and motives of the Deity by the narrow conceptions of human reason. For this the Doctor justly ridicules the others, though he also uses it when it serves his own purpose.

The presumptive evidence which I propose to bring is founded upon solid facts, recorded for our instruction by the authority of God Himself, and from which the conclusion flows with undoubted certainty; so that, though I term it presumptive evidence, yet when the force of it is well considered and fully comprehended, it must be allowed to be evidence of the highest kind, even bordering upon absolute proof.

IV. But though the Doctor, as a Christian, is justly blamed for restricting to the works of the creation the means of knowing what God has actually done, and for excluding, by that limitation, all our knowledge from His holy Scriptures, yet doubtless the works of creation are not to be rejected. On the contrary, they afford us a noble field for such contemplation, and a strong presumptive proof for the continuation of miracles.

When treating of the ends of miracles as manifested by the light of reason, we considered the glorious fabric of this visible creation; we examined the nature of good and evil with relation to different creatures; we compared the material part of the creation with the rational and intelligent, in order to know their respective value. We considered the intention and views which God had in the inanimate creation, and in all those laws by which the material world is governed. We reviewed the beneficent purposes which are manifest throughout the whole creation; and from our reasonings on these heads, confirmed by revelation, we drew as a necessary consequence, "That the rational and intelligent creatures are the chief, and by far the most excellent, part of the creation; that without them the others are of little or no value; that they are the principal object of the care and attention of the Creator; that other inferior beings are made only to serve, either mediately or immediately, to their happiness and perfection;—and therefore, as the present order and laws of nature are established only as subservient to these great ends, and for promoting by them the glory of the Creator, it is not only reasonable, but highly becoming the infinite wisdom and goodness of God, to suspend any of these laws, and alter the present order of things, or to perform any other miraculous effects, either by procuring the happiness and perfection of His rational creatures, or by averting their misery and moral turpitude, or even by inflicting just punishment upon them, as His own honour and glory may require. Nay, should it happen that these ends could not be so perfectly acquired by ordinary means, it would then not only be becoming Almighty God, but even in a manner incumbent on Him to work a miracle in order to procure them."

In the same chapter we showed that miracles are always much more effectual for procuring happiness and moral good, and for preventing misery and moral evil in intelligent creatures, than ordinary means by the agency of second causes; and therefore, not only that Almighty God may, but that it is most becoming His divine goodness that He should, from time to time use them for such ends. Our reasoning on this subject is not restricted to time nor place; it has equal force in all countries and in all ages. It is as convincing under the Gospel as under the law; in the eighteenth century of Christianity as in the times of the apostles. Wherever, therefore, the happiness or moral perfection of rational creatures is to be promoted, and especially where the ordinary means for doing so are ineffectual or less proper, it is highly becoming the divine goodness to interpose by miracles for so worthy and laudable a purpose; and therefore it is highly reasonable to presume that He will from time to time continue to do so throughout all ages to the end of the world.

Even from the limited view of the divine conduct taken by Dr Middleton in the contemplation of the visible creation, we find a strong and just presumption to believe that the Divine Wisdom has by no means confined the working of miracles to any particular period of time; but that as the happiness and perfection of His rational creatures will be a continual object of His desire while time endures, so it will at all times be highly becoming His goodness to perform miracles in order to procure them. But if we consider that more extensive view which God Himself has unfolded to us in His holy Scriptures, we shall there find stronger grounds to believe that miracles will never cease in the Church of Christ. These grounds are taken from the following sources: 1. From the conduct of God in the old law; 2. From the conduct of Jesus Christ in the Gospel; 3. From the promises of Christ; and 4. From what we are told will happen at the end of the world;—each of which we must consider separately by the light of revelation.

V. By revelation we are informed that when man was lost by sin, and had become a prey to the delusions of Satan, this impious spirit endeavoured to extend his empire over the entire world, and to become sole master of the hearts of men. That although Almighty God, in His infinite mercy, had determined to redeem lost man, and restore him to that happiness of which he had been deprived by sin, yet, for just and wise purposes, He delayed this great work for many ages, and in the mean time permitted man to be deluded by the devil, and hurried on by him to every excess of wickedness and vice, that his pride might be confounded, and that experience might convince him of his extreme misery and weakness, and his great need of a Redeemer. But whilst mankind in general were thus abandoned to themselves, Almighty God was pleased to select one nation, which He preserved from this general corruption, and to which He made an express revelation of Himself and of His will, of the religious worship which He required from them, and of the law by which He commanded them to walk. This revelation was made by Moses and the prophets, to whom God communicated His will, and gave authority to announce it to His people. But it was imperfect compared to what was afterwards to be made known by our Redeemer, of Whom the holy prophets predicted that He would come in the fulness of time to give a perfect revelation of the will of God to men, to disclose to them the secrets of the divine wisdom, to bring all nations to the knowledge of the true God, and to teach them a more holy law and a more perfect worship, of which all that had been taught by Moses was only a shadow, a figure, and an emblem.

God in the mean time showed a peculiar care of His chosen people, whom He made the depositaries of His divine oracles, sending from time to time His servants to teach, instruct, exhort, and preserve them in His service. At last the Redeemer Himself appeared, clothed with the omnipotence of God, by which He gave the most convincing proofs of His mission, fulfilled and abolished the Mosaic institution, and manifested to the world that pure and holy religion which was to be the only means of salvation to mankind, and which therefore was to be the religion of all nations, and to continue to the end of the world.

Here then we find that Almighty God has made two separate external revelations of His will to men, the one by Moses, the other by Jesus Christ His Son. The former was imperfect both with regard to the knowledge which it imparted of God and of heavenly things, and with regard to the nature of the worship required by it from man. The latter was full and ample in both respects, giving us a glorious knowledge of God and of a future world, and discovering to us a most pure and holy worship due to the sovereign Being from us His creatures. The Mosaic institution, with all its sacrifices and ceremonies, was only a shadow of the good things to come, a figure and emblem of the religion of Jesus, and was therefore incapable of cleansing the soul from sin, and of perfectly reconciling man with his offended Creator.

The Christian religion is the substance, of which the former was only the shadow, and it contains in itself every celestial grace and benediction necessary for the perfect sanctification of our souls, and for bringing us to the possession of eternal happiness. The religion of Moses was temporary, and to continue only till the Redeemer should appear, being intended to prepare the world for receiving the more perfect religion of Jesus. But this was confined to no space of time; it is to last till the end of the world, while the sun and moon shall endure. Finally, the law of Moses was given only to one nation, and confined to one people; the law of grace under Jesus Christ is intended for all nations, to bring all to the knowledge and service of the true God, and to be established from the rising of the sun to the going down thereof.

VI. Jesus Christ being come into the world, the law

of Moses was abolished, and an end put to his institution, that the more perfect religion of Jesus might be established in its place. Now Almighty God has been pleased to give us a particular history, authorised by Himself, of the conduct of His divine providence during the whole time of the Mosaic institution. In this history we have an account of vast numbers of miracles performed by God on various occasions, and for many different ends, during that period. From this we evidently see, by the authority of God Himself, on what occasions and for what ends it is worthy of Almighty God, and becoming His divine goodness, to work miracles. If, therefore, we find that the same occasions must frequently occur, and the same or similar ends come every day to be promoted in all ages of Christianity, it must follow that it will at all times be equally worthy of Almighty God, and equally becoming His goodness, to perform miracles on these occasions. We have therefore the strongest reason to presume that from time to time God will continue to do so in every age to the end of the world. Nay, we shall find, when we come to consider the particular cases, that there is much greater reason to expect this in the Christian Church than there was under the Jewish law.

VII. In explaining the ends of miracles from revelation, I have given an ample detail of the various occasions on which Almighty God wrought miracles under the old law, and of the several ends which he had in view. Some of these tended more immediately to promote the divine glory by the general good of the whole people; others seemed to have for their more immediate object the perfection or happiness of particular persons only; though by being afterwards published to the world, they contributed no less than the former to the divine glory and the good of mankind, as to their grand and ultimate end.

Of the first kind were chiefly these following : 1. To convince mankind that the doctrine preached to them by those who wrought these miracles in the name of God was truly His doctrine, and thereby to engage them the more readily to receive it, and the more steadfastly to adhere to the belief and profession of it. 2. For defending the doctrine thus revealed to them, and for preserving the religion which He had given to His people against all attempts in after-ages to corrupt and destroy it. 3. For asserting His own honour against all false gods, and their idolatrous worship. 4. For engaging His people to believe and trust in Him, to love Him, to obey Him, and to serve Him only, and thus to promote the sanctification and perfection of their own souls. 5. To assert and vindicate the honour of His priesthood, and of all holy things more immediately used in His service, and to procure for them due respect and veneration. 6. To manifest the sanctity of holy persons, whom He sends from time to time as His messengers to men, and to gain for them due credit and respect, that, by their words and example, others may be excited to greater piety and fervour. 7. To convince idolaters, and those who know Him not, that He is the only true God, when He is pleased to communicate the knowledge of Himself and of His holy will to them.

Of the second kind, where the immediate end intended was the benefit of particular persons only, we considered four different classes. The first contains those cases where Almighty God, in communicating any truth, commission, or promise to a particular person, either immediately or by others, was pleased to convince them by miracles that those things were really from Him, and not delusions. The second contains those cases where we find Almighty God condescending to work miracles in favour of particular persons, as a reward of their virtuous actions, particularly their acts of charity, their confidence in His goodness, and constancy in His service. In the third class, I collected those examples where we find the divine goodness working miracles, and frequently of the first order, merely to supply the corporal wants of particular persons, and sometimes where these were so little important as might, to unassisted natural reason, appear unworthy of such divine interposition. The last class contains those cases where the Divine Wisdom was pleased to work miracles for the punishment or correction of sinners, as the immediate end intended, and for the manifestation and exaltation of His justice in those who rejected the offers of His mercy.

VIII. No Christian can deny that all these ends of miracles were worthy of God, and that it was becoming His divine wisdom to perform the most stupendous miracles in order to procure them. Now, if it was thus worthy of God to perform miracles for these ends in the old law, it must at least be equally so in the new. To illustrate this in each particular case would carry us to too great a length, so I shall confine myself to a few of the most remarkable examples.

IX. The Christian religion assures us that Almighty God has been pleased to make two different revelations of Himself to man; the one, less perfect, by Moses—the other, most ample and perfect, by Jesus Christ. In the first of these He declared several important truths to mankind concerning Himself, and delivered a body of laws to His people, of which He demanded the most exact observance. It was necessary, therefore, that they should be thoroughly convinced that this revelation was from Him, the Creator and sovereign Lord of the universe.

He could, undoubtedly, have infused into their minds a thorough knowledge and full conviction of these things without having recourse to any external means whatever. But this would have been acting in a manner supernatural, and by no means suited to the state and condition of mankind. Moreover, this would have been forcing conviction upon them, and depriving them of all exercise of free-will. This method, therefore, God did not employ; but, giving commission to His servant Moses to declare His will to His people, He thought it worthy His infinite goodness to work surprising miracles by the hand of Moses in their presence, as convincing proofs that he was authorised by Him. These were proofs exactly suited to their state and condition, falling under the scrutiny and examination of their senses.

But though these proofs carried with them the strongest conviction of the truth of what Moses taught, yet they did not deprive the people of their free-will, nor force them to believe. Nay, we find that, notwithstanding those proofs, they frequently rebelled against the light attending them, and murmured against Moses, as if he had deceived them. Hence, in receiving this revelation as from God, and subjecting themselves to this law as coming from Him, their service was reasonable, free, and voluntary, and such as God requires from His rational creatures. It was not only becoming the Divine Wisdom, then, to confirm this revelation by miracles, but it was even necessary that He should do so, on the supposition that He desired such a voluntary service from His people.

X. Now, if this was the case with the first revelation which God made of His will to mankind; if it was even necessary, in order to obtain a reasonable and voluntary service from His people, it must be no less becoming His divine goodness when making His second and more perfect revelation to the world. A little reflection will show that this was even much more necessary in the latter case than in the former. In the first place, the truths which He revealed by Jesus Christ concerning Himself and supernatural things, were far more sublime, more incomprehensible, more spiritual than those which He revealed by Moses; and yet He demands the most submissive belief in them. The law promulgated by Jesus Christ was far more holy, more opposed to self-love, to all the desires and inclinations of our corrupt nature, than the law of Moses, and yet He requires the most complete obedience to it. The sacrifice of our heart, of our affections, the mortification of all our carnal desires, and the sanctity and perfection which God demands under the Gospel, are greater and more sublime than He required under the old law. If, then, miracles were necessary in order to procure credit to the revelation of the less perfect law, requiring the belief and practice of things less difficult to flesh and blood, much more necessary must it be to employ the same powerful means, in order to convince mankind of the divine revelation of the Gospel, where truths so much more incomprehensible are proposed to our belief, and greater perfection is required from us in practice.

In the revelation made by Moses, the people were expressly forbidden so much as to give ear to any one who should invite them to leave their religion, even though he should appeal to signs, and those signs should come to pass. Most necessary, therefore, was it on the revelation of the Gospel, by which the law was abolished, and a more pure and holy worship substituted in its place, not only that miracles should be performed in confirmation of it, but even that these miracles should be so extraordinary, both in greatness and in number, as to overrule the above prohibition, and convince the Jews that the author of this revelation was the expected Messias. Lastly, the revelation made by Moses was made to a people already acquainted with the true God, the children of the patriarchs, who had preserved the memory of the promises made to their fathers, and who were at the time in a state of cruel slavery, from which the first step of this revelation was to deliver them. All this, of course, powerfully disposed their minds to receive and embrace it. The revelation of the Gospel, on the contrary, was chiefly intended for the heathen world, a people absolutely ignorant of the true God, sunk in gross idolatry, vice, and wickedness, and whose principles, practices, and affections were all directly opposed to the pure maxims contained in that revelation. Consequently, if it was not only worthy of God, but even necessary, to work miracles for the establishment of the Mosaic revelation, how much more worthy of the divine goodness, how much more necessary, was it to work more and even greater miracles in order to establish the Gospel among a people from whom, on so many accounts, it was to find the most inveterate opposition! If, therefore, it was so worthy of God to do this, and so necessary for the purpose He intended of subjecting all nations to the yoke of Christ, this affords a strong and well-founded presumption that He would actually do so.

XI. We may further observe that, as the Gospel revelation was intended not for one people only, as was that of Moses, but for all the nations of the world—and as these were equally ignorant of the true God, and guided by principles and affections equally opposed to the rules of the Gospel—the necessity of miracles to overcome all opposition, and conquer the force of prejudice and self-love, was not confined to its first appearance in one or two nations only, but was equally great in every nation wherever it was first preached. It was therefore equally worthy of God to introduce the knowledge and belief of the Gospel among all these different nations, by working miracles for that end. Besides, as the knowledge of the Gospel was not to be communicated at once to all nations, but, by the disposition of the divine providence, was to be the work of many succeeding ages, even till near the end of the world, we have the same strong and well-founded presumption, as above, to expect that the miraculous powers will therefore continue in the Church of Christ throughout all ages, and will never fail to be exerted when new heathen nations are to be brought to the knowledge and belief of the Gospel, by those holy souls whom God shall be pleased to raise up and employ as His instruments for that purpose.

XII. Dr Middleton, indeed, makes much parade of the genuine strength of the Gospel, and of the natural force of the divine graces with which it was so richly stored—faith, hope, and charity; and he pretends in his preface to the Free Inquiry, that as soon as Christianity had gained an establishment in every quarter of the known world, which he thinks might have happened before the death of all the apostles, there was no longer any need of miracles. He concludes, therefore, that they were then finally withdrawn, and that the Gospel was left to make its way by its own strength and the above divine graces. This is an argument used not only by Dr Middleton for the cessation of miracles in the apostolic age, but also by some of his Protestant adversaries to prove their cessation after the respective periods assigned them; for they all pretend that the exigencies of the Church being the only reason why miracles were wrought, and these exigencies continuing as long as they are pleased to allow, and no longer, they assert that on their cessation miracles must have ceased also. This argument has a specious appearance, and therefore it is proper to examine its real worth.

XIII. I would ask these gentlemen what they understand by the genuine strength of the Gospel and by the divine graces, faith, hope, and charity, with which it is so richly stored? If they mean that when the Gospel is cordially received and embraced by any persons or people, and when these divine virtues take full possession of their hearts, it is capable of producing the most admirable effects, by the change it works in their hearts, affections, whole conduct and behaviour—it will be readily admitted that its strength in this respect is admirable. To be convinced of this we need only read the wonderful effects which it produced in the apostles themselves, and in the first Christians, as related in the holy Scripture; but in this sense it is nothing at all to their purpose.

If they mean that when the Gospel is thus received by a whole nation, and established in it by law, there is no longer any need of miracles to induce that nation to embrace it; this also will be readily granted, but it is as little to their purpose as the former. If they mean that when a considerable number in any nation have cordially embraced the Gospel, the strength of their faith, hope, and charity will suffice to enable it to make its way through all the rest of that nation, and to convert the whole without the help of miracles; this is certainly false, and contrary to experience. No doubt the sanctity and virtues of Christians are great arguments in favour of their religion; but alone, they are too weak to induce heathens, who have little idea of true virtue, to embrace it. Were there ever more holy, more virtuous and perfect Christians than the apostles and the first converts? Yet their virtue and holiness were not the means by which they converted others, but the miracles which they wrought, and to which they always appealed in proof of their doctrine.

If they mean that were Christianity once fully established in any large country, such as the Roman empire, it then acquires sufficient strength to spread itself throughout the other nations by the divine virtues of faith, hope, and charity, without the further aid of miracles; this is no less false and contrary to experience than the former case. Lastly, if they mean that, when Christianity is fully established in any country, the solid reasons that can be given to prove its truth, and the motives of credibility adduced in its favour, are sufficient to convince any reasonable man of its divine origin; this will readily be acknowledged with regard to the people of that country who have been brought up from infancy in the knowledge of it, provided they believe all the motives of credibility on which it is founded, of which the miracles wrought at its first establishment are certainly one of the most essential.

But experience shows that all these motives of credibility are too weak to convince even those who, having been educated in the knowledge of Christianity, afterwards become atheists or deists, deny the existence of miracles at its first establishment, and would require other miracles performed before their own eyes to convince them. Now, if this be the case, even in those who have enjoyed the advantage of a Christian education, what can be expected from a barbarous, heathen nation, sunk in ignorance and vice, and whose principles, affections, and practices are as much opposed to the pure maxims of the Gospel as those of the Romans were when it first appeared among them?

We may illustrate this by a particular case, which will at once show the force of the argument. Let us suppose that not only the Roman empire, but that all Europe had cordially embraced the Gospel; that, like the first Christians, they continued "steadfast in the doctrine of the apostles, and had all but one mind and one soul;" that faith, hope, and charity had taken root so deeply in their hearts that they were all perfect Christians. Surely if ever the genuine strength of the Gospel appeared in the world it would appear in this case. Let us suppose, further, that many learned men among them had displayed in the strongest light, and with all the power of eloquence, the motives of credibility in proof of the truth of their religion. Yet what would all this serve to the conversion of the people of China or Japan, or of the wild Indians of America?

Let a number of European missionaries go among these people, burning with zeal, and full of faith, hope, and charity; suppose them to learn their language and preach the Gospel among them,—would all that they could say, without the aid of miracles, be more effectual to convert these people, than the zeal of the apostles was in their fervent preaching to the heathen world in their days? And if miracles were necessary to give a sanction to what the apostles taught, notwithstanding their sanctity and zeal, will they not be at least equally so in the other case, even though we suppose the sanctity and zeal of these preachers equal to that of the apostles? Will not the doctrine of the cross, on being proposed to the Chinese and Indians, appear as great folly as it did when proposed to the Romans? Would not all the mysteries of the Gospel be as incomprehensible to them as they were to the Gentiles in the days of the apostles? Would not the passions, prejudices, and vices of these nations, be as great an obstacle to their embracing the pure maxims of the Gospel as those of the heathens were at its first promulgation?

If it be said that the solid reasons and motives of credibility could be displayed to these people to convince them, it must be remembered that the chief and most essential of these motives are the miracles wrought at the first establishment of Christianity. And must not these appear as incredible to a nation that never heard of them before as the very mysteries themselves, of which they are the proofs? Besides, the motives of credibility would be only for the learned; the great multitude of the people could not penetrate nor comprehend them. If, therefore, when the Gospel is first proposed to any heathen nation, its obstacles and difficulties, both from its doctrines and maxims, and from the passions, prejudices, and vices of men—and we may add also, from the efforts of the devil to oppose it—must be as great in all succeeding ages as at its first appearance in the world, it must of course be no less worthy of God, and no less necessary for converting any nation, to work miracles in every succeeding age to the end of the world, than it was at the first establishment of Christianity.

XIV. This will appear still further if we consider that, under the Mosaic dispensation, when Almighty God would bring even particular persons among the heathens to the knowledge of Himself, and of what was then His true religion, He made use of miracles as the proper means; and we have seen above, that

He regarded this as an end most worthy of such divine interposition. Thus He miraculously cured Naaman's leprosy to procure his conversion. The miraculous preservation of the three children in the fiery furnace, and of Daniel in the lions' den, effectually convinced two great and powerful heathen kings, that the God Whom these holy men served was the only true God, the sovereign Lord of heaven and earth. If, therefore, it was worthy of Almighty God to work such glorious miracles under the law, for convincing individuals of His being the true God, even so many ages after that law was established among His people, how much more worthy of Him must it be to work miracles in every age of His Church, when the conversion of whole nations to the faith of Christ is the end to be gained by them!

XV. The preservation of the true religion, once established, from all attempts to corrupt or to destroy it, is another end which Almighty God judged worthy to secure under the law by working surprising miracles. This He did, whether those were the attempts of open force or secret fraud; whether the danger arose from heathens persecuting from without, or from the designs of impious men among the people of God themselves. See this illustrated by numerous examples in chap. vi. Now, from this conduct of the divine wisdom under the law, the probability of the same under the Gospel is exceedingly strong. The works of God are not like the works of men, subject to be corrupted and destroyed by numberless accidents, contrary to the will and design of those who perform them. When Almighty God performs any work, no power of man, no malice of hell, can destroy it against His will, or frustrate His views and designs in performing it; not a hair of your head falls to the ground without your heavenly Father, as we are assured by Christ Himself.

When the law was given by Moses, and the whole ceremonial of religion ordained among the Jews, the design of Almighty God was that this religion should continue to be professed and practised by them till the coming of the Messiah; that whilst the rest of mankind were, by His incomprehensible judgments, permitted to follow their own inventions, and to be led away by the delusions of Satan, there might never be wanting one nation at least wherein the worship of the true God should be preserved and practised. Almighty God, then, having thus determined that this religion should continue on the earth among His chosen people till the promised Redeemer should come to perfect it, never failed to protect and defend it by miracles whenever any attempt was made against it.

If we examine the idea which the Scriptures give us of the doctrine taught by Christ, and of the duration of the Christian religion in the world, we shall find, from the declarations of God Himself, that it was His express design and resolution that the purity of His true doctrine should never be corrupted in His Church, but that this holy religion should remain to the end of ages, in spite of every attempt to destroy it. Among the many testimonies of Holy Writ on this point, the following are particularly beautiful. In Isaiah, lix. 19, Almighty God makes this glorious promise to the Christian Church: "So shall they fear the name of the Lord from the west, and His glory from the rising of the sun. When the enemy shall come in like a flood, the Spirit of the Lord shall lift up a standard against him. And the Redeemer shall come to Zion, and unto them that turn from transgression in Jacob, saith the Lord.

And as for me, this is my covenant with them, saith the Lord. My Spirit that is upon thee, and my words which I have put in thy mouth, shall not depart out of thy mouth, nor out of the mouth of thy seed, nor out of the mouth of thy seed's seed, saith the Lord, from henceforth and for ever."

Let any person consider these words attentively, and say if it was possible to declare in stronger terms that the Spirit of God should never leave the true posterity of Jesus Christ, and that the pure doctrine once revealed to them should never depart from among them while the world endures. Almighty God expressly declares, that "when the enemy shall come in like a flood," and attempt to corrupt or destroy the work of God, His Holy Spirit, always abiding with His Church, "shall lift up a standard against him," to preserve the purity of the truth once put in her mouth, against all the rage and fury of the enemy and his utmost efforts to destroy it.

Another glorious promise to the same purpose we have in Psalm lxxxix. 3, where God says, "I have made a covenant with my chosen, I have sworn unto David my servant. Thy seed will I establish for ever, and build up thy throne to all generations." Verse 27, &c.: "I will make him my first-born higher than the kings of the earth. My mercy will I keep for him for evermore, and my covenant shall stand fast with him. His seed also will I make to endure for ever, and his throne as the days of heaven. Once have I sworn in my holiness, that I will not lie unto David. His seed shall endure for ever, and his throne as the sun before me. It shall be established for ever as the moon, and as a faithful witness in heaven."

This beautiful promise, confirmed by a solemn oath, that Christ, the true David, should reign for ever—that the Church, His kingdom, should last to the end of ages—

and that His seed should endure whilst the sun and moon have their being,—needs no application; it speaks for itself in the plainest terms. This is again confirmed by the angel Gabriel, and expressly applied to Christ, when he tells the blessed Virgin that her Son should sit on "the throne of His father David, and reign over the house of Jacob for ever; and of His kingdom," said he, "there shall be no end," Luke, i. 33. Christ Himself also assures us of the same truth, when He says, "Upon this rock will I build my Church, and the gates of hell shall not prevail against her," Matt. xvi. 18.

In these words He declares the perpetual stability of His Church by the solid foundation on which she is built. He foretells, indeed, that the gates of hell will continue their attempts to destroy her, but in vain; for He at the same time pledges His sacred word that they shall never be able to prevail against her—nay, in the fourteenth and sixteenth chapters of St John, He assures us, that after His ascension into heaven He would send the Holy Ghost, the Spirit of truth, upon His followers, who should abide with them for ever; and that His office should be to teach them all truth. In this promise He verifies what Almighty God had said by Isaiah many ages before, that the Holy Spirit to be given to the Redeemer, and the words once put in His mouth should never depart from the mouth of His seed, from henceforth and for ever.

XVI. From these testimonies of the Word of God the following truths manifestly flow: 1. That the kingdom of Christ, His Church, shall continue till the end of ages, whilst the sun and the moon endure. 2. That the true doctrine revealed by Him to His Church, the words which He puts in her mouth, shall never depart out of her mouth, but continue to be constantly taught and professed by her from henceforth and for ever. 3. That the enemy, the gates of hell, will assault her with all their power, coming upon her like a flood, and like a torrent to overwhelm and destroy her. But, 4. That God will never fail on all occasions to protect and defend her; that the Spirit of the Lord, her guardian and teacher, shall lift up a standard against the enemy which will baffle all his attempts, so that hell's proud gates shall never prevail against her—nay, instead of prevailing, we are further assured that those wicked men, whom the enemy will stir up as his instruments to fight against Christ and His Church, shall themselves be brought to ruin and desolation, as the just punishment of their impious attempts. "Behold," says Almighty God, foretelling the attempts of wicked men against His Church—"behold, they shall surely gather together, but not by me;" and He immediately adds their doom— "Whoever shall gather together against thee, shall fall for thy sake. No weapon that is formed against thee shall prosper, and every tongue that shall rise against thee in judgment thou shalt condemn," Isa. liv. To the same purpose He speaks in Ps. lxxxix. above cited, where, after the promises made to Christ, the true David, He adds, ver. 22, "The enemy shall not exact upon him, nor the son of wickedness afflict him, and I will beat down his foes before his face, and plague them that hate him."

XVII. That these prophecies of the attempts of the enemy against the Church of Christ have been literally fulfilled we are assured from the histories of all ages. No sooner did she appear in the world, and send forth her zealous pastors to declare the glad tidings of salvation to mankind, than immediately the most violent and cruel persecutions were raised against her. Hell seemed let loose, and, having engaged the greatest powers of earth on its side, and inflamed the violent passions and malice of the human heart, aimed at nothing less than her entire ruin. But in vain; her divine Master lifted up His standard in her defence, her foes were beaten down before her face—idolatry, that rose up against her, fell for her sake, and she at last gloriously triumphed over all her enemies.

Scarcely was peace restored to the Church by the conversion of the Roman emperors, when the powers of hell attacked her in another and more dangerous manner. Though driven out of one stronghold, they did not desist from their attempts; they shifted their ground, but laid not aside their malice. Finding her an overmatch in the open field, they hoped to accomplish by secret fraud what they could not achieve by open force; and as they were not able by persecutions to extinguish her faith, they endeavoured by heresies to change and to corrupt it.

St Paul, foreseeing the unrelenting attempts of Satan, foretells that "there must be also heresies among you, that they which are approved may be made manifest," 1 Cor. xi. 19; thereby pointing out the reason why the Divine Wisdom would allow these things, for the greater merit of His faithful servants, who should stand fast under all these dangers. Now, to promote this his design against the Church with the greater certainty, Satan makes use of her own rebellious children— "Men," as St Paul describes them, "lovers of their own selves, covetous, boasters, proud, blasphemous—incontinent, fierce, despisers of them that are good, traitors, heady, high-minded, lovers of pleasures more than lovers of God." These, the better to accomplish their ends, though rapacious wolves, clothe themselves with sheep's clothing; put on a form, an outward show, " of godliness, but denying the power thereof; men of corrupt minds, and reprobate concerning the faith," 2 Tim. iii.

Men of this kind the devil stirs up from among the children of the Church, who, as the same great apostle tells us, " Depart from the true faith, giving heed to seducing spirits and the doctrines of devils, speaking lies in hypocrisy, and having their consciences seared as with a hot iron," 1 Tim. iv. Having corrupted their faith, and hardened them in his service, he uses them to spread his doctrines among others, to seduce the faithful by false doctrines, and, if possible, to make lies and falsehood triumph over the truths of Jesus. But in vain; the same divine power which protected the spouse of Christ from open force, will, we are assured, equally defend her from these secret snares. Through the unsearchable judgments of God these dangerous attempts shall prevail with many, but, when they have come to the length permitted by divine providence, we are assured, by the same great apostle, that then " they shall proceed no further, for their folly shall be made manifest to all men," 1 Tim. iii. 9.

St Peter also, describing these attempts of Satan against the truth, speaks thus: " There shall be false teachers among you, who privily shall bring in damnable heresies;" but he immediately assures us that " they bring upon themselves swift destruction;" and though he also lets us know that " many shall follow their pernicious ways by whom the way of truth shall be evil spoken of," yet he immediately adds, that " their judgment now of a long time lingereth not, and their damnation slumbereth not," 2 Pet. ii.

In the description given us by these two apostles, we

see displayed the nature of those violent and dangerous snares which the gates of hell will use in all ages against the Church; but we are assured that they never shall prevail against her, that they shall proceed no farther, that they shall fall for her sake, and their damnation shall not slumber. That is to say, we are assured that whilst God permits the devil to rage against His Church, and to endeavour to corrupt the purity of her doctrine by heresies, He never fails at the same time to defend her truth, to manifest their folly, and to give her in the end a triumphant victory over all their efforts.

XVIII. Now, what are the means which we may expect the divine wisdom will employ for this purpose? The invincible fortitude of martyrs? the heroic constancy of confessors? the zealous labours of the Church pastors? All these, no doubt, will greatly contribute to confirm the faithful and defend the purity of the true doctrine. But these alone will not suffice. Nay, all these in some degree are to be found even among heretics. Heresy has had its martyrs, who, blinded by their passions, and excited by enthusiasm, have gone to death in profession of their false doctrines. Heresy, also, has had its confessors, who have suffered imprisonment and banishment for its sake; and among the characters which St Paul gives of heretics, one is the putting on a form of godliness, an outward show of piety, of zeal, of virtue; and experience shows the indefatigable labours which many heretics have undergone to propagate their sects, and corrupt the minds of the faithful. In fact, we find in the sacred Scripture that these things alone did not suffice to defend the true religion under the law when exposed to such dangers; and that therefore Almighty God Himself judged it necessary, and becoming His divine wisdom, to raise up another more efficacious standard to preserve it.

During the attempts of Jezebel and Achab against the true religion there were martyrs, for "Jezebel slew the prophets of the Lord;" there were confessors, for Obadiah "hid a hundred of them by fifties in a cave, and fed them with bread and water," 1 Kings, xviii. 13; there were zealous pastors; the great Elijah, who alone was worth thousands, who did not fail to stand up as a wall in defence of the truth, and to reprove the king for his impiety, threatening him with the divine justice if he persisted in it; but were these sufficient to confirm the people and defend the truth? No; they still halted between two opinions, many of them bowed their knees to Baal, and were on the point of entirely forsaking the God of their fathers. The holy prophet, full of zeal for the glory of his Master, had recourse to the all-powerful standard of miracles; and no sooner did these appear, than the clouds were dispelled from the minds of the people, their doubts removed, their faith confirmed, and with one voice they cried out, "The Lord, He is God! the Lord, He is God!"

Miracles, then, are the proper arms to defend the truth when attacked by error; they are the natural and effectual means to convince the human heart, because they are the language of God Himself, which can never be spoken by His enemies; they are the broad seal of heaven, confirming the doctrine of God beyond all reply. Hence we find, as we have seen above, that during the whole period of the Mosaic institution, whenever the true religion was attacked, God never failed to use these powerful means to defend it. From this we draw the undeniable conclusion, that if it was worthy of God to defend His true religion under the law, by working miracles on every occasion when it was in any danger, much more becoming His infinite wisdom and goodness must it be to perform miracles in defence of the Christian faith on similar occasions, to the end of time, when the gates of hell and the malice of man combine with united rage to destroy it.

That He will defend the true doctrine of His beloved Son from all such attempts to the end of the world is undoubted. He has repeatedly promised, and sworn by Himself, that He will do so. That miracles are the most proper, natural, and effectual means for this purpose is self-evident; that the using them for this end is worthy of Almighty God, and highly becoming His divine wisdom, is most certain, from what He actually did on all such occasions under the law; therefore we have the highest presumption, and the strongest probability, that He will actually continue to work miracles in defence of His truth throughout all ages, even to the end of the world.

I go a step further: we have seen that, under the law, the other means of defending the truth were insufficient; that miracles were therefore necessary for that purpose. Are they less so under the Gospel? At least it cannot be denied that, if not absolutely necessary, they are the most proper, the best suited to convince the human heart, and therefore the most effectual means for the above purpose. We conclude, therefore, that the conduct of Almighty God under the law, in defending the purity of His holy religion by miracles, not only gives us the highest probability, but even absolute certainty, that He will never fail under the Gospel to use the same glorious means from time to time in defence of His truth so long as the world endures.

XIX. Here I cannot help expressing my astonishment

at the conduct of those who pretend to restrict the duration of miracles in the Church to any certain period. Their reasoning seems one of the most humiliating examples of the weakness of human reason when engaged in a bad cause. However they disagree among themselves as to the precise period to be assigned for the cessation of miracles, they are most unanimous in giving the same reason for this pretended cessation at the different periods they assign. As long, say they, as the Church continued pure, the gift of miracles continued with her; but when the corruptions of Popery crept in, when her doctrine became infected by superstition, when "the Athanasian heresy," says Mr Whiston, "was established by her councils, and she became Athanasian, anti-Christian, and Popish," then that glorious gift of miracles was withdrawn from her, and the devil substituted his lying wonders in their place.

Is it possible to hear men arguing thus without astonishment and indignation? astonishment that men of sense and learning should speak in a manner so unworthy; indignation to hear expressions so injurious to Almighty God, and so contrary to every part of His conduct which He has been pleased to reveal? Can a serious Christian allow himself to believe, after what we have just now seen, that at the very time when the truths of God are supposed to stand in the greatest need of His protection; when the gates of hell are striving to prevail over the Church of Christ; when the enemy, like a torrent, seems upon the point of carrying all before him; that at that very time Almighty God should abandon His truth to be totally corrupted and defaced, and give up His Church as a prey to the enemy? Is it possible that a serious Christian can harbour such a thought, and not be shocked at the blasphemous supposition?

Yet it is upon this blasphemous supposition that Almighty God has altogether abandoned His Church to the tyranny of Satan, that He has proved false to all the solemn promises made to her, that He has allowed the devil for ages to work lying signs and wonders to delude mankind without giving them the least defence against them; it is upon this blasphemous supposition that all the various systems of Protestants are chiefly founded. Thus the main reason alleged by them is the very one from which we ought to draw the contrary conclusion, if we argue from the conduct of God in the old law, from the perpetuity of the Christian faith, the stability of the Church, and the solemn promises of Almighty God, made and confirmed by oath in the prophets, and the like sacred promises made by Christ Himself in the Gospel.

XX. Another great end which Almighty God judged worthy to procure by His divine interposition under the law was, "to assert and vindicate the honour of His priesthood, and of holy things which were more immediately used in His service, and to cause a proper respect and veneration to be paid to them." The sacred Scriptures are full of most surprising miracles wrought for these ends. Now, from this, we have another strong presumptive argument for the perpetual continuation of miracles throughout all ages under the Gospel; for the priesthood of Aaron, and all the holy things used in the externals of that religion, were only shadows of the good things to come; but the priesthood instituted by Jesus Christ was the substance of which the other was only the figure.

The priesthood of Aaron, and all its sacrifices and ceremonies, were incapable of cleansing consciences from sin, or of conferring the grace of God upon the soul; the functions annexed to the priesthood of Jesus Christ, by applying to us the merits of His passion and death, cleanse us from our past sins, adorn our souls with the grace of God, and enable us to avoid sin for the time to come. The priesthood of Aaron and its functions were confined to one nation; that of Jesus Christ is extended to all nations from "the rising of the sun to the going down of the same." The priesthood of Aaron was to last only for a time, till the better things should come; that of Jesus Christ is to last till the end of the world, "whilst the sun and moon endured."

Now, if it was worthy of Almighty God to work miracles to vindicate the sanctity of the priesthood, and of the holy things used in its ministry under the law, though but a shadow, a figure, a temporary institution, and incapable of conferring grace or cleansing away sin—how much more so must it be in order to vindicate the sanctity of the priesthood of Jesus Christ, and of all the sacred vessels used in its functions, which so immensely exceed that of Aaron in holiness, excellence, and utility to our souls! We have therefore a well-founded presumption that God will be no less ready to do so in defence of the latter, in all ages and in all nations, wherever the circumstances may require it.

XXI. The second source of presumptive evidence for this truth, is "the conduct of Jesus Christ Himself in the Gospel." In all I have hitherto said, I have taken no account of anything related in the New Testament; I have considered only what God has done under the Mosaic dispensation, and from that have concluded what we may reasonably presume He would do under the Gospel. If now we go a step further, and take a view of what the holy Scriptures assure us Jesus Christ has actually done, both by Himself and after His ascension by His apostles, we shall find another strong reason to expect the continuation of miracles in the Church of Christ till the end of the world. For if Jesus Christ judged the ends worthy of miracles in His own days; if He continued to judge them worthy of miracles in the days of His apostles after He Himself had left them—how could it be asserted that He would not judge them equally worthy of such divine interposition during every subsequent age of Christianity? Let us examine what the Gospel teaches us on this head.

XXII. In reasoning from the conduct of God in the old law, we concluded that we had the most just grounds to presume that when the new and more perfect revelation was made by Jesus Christ, it would be introduced into the world by miracles; nay, that the nature of the Gospel, and the difficulties it had to encounter from the passions and prejudices of men, made it necessary that it should be confirmed by miracles at its first appearance. And, lastly, as these difficulties were the same in all nations wherever it should first be preached, that it was a just presumption that miracles would continue to the end of the world whenever the introduction of the Gospel into any new nation or kingdom required it. Now, this conclusion we find literally verified by Jesus Christ and His apostles in the first age of Christianity. The miracles which He Himself wrought during His first publication of it among the Jews were innumerable; all nature was at His command; the heavens and the earth, men, angels, and devils, were subservient to His will. After His ascension, the apostles, whom He left to carry on the work which He had begun, acted in the same manner. Miracles of the most astonishing kind were wrought by their hands in proof of the heavenly doctrine which they taught. Their miracles converted multitudes, both Jews and Samaritans, of all states and conditions, and even many of the priests themselves became obedient to the faith. The change of their manners was no less remarkable than that of their faith. They became Christians in practice as well as in belief, and no force of persecution could shake their constancy and perseverance.

XXIII. When the Gospel had thus gained ground in Judea and Samaria; when a numerous and flourishing Church of Christians was established there; when these holy persons had arrived at the highest perfection, and breathed nothing but fervour and zeal for the glory of God and the good of souls,—did Jesus Christ consider their good example, their fervent preaching, piety, and zeal, sufficient to carry the Gospel to other nations, or even to those immediately around them? By no means. He well knew that the opposition which the Gospel would encounter everywhere at its first appearance would be insurmountable by natural means, unless accompanied with His seal and confirmed by miracles, as the incontestable proofs that the doctrine was divine.

Into whatever nation, therefore, the apostles went to introduce our holy religion, Almighty God never failed to accompany and confirm their words by signs and wonders. Thus, in the short account which St Mark gives us of the propagation of the Gospel after our Lord's ascension, he tells us that the apostles "went forth and preached everywhere, the Lord working with them, and confirming the Word with signs following," Mark, xvi. 20. St Paul also assures us that wherever he went to plant the Gospel, he did it "by mighty signs and wonders," Rom. xv. 19; and puts the Corinthians in mind that his preaching among them was "in demonstration of the Spirit and of power," 1 Cor. ii.

If, therefore, Jesus Christ judged it necessary, in introducing the Gospel into any heathen nation, to work miracles, even though the persons He employed were the apostles, those fervent, zealous, holy men upon whom He had poured out the plenitude of the gifts of the Holy Ghost, how much more must He judge it necessary to work miracles for the same end in after-ages, when the opposition and difficulties would be equal, and the instruments employed so much inferior to those great men who first planted the Gospel in the world! It is, then, most just and reasonable to conclude that He will continue so to propagate it throughout all nations to the end of the world.

XXIV. To convince mankind of the sanctity of His servants; to procure credit and authority for them, that by their words and examples others might be excited to greater fervour and devotion; to restore and preserve a spirit of piety,—is an end which we have seen Almighty God, under the law, judged worthy to procure by the most splendid miracles; and thence we justly conclude it to be no less so under the Gospel. Indeed we find that this was admirably procured, both by Jesus Christ Himself and by His apostles. How were the people filled with gratitude and love to God! how did they break forth into His praises when they saw the miracles of our Saviour! "And there came a fear upon all, and they glorified God, saying, A great prophet is risen up amongst us, and God has visited His people." How were they astonished at the miracles of the apostles, so that none of the "others durst join to them, but all the people magnified them"!

If, therefore, this was one of the principal fruits gained by the miracles of Christ and His apostles in their days, can it be doubted that the infinite goodness of God will continue to the end of ages, at proper times, to send His holy servants to recall mankind to their duty, to excite in them a spirit of devotion, to restore decayed piety, and to promote a greater fervour and zeal in His service, and that He will confirm their words and examples, even by miracles wrought from time to time by their means, for so noble an end?

XXV. Another great end which we have seen to be most worthy of a divine interposition by miracles, was to procure a just respect and veneration for persons in priestly orders, and for holy things. How does the conduct of Jesus Christ, by His apostles, lead us to infer that He will esteem this an end worthy of miracles throughout all ages! What respect, what veneration must not the punishment of Ananias and Sapphira have procured to St Peter, particularly when their crime in telling a lie to the chief pastor of the Church was declared to be telling a lie to the Holy Ghost Himself! What an exalted idea must it not have given the people of the sanctity and of the sacred dignity of this great apostle, when they saw that his very shadow passing over the sick cured them of whatever diseases they laboured under! What must they have thought of the sanctity of St Paul, when handkerchiefs and aprons, after touching his sacred body, also cured diseases! With what respect must they not have kept these sacred relics! What veneration must they not have paid to them, when they saw them so much honoured by Almighty God as to be the miraculous instruments of so great benefits to men!

Now, if from the conduct of Almighty God, in the old law, we found reason to expect that He would at all times, under the Gospel, judge it worthy of Himself to work miracles in order to procure respect to the priesthood and holy things; and if we find that Jesus Christ actually did so in the apostolic age, does not this afford the strongest presumption that He will continue to do so from time to time, as He sees occasion, in all future ages? In the old law Almighty God was pleased to give such a proof of the sanctity of His holy servant Elijah, that, after he was taken from among men, the very mantle which he had worn, upon touching the waters of the Jordan, became the instrument for dividing these waters into two parts, and leaving a passage for Elisha upon dry ground. After the death of Elisha, a dead corpse cast into his grave, and touching his sacred bones, was immediately restored to life. And, under the Gospel, in the apostolic age, God continues to act in the same manner, using the very shadow of St Peter, and handkerchiefs and aprons that had touched the body of St Paul, as instruments for miraculously curing all diseases. May we not therefore reasonably presume that He will in all succeeding ages continue to attest the sanctity of His holy servants, by making use of things belonging to them in their lifetime, or of their relics after death, as instruments for performing miracles?

XXVI. If we apply this to the other objects of miracles, as, rewarding the heroic virtues of His servants, supplying their temporal wants and necessities, especially such as they incur from their adherence to His service, or punishing sinners, either for their own correction or as a warning to others, we shall find that our present argument avails with equal strength in these as in the above examples. We have seen that the ends just mentioned are most worthy of a divine interposition; we have seen numbers of glorious instances in the old law, where Almighty God was pleased to perform most wonderful miracles to procure them; and hence we inferred that at all times, and in all ages under the Gospel, He would be ready to act in a similar manner when the like ends should require it. That this was a just presumption we are assured from the conduct of Jesus Christ.

If He cures the woman of her bloody flux, He declares it a reward of her great confidence in His goodness. If He cures the daughter of the Canaanean woman, He assures her it is in consequence of her faith and perseverance. If the multitudes, charmed with His heavenly conversation, follow Him to the wilderness, and continue there for three days without eating or drinking, He is moved with compassion towards them, and in reward of their love and affection, He once and again so multiplies a few loaves that they suffice to feed some thousands. If St Peter is thrown into prison, and loaded with chains, for his ardour and zeal in His service, an angel is sent from heaven to deliver him, the chains fall off his hands, and the iron gate opens to give him a safe passage out of prison, and to deliver him from the hands of Herod. If Elymas the magician strives to oppose the progress of the Gospel, and to prevent the proconsul Sergius from giving ear to the words of St Paul, at one word of that apostle he is struck blind, in punishment of his impious opposition to the work of God. It were endless to adduce all the examples related in the New Testament. But these are fully sufficient to show that the conduct of Jesus Christ under the Gospel confirms our conclusion from what Almighty God did under the law; and that as He has actually wrought many splendid miracles for these ends in the apostolic ages, we have the strongest grounds to conclude that He will continue from time to time to do so while the world endures.

XXVII. This shows wherein the force of this second

presumptive argument properly consists. In the former argument we concluded, from the ends of miracles in the old law, that they were worthy of that divine interposition; and therefore that we might reasonably presume that God, in all ages under the Gospel, would continue to work miracles for such ends, when the obtaining them should at any time require it; for here difference of time or place can have no weight. Nay, we considered several circumstances of the Gospel, showing that the necessity of working miracles for such ends was much greater under the Gospel than under the law; and therefore, that under it we might with greater reason expect them.

In the second argument we go a step further; we consider the conduct of Jesus Christ and His apostles as related in the New Testament, and of which, therefore, we are absolutely certain. We find this conduct precisely such as the conclusion in our former argument led us to expect; we see numbers of miracles wrought for the very same or similar ends. Hence we inferred the justness of our conclusion in the former argument, and, from the conduct of Jesus Christ in the apostolic age, we have a still stronger reason to presume that as He began the Gospel period by working so many miracles for the above ends, and by instruments similar to those which He used under the law, so He will continue in all succeeding ages to act in the same manner when similar circumstances may require it.

XXVIII. I come now to the third argument, which is taken from Christ's own sacred promises. At first I was in some doubt whether I should use these promises only as a presumptive proof, and not rather as positive evidence; because in themselves they are most ample, unlimited, and confirmed with His usual solemn asseveration; and the conditions annexed are such as must be found among Christians till the end of time. From this we might justly conclude, that these promises are not mere presumptive arguments, but strong and positive proofs; that the power of miracles will never be withdrawn from the Church while she has a being; for the express promise of God that anything will be, is as strong a proof beforehand that it will happen, as any positive human testimony can be afterwards that it has occurred. However, as our adversaries are obliged to put a limitation to these unlimited promises of our Saviour, I deemed it best to give them a place here among the presumptive arguments, and we shall see how unjust our adversaries are in presuming to limit or restrict them.

XXIX. The first promise I shall notice is from our Saviour's last sermon to His apostles on the night before His passion; where, after exhorting St Philip to believe in Him as God, equal to the Father, and appealing to His works as the testimony given by the Father to this truth, He immediately adds, with His usual asseveration, "Verily, verily, I say unto you, He that believeth in me, the works that I do shall he do also; and greater works than these shall he do, because I go unto my Father. And whatsoever ye shall ask in my name, that will I do, that the Father may be glorified in the Son," John, xiv. 12, 13.

Now, whether we consider the obvious sense of these words, the intention for which this promise was made, or the reasons upon which the performance of it was grounded, we clearly see that it does the greatest violence to the sacred text to affix any restriction or limitation to the duration of this glorious promise. For, in the first place, there is not the slightest insinuation of any such limitation either in the passage itself or in the context. He promises that His faithful followers, "he that believeth in me," shall perform miracles equal and even greater than He Himself had done. The only condition is, that the person should believe in Him—that is, should have that strong faith to which the grace of miracles is particularly attached. Now, as Almighty God will never be without true, holy, and faithful servants in every age to the end of the world, whose souls will be endowed with this sacred faith and every other divine virtue; and as, in the words of the promise itself, there is no insinuation of any limit to its duration where this faith is found, so there is every reason to conclude that the duration of the promise will never suffer limitation.

In the second place, the intention of the promise shows this still more fully. Our Saviour is here proving His own divinity, that He Himself is God equal to the Father. The argument to which He appeals as the most convincing proof of this truth is the working of miracles. This He proposes in two different lights. First, He appeals to the works which He had done: "Believe me that I am in the Father, and the Father in me; or else believe me for the very work's sake," ver. 11. But as His divinity was to be the object of our faith in all times to the end of the world, and as His miracles were seen only by those of His own days, and might be called in question or denied in after-ages, as they have been, and still are, by many; therefore He proposes a second proof both of His divinity and of His miracles—namely, that He would confer this very power on His faithful followers, who should be enabled to perform the same, and greater works than He Himself had done.

This was a proof beyond exception; for though an impostor might deceive the multitude by false signs and wonders, yet it is manifestly impossible that an impostor should confer upon his followers the power of working greater miracles than He Himself had done, and foretell this with certainty. It is true that the apostles at the time did not see this fulfilled, and therefore the argument could not have its full influence upon their minds; but they afterwards found it verified in themselves, and in their disciples, and then they both felt and were enabled to impart to others the fullest conviction of the divinity of their Lord and Master.

The intention of the promise clearly shows that it admits of no limit as to its duration. For it was made to His faithful followers as a proof of His divinity, especially where the miracles wrought by Himself might not suffice either from being unknown or disbelieved; and as these circumstances must frequently occur, especially when the Gospel is first proposed to heathen nations, it follows that this promise will hold good in every age, and be performed as the divine wisdom shall deem necessary for the end intended. Lastly, If we consider the reasons of this promise, we see the same conclusion more and more confirmed. He gives two. First, because He was soon to leave this world and return to the Father: "Greater works than these shall he do, because I go to the Father," ver. 12. Now, what connection has this reason with the promise? The connection is evident and natural: "Hitherto, whilst I was visibly present upon the earth, I have wrought such miracles as I knew were fully sufficient to convince you, my faithful followers, of all I have taught you; I also, by my own presence, have instructed, comforted, and assisted you in your necessities: but I am about to leave you and return to the Father; and after I am gone you will be exposed to innumerable trials, persecutions, and afflictions, from the fury of hell and the malice of the world; but I will not leave you Comfortless," ver. 18. "I will pray the Father, and He will give you another Comforter, that He may abide with you for ever, even the Spirit of truth," ver. 16. "And this Comforter, which is the Holy Ghost, He shall teach you all things," ver. 26. "And when they bring you into synagogues, and magistrates, and powers, take ye no thought how or what thing ye shall answer, or what ye shall say: for the Holy Ghost shall teach you in the same hour what ye ought to say," Luke, xii. 11. "And I will give you a mouth and wisdom, which all your adversaries shall not be able to gainsay nor resist," Luke, xxi. 15. And, lastly, for your further support and comfort under your afflictions, to enable you to overcome all your adversaries, to convince them that your doctrine is from me, that I am the true God equal to the Father, and that when I leave this world I go to the Father, and have the same power with Him in all things, I will bestow upon my faithful followers the power of working miracles, even greater than I myself have done; "he that believeth on me, the works that I do shall he do also; and greater than these shall he do, because I go to the Father."

It is plain that all these promises were intended, after our Saviour's departure from this world, for the support, encouragement, and comfort of the apostles, of their successors in the ministry, and of all faithful Christians, who must suffer persecution if they wish to live piously in Christ Jesus. Now, the former of these promises, of the coming of the Holy Ghost to teach them all things, and suggest to them what to answer when called before civil powers, was immediately addressed to the apostles; yet no one doubts but this will continue to be fulfilled to the end of the world whenever circumstances should require it. Nay, it is expressly declared that the Holy Ghost will abide with His Church for ever for this very purpose. But this latter promise of the power of working miracles was not addressed to the apostles immediately in their own persons, but to all true believers, "he that believeth on me;" consequently, if the former promise, though addressed immediately to the apostles, is yet justly understood as admitting no limitation, much more ought the latter to be taken in the same unlimited sense, being addressed to the faithful in every age. With greater reason, therefore, must we believe that the Holy Ghost, to whose grace and operation the gift of miracles is chiefly attributed, abiding with His Church, will never fail to fulfil this latter promise also in the absence of our Saviour, when the support of the faithful, the propagation of the Gospel, or any other end which Almighty God judges worthy, shall require His doing so.

The second reason of the above promise is given by our Saviour in these words: "And whatsoever ye shall ask in my name, that will I do, that the Father may be glorified in the Son," ver. 13. This promise was designed to be a proof of the divinity of Jesus Christ. The performance of it served powerfully in His absence for this purpose; but the manner of performing it serves still more: "Whatsoever," says He, "you shall ask in my name, that will I do." When any of you, my faithful followers, shall perform a miracle, you must do it "in my name,"—you must ask the Father, "in my name," to grant it; and I here pledge my sacred word, that whatever you ask in this manner, "in my name," and with a full faith, I will undoubtedly perform. We have seen above, in the rules of the criterion, how unanswerable a proof it is that a miracle is truly the work of God when it is done in His name. Here, then, Jesus Christ promises, without any limitation, to perform this proof of His divinity when His faithful servants, in suitable circumstances, shall demand it of Him, in order, as He adds, "that the Father may be glorified by the Son." Now, as these circumstances will occur in every age, especially in converting heathen nations, we justly conclude that this promise admits of no limitation of time, but will be performed to the end of the world, when required to convince mankind of the divinity of Jesus Christ, and to glorify the Father by the Son.

XXX. In the two preceding arguments of presumptive evidence we have seen that it is worthy of Almighty God to perform miracles in any age when the above ends shall require it. We have seen that some of these ends will never be wanting while the world endures. We have seen that Jesus Christ has actually wrought many miracles by Himself, and by His followers, for these ends, during the first age of Christianity, and therefore we conclude that we have just reason to expect that the miraculous powers will continue in the Church to the end of time. If to these presumptive arguments we add the above solemn promise of Jesus Christ, and the reasons which prove that it can admit of no limitation, I appeal to common-sense whether this does not afford us, I do not say merely a presumptive evidence, but even a positive assurance, that the power of miracles will never be withdrawn from the Church of Christ while the world endures.

XXXI. As the above promise confirms the presumptive evidence of the two preceding arguments, so they afford another convincing proof that the promise ought to be understood in the unlimited sense in which I have explained it. From the presumptive arguments we have the strongest reason to expect that Almighty God will from time to time work miracles in His Church to the end of the world. Jesus Christ makes a solemn promise to His faithful followers, "he that believeth in me," to bestow upon them the power of working even greater miracles than He Himself had done. He makes it in general terms; He puts no limitation either of time or place. The question is, How long is this promise to continue? If, as we have seen above, there be the strongest presumption to expect that miracles will be wrought in every age to the end of the world, this plainly shows that the promise of Christ, to which He Himself has attached no limitation, is most certainly so to be understood as we have proved by other intrinsic reasons, which together amount to an unanswerable proof that the power of working miracles will continue to be exerted in the Church from time to time to the end of the world.

XXXII. The next promise made by our blessed Saviour on this subject is mentioned in the last chapters of St Matthew and St Mark, when, before His ascension, He gave His apostles their commission to publish His Gospel throughout all nations. In St Matthew it is thus related: "And Jesus came and spake unto them, saying, All power is given unto me in heaven and in earth: go ye therefore and teach all nations, baptising them in the name of the Father, and of the Son, and of the Holy Ghost; teaching them to observe all things whatsoever I have commanded you: and, lo, I am with you alway, even to the end of the world," Matt. xxviii. In St Mark several other circumstances not noticed by St Matthew are added as follow: "And he said unto them, Go ye unto all the world, and preach the Gospel to every creature. He that believeth and is baptised shall be saved, and he that believeth not shall be damned. And these signs shall follow them that believe: In my name they shall cast out devils; they shall speak with new tongues; they shall take up serpents; and if they drink any deadly thing it shall not hurt them; they shall lay their hands on the sick, and they shall recover. So then after the Lord had spoken unto them, He was received up into heaven, and sat on the right hand of God. And they went forth and preached everywhere, the Lord working with them, and confirming the word with signs following," Mark, xvi.

On these two passages we may observe, First, That our Saviour begins by assuring us, that all power is given unto Him in heaven and on earth, and thereby removing all doubt as to His performing whatever He promises. Secondly, He gives the apostles the commission to teach all nations the sacred truths which He had revealed to them, and absolutely requires that all nations should receive and believe these truths under pain of damnation. Thirdly, To remove all ground of complaint, as if He had not given mankind sufficient evidence that these truths were really from Him, He solemnly promises the gift of miracles to His faithful followers, as the undoubted proof that what they taught were the truths of God; so that whosoever refused to believe should be altogether inexcusable. Fourthly, He promises to be always with His apostles in this great work to the end of the world, thereby showing that this commission and these promises were not confined to the apostles, who were soon to leave the world, but were made to them and to their successors to the end of time. Fifthly, We are assured that, immediately upon the apostles' beginning to execute their commission by preaching the Word, the

Lord fulfilled His promise, confirming their words with signs following; thereby showing that He will continuously perform it in its full extent in every succeeding age. Sixthly, It is also to be observed that though the commission of teaching was directly conferred on the apostles, yet the promise of miracles was given to those that believe.

The plain and natural consequence of these observations is, that miracles, without restriction of time or place, are here promised to true believers, as a proof of the truth of the Gospel when taught to the nations, as Christ's presence for assisting the pastors of His Church in this great work is expressly promised to the end of the world; and, finally, as this great work will not be fully accomplished till towards the end of the world, this promise of miracles will therefore continue to be fulfilled from time to time till that period, as often as the end for which it is here made shall require it. If we add to this what we have said above upon the former promise from John, xiv., and what we have seen in the two first arguments of presumptive evidence, I appeal to our adversaries themselves whether it be not a manifest wresting of the sacred texts, and the utmost presumption, to pretend to limit these divine promises to any age or period whatever.

XXXIII. The last promises I shall notice are those made on different occasions to a strong faith, and related in the different Gospels. When the disciples saw the fig-tree wither away upon their Master's commanding it, "they marvelled, saying, How soon is the fig-tree withered away! Jesus answered and said unto them, Verily I say unto you, If ye have faith and doubt not, ye shall not only do this which is done to the fig-tree, but also, if you shall say unto this mountain, Be thou removed, and be thou cast into the sea, it shall be done. And all things, whatsoever ye shall ask in prayer, believing, ye shall receive," Matt. xxi. 21; Mark, xi. 23. Again, when the disciples could not cure the lunatic child, and asked their Master the reason, "Jesus said unto them, Because of your unbelief: for verily I say unto you, If you have faith as a grain of mustard-seed, ye shall say unto this mountain, Remove hence to yonder place, and it shall remove, and nothing shall be impossible to you," Matt. xvii. 20. Lastly, When the apostles begged their Master to increase their faith, He said, " If ye had faith as a grain of mustard-seed, ye might say to this sycamore tree, Be thou plucked up by the root, and be thou planted in the sea, and it should obey thee," Luke, xvii. 6.

On these texts I shall only observe, that in them we find the working of the most stupendous miracles attached to a strong faith and confidence in God, without the slightest hint of restriction or limitation of any kind, either as to time or place. As there is not, therefore, the smallest reason to imagine that such faith may not be found in some holy servants of God in all ages of the Church to the end of the world, we may conclude that the miraculous powers will never be withdrawn from the Church in any age whatever.

XXXIV. I come now to the last source of presumptive evidence taken from what we know will happen at the end of the world. We are assured then, in the Book of Revelation, that during the dreadful times of Antichrist, the two witnesses will appear to oppose him, invested with the most ample power of miracles: " If any man will hurt them, fire proceedeth out of their mouths and devoureth their enemies. These have power to shut heaven, that it rain not in the days of their prophecy, and have power over waters to turn them into blood, and to smite the earth with all plagues as often as they will," Rev. xi.

Here, then, we are assured that miracles most amazing, and in great numbers, will be performed by these defenders of the cause of God in the last age of the Church. It is acknowledged by all that they were performed in great abundance in the first and some following ages: there is not the smallest insinuation in the Scriptures that the power of performing them should, after any period of time, be withdrawn from the Church, and at the end be restored. Therefore we may justly conclude that no such interruption ever was or ever will be made. On the contrary, with great reason we assume that, as these powers most certainly were in the Church at the beginning, and undoubtedly will be at the end, so they will never be taken from her at any intervening period, but will continue to be exerted in every age, whenever the promotion of the divine glory shall require it. Join this presumptive argument with all the former, and let common-sense pronounce upon their combined strength.

XXXV. I shall now sum up what I have advanced on this head of presumptive evidence for the continuation of miracles in all ages, in the manner that Mr Brook has done for the first three centuries, and as nearly as possible in his own words: "Thus it will appear, I think, from the history of these extraordinary and divine powers with which the saints of God were endowed in every age during the old law, from the ends for which these powers were given them, from the conduct of Jesus Christ during the first age of the Gospel, and from the several unlimited promises of bestowing these powers upon His faithful followers, that there is a strong, even the strongest, presumption for the continuance of miracles in the true Church of Christ till the end of the world. This presumption is much heightened by considering that all and every one of those ends for which Almighty God wrought so many miracles under the old law, and for which many were also wrought by Christ and His apostles in the first age of the Gospel, must necessarily occur on numberless occasions in every succeeding age, and very frequently in circumstances which render the aid of miracles much more necessary than it was in those former times in which he actually wrought so many miracles on their account."

XXXVI. Dr Middleton, and every other man who professes himself a Christian, must allow that miracles were wrought in great abundance, not only at the first establishment of the Mosaic institution, but on many different occasions in every period during its existence. They must allow that miracles were wrought in great numbers during the lives of the apostles, and that the Christian religion was first propagated by an extraordinary providence. Mr Brook will also allow, and has indeed fully proved, that the same extraordinary providence continued, and that miracles were wrought in no less abundance during the first three ages of Christianity.

Other Protestant authors, with equal reason, have ascertained the continuance of miracles in the Church of Christ for several succeeding ages. The question then will be, Whether we have reason to conclude that the same extraordinary providence has continued ever since, and will continue to the end of the world? If the probability of an event is to be determined by the likelihood of its happening, and if that thing is allowed to be likely to happen, which has frequently, and in a variety of instances, already come to pass, then it may reasonably be presumed, that if there were such frequent interpositions of the Deity for the several ends above specified, in every age during the law, and for several ages at the beginning of the Gospel, it is likely that in all succeeding ages the same extraordinary interpositions would from time to time be continued in similar cases, and where the same important ends present themselves.

If to this be added the several promises of Christ, of bestowing the gift of miracles on His faithful followers,—the reasons of these promises, the ends proposed, the unlimited terms in which they are conveyed—and, lastly, what we know will undoubtedly happen at the end of the Church in this world,—I think every man of common-sense will readily agree that they amount not only to the greatest probability, but even to a certainty, that the power of working miracles will never be taken from the Church of Christ, but will continue to be exerted by the holy servants of God in every age to the end of the world; and therefore that if a particular miracle in any age be properly attested, it is justly worthy of credit. The nature of this attestation I now proceed to consider.

CHAPTER XV.

POSITIVE EVIDENCE FOR THE CONTINUATION OF MIRACLES THROUGHOUT ALL PRECEDING AGES DOWN TO THE PRESENT TIMES.

I. THE result of our observations upon the criterion and continuation of miracles is, that the evidence of testimony is the only natural and proper proof for the existence of miracles to those who were not eye-witnesses of them; and that no metaphysical arguments *a priori*, can, in the smallest degree, weaken the force of this evidence when the testimony is trustworthy. That the miraculous powers will be continued in the Church of Christ throughout all ages to the end of the world we have the strongest presumptive evidence: and there is not the smallest weight in any argument brought to the contrary. If the positive testimony, therefore, be unexceptionable, it is the height of folly to call the existence of miracles in question.

II. Before we examine the nature of this testimony, it will be proper to notice an instance of unfair dealing on this subject in some of the adversaries of the Catholic Church; for we must distinguish three different classes of miracles with respect to the testimony on which they they are founded. First, those which have no other ground than popular report, or mere oral tradition, without any proof of their existence from history, authentic testimony, ancient monuments, or the like.

Now, on miracles of this class no stress whatever is laid; for though the mere want of proper evidence is not absolute proof that such miracles never did exist, yet it is a just reason for not appealing to them on the point in question, and accordingly it is never done. But when they have a good moral tendency, serving to illustrate points of religion, or to enforce any practical duty, they are justly used as parables, after the example of our blessed Saviour Himself in the Gospel. And experience teaches those who are conversant with the care of souls, how much a well-timed example or parable of this kind serves to influence the minds of the unlearned, and to render the great truths of religion intelligible to them. Neither can this use of such parables be reasonably objected to; since, besides the example of Jesus Christ who authorises it, we see that nothing is more common, even among those who declaim against them, than to propose moral duties for the instruction of others, by narratives professedly false, by fables, novels, romances, and the like; whereas the examples and parables of which we speak, though not attested by positive proof, may yet have been true and real—and many of them undoubtedly are so. For it is well known that many extraordinary favours done to the saints of God are studiously concealed by them through humility, and though afterwards discovered and published, are not always so properly attested as to carry evidence to posterity. Besides, many things have been fully attested when they happened, though the testimony has by length of time been lost, whilst the memory of the fact has been preserved by oral tradition to after-ages. But whatever may be thought of this, miracles of this class are entirely set aside when there is question of proving the continuation or existence of miracles in the Church, and only those of the two following classes are regarded.

The second class contains those miracles which are properly attested by judicious historians, or other writers of credit and authority; who either were themselves eye-witnesses of what they relate, or had ample means of knowing the truth, and published their works in such circumstances as render their testimony above suspicion.

The third class contains those miracles which have undergone the rigorous examination of the Church in her process for the canonisation of saints, and have been authentically published to the world as true and incontestable, after such examination.

III. Now, right reason and common justice require that, when the adversaries of the Catholic Church attempt to disprove or ridicule her miracles by examining any particular case, they should select one belonging either to the second or third class. But this justice they seldom do. Nay, we find that two of her most declared modern adversaries, Mr Hume, in his Essay on Miracles, and Dr Campbell, in his Dissertation against that Essay, have not so much as attempted to examine any one particular miracle authentically approved by the Church, belonging either to the second or third class, but have only attacked and ridiculed a mere popular hearsay, and a collection of pretended miracles, the forgery and falsity of which have been detected and exposed by her own pastors. The reason of this conduct will easily be intelligible when we consider the character of miracles of the second and third class, the nature of the testimony, and the solid ground on which they stand. This I now proceed to examine.

IV. In examining miracles of the second class—that is, those which are properly attested by judicious historians of credit and authority, I do not intend to adduce examples in the different ages of the Church, and to point out in each the strength of the testimony on which we receive them. This would lead me to an unreasonable length; neither is it necessary, as it has already been ably done by the learned author of 'The Miraculous Powers of the Church,' &c., in that masterly performance. I shall therefore confine myself to a general view of the nature and circumstances of the testimony, which will fully answer my purpose, and which I chiefly take from the judicious observations of that pious author.

V. First, then, if we consider the characters of those persons who attest the existence of miracles in their own days throughout every age, we shall find them above all suspicion, the holy fathers and chief pastors of the Church, men raised up by Almighty God from time to time as the great luminaries of the Christian world, replenished with a superabundant measure of the divine Spirit, and whose lives were spent in the most perfect exercise of all Christian virtues. The many excellent and justly-admired writings which they left behind them, and which still remain, are unexceptionable proofs of their deep penetration, acute judgment, and extensive learning. The position which many of them held in the Church gave them every opportunity to search into the truth, and their duty required them to use every precaution to prevent their flock being deceived by impostors. We cannot, therefore, doubt either their ability or diligence in investigating the truth, much less can we suspect that they would wilfully deceive by publishing to the world anything as true which they knew to be false.

They were Christians, exemplary Christians, whose whole study was to live up to the perfection of Christian virtue. They well knew that it was absolutely unlawful to deviate from the truth for any cause whatever. They preached this doctrine to their people; they have left it on record in their writings; and whenever occasion offered, they always protested their attachment to the truth in whatever they related.

Thus St Justin Martyr declares that he would rather lose his life than save it by a lie; St Sulpicius Severus, in his life of St Martin, does the same: "I entreat those who shall read it," says he, "that they would believe what I say, and be persuaded that I have written nothing but what is well attested and assured; for I had rather be silent than tell an untruth." St Augustine, also, who relates many remarkable miracles as within his own knowledge, and of which he was an eyewitness, shows his utter abhorrence of all lies in many different parts of his writings, particularly in his book to Consentius, where he says, "All lies, without exception, are to be excluded from the doctrine of religion, and even from every proposition which is uttered concerning that doctrine in the teaching and learning of it. And let it not be imagined that there can possibly be any reason found for telling a lie in such matters; since it is not justifiable to tell a lie about religious doctrines, even for the sake of converting a person more easily by them; for if the fence of truth be once broken down, or even but slightly weakened, everything will be rendered uncertain," c. x.

This doctrine is held and professed by the saints in all ages. Their cause was the cause of truth; they believed themselves, and laboured to impress on others, that to deviate from the known truth, or to propagate a known falsehood, is a crime for which we must account to Almighty God, by whom it will be severely punished. We cannot, then, suppose them capable of attesting and publishing to the world as truth the smallest thing which they were conscious was a falsehood. Witnesses of this character are above suspicion, especially when we consider that they are numerous, of different countries, in different ages, and that they give their testimony to facts that happened in the very times in which they themselves lived : "Such a general attestation of matters of fact," says Mr Brook, speaking of this testimony in the first three ages, but which is perfectly applicable to every succeeding age—"such a general attestation of matters of fact, which are in themselves unexceptionable, is ever thought authentic and substantial. Nothing, indeed, but the force of truth itself, and the reality of the things themselves thus related, is able to create so unanimous, so universal a consent."—Brook's Exam., p. 145.

VI. But the weight of this universal testimony of such witnesses in every age is increased when we consider the manner in which it is given, and the circumstances attending it. Under this head there are several things worthy of attention. The witnesses do not mention the miracles they speak of as popular reports or mere hearsays; they attest them as facts strictly consistent with their own knowledge, of which they either were themselves eyewitnesses, or had them from such as were. Thus Origen, in his first book against Celsus, declares that the Christians in his days "drive away devils, perform many cures, foresee things to come, according to the will of the divine Word." And a little after he adds : "I have seen many examples of this sort, and should I only set down such of them as took place in my presence, I should expose myself to the ridicule of the unbelievers, who imagine that we, like others whom they suspect of forging such things, are imposing our forgeries also upon them: but God is my witness that my sole purpose is to recommend the religion of Jesus, not by fictitious tales, but by clear and evident facts."

In like manner, the great St Athanasius, in his preface to the life of St Anthony, relates many extraordinary and miraculous effects of the divine power, and says: "The facts which I have inserted are partly from my own knowledge, for I often went to see him, and partly from the information of one who had long attended on him; in all which I have carefully adhered to truth." And in the course of the history itself he relates several of these miracles done by the saint in his own presence. St Paulinus also relates miracles performed by St Ambrose before his own eyes; and the celebrated miracles wrought in Milan by the relics of the holy martyrs, Sts Gervase and Protase, are related both by St Ambrose and St Augustine, as facts of which they themselves, as well as thousands of others, were eyewitnesses.—See St Ambr. Ep. 2, ad Sororem Marcellin, et St Aug. Confes. l. ix., c. 7.

St Chrysostom, speaking of the sign of the cross, says: "This sign, both in the days of our fathers and in our own, has thrown open gates that were shut, destroyed the effects of poisonous drugs, dissolved the force of hemlock, and cured the bites of venomous beasts," t. vii. p. 552. St Paulinus has celebrated, both in prose and verse, many miracles performed by the relics of St Felix the martyr; and, poem 23, he declares that many of them were actually performed in his own presence. St Augustine, in his excellent work on the city of God, relates many extraordinary miracles done in his time and before his own eyes, at which, says he, *nos interfui-*

mus et oculis aspeximus nostris: "I myself was present, and beheld with my own eyes;" and coming to the famous cure of two persons at the shrine of St Stephen, he gives a most circumstantial account of it as having been performed before the whole people, and says: "It is so public and celebrated that I do not think there is one of all the inhabitants of Hippo who did not see it, or hath not been informed of it; nor one that can ever forget it."

Theodoret, bishop of Cyrus, declares himself to have been eyewitness to several miracles wrought by the holy monks of his time. He was intimately acquainted with many of them, and has transmitted to posterity a circumstantial account of the wonderful works which God performed by their means. Speaking of St Simeon Stylites, he says: "I myself saw another most celebrated miracle," which he relates in the cure of a sick man; and adds, "I was not only a spectator of his miracles, I was also a hearer of his predictions;" several instances of which, and their full accomplishment, he describes.

Æneas of Gaza, in his dialogue between Theophrastus and Aritheus, speaking of the African confessors, whose tongues had been cut out by the Arians, but who miraculously retained the perfect faculty of speech, says: "I myself saw these men, and heard them talk, and was astonished that they could speak so articulately; I looked for the organ of speech, and, not trusting my ears, I examined the matter with my eyes, and having opened their mouths, saw that their tongues were entirely cut away, root and all. Upon which I was amazed, not only that they could speak, but even that they had not expired in the execution." Procopius also attests that he had seen them at Constantinople.

The same language we find used in every age by those

who attest these matters; but as it would be tedious to collect all, I shall conclude with Geoffroy, one of St Bernard's disciples, who writes his life, and declares, "I was present at almost all the transactions I relate; some few things to which I was not an eyewitness have been attested to me by brethren on whose veracity I can depend." But, 2. What makes this declaration still more worthy of credit is, that they often call God Himself to witness the truth of what they attest. This we have seen above was done by Origen. Palladius also, in his history of the fathers of the desert, relates numerous miracles performed by those great saints, not only from the report of credible witnesses, but from his own certain knowledge, declaring that he had seen the wonderful works himself, and assures us that, by the grace of God, he tells the truth.

St Sulpicius Severus was a learned and pious priest, who wrote the life of that great prelate, St Martin of Tours, in which numbers of splendid miracles wrought by the saint are related; and in the beginning of it he says: "I entreat those who shall read it that they would believe what I say, and be persuaded that I have written nothing but what is well attested and assured; for I had rather be silent than tell an untruth." And in the fifth chapter he declares that he should esteem it a crime to tell a lie in favour of St Martin; and calls Christ to witness that he has related nothing but what either he himself had seen or received from known witnesses, and for the most part from St Martin himself.

The sixth book of the life of St Bernard, written by his disciple Geoffroy, is an attested narrative of a number of miracles wrought by the saint in different places, supported by unexceptionable witnesses, the bishop of Constance, his chaplain, two abbots, two monks, and three clergymen, who accompanied the saint, and day by day attested and attached their names to what they were eyewitnesses of; and in their attestation they thus express themselves: "We that were present have judged it necessary to specify the miracles as well to prevent confusion as to preclude all doubt: we have each of us signed our names, and do solemnly attest what we have seen and heard."

To mention one instance more: In the fourteenth century lived St Catherine of Sienna, remarkable for the many miracles wrought by her means. Her confessor, F. Raymond, General of the Order of the Dominicans, wrote her life, with which he was well acquainted, and candidly acknowledges that for a long time he doubted of the reality of those heavenly things which he saw in her; till, having maturely examined them, and experienced in himself the wonderful efficacy of her prayers, he was fully satisfied, and therefore in the presence of God avers the truth of what he relates.

What confirms still more the veracity of this their testimony is, 3. That they often appeal to their very enemies for the truth of what they attest, as a thing public and perfectly consistent with their knowledge. Thus St Justin Martyr, in his second apology to the Roman Senate, says: "This you may understand by what happens before your own eyes: for many persons possessed with devils, through the whole world, and in this very city, have been delivered, and are even now delivered, by several of our Christians adjuring them in the name of Jesus Christ." Tertullian challenges the heathen magistrates "to call before their tribunals any person manifestly possessed with a devil; and if the evil spirit, when exorcised by any Christian whatsoever, did not own himself a devil, as truly as in other places he would falsely call himself a god, not daring to tell a lie to a Christian; that then they should take the life of that Christian. And what is more manifest, says he, than this work? what more convincing than this proof?" Apol. c. 23. St Jerom also, writing against Vigilantius, who denied that any veneration was due to the relics of the martyrs, appeals to the very miracles done by those relics, as evident and manifest proofs against that heretic: "Answer me," says he, "how comes it to pass that in this vile dust and ashes, as you call them, of the martyrs, there is so great a manifestation of signs and miracles?"

Again, 4. In several cases the testimony, the miracles themselves, and the opposition made against them by the adversaries of the Catholic faith, have been examined at the very time; but this had only the effect of establishing them the more firmly. Thus the celebrated miracles wrought at Milan by the relics of the two holy martyrs, Sts Gervase and Protase, had such influence on the minds of the people that it greatly alarmed the Arians, who made every effort to discredit them, both by lies and misrepresentations, and by the interest of the court, then residing in that city. But all in vain. The people knew what they had seen. The notoriety of what was done prevailed over all these efforts, and in spite of the rage of the empress and her party, gave a check to the persecution against the Catholics.—See St Ambr., Ep. 2. ad Marcellinam.

In like manner, in the Arian persecution in Africa, under Hunneric, King of the Vandals, we have the celebrated miracle of restoring sight to a blind man, before the whole people, by Eugenius, Bishop of Carthage, which is related at length by St Victor, Bishop of Vite, in his history of this persecution. This created such a sensation, "that the news," says St Victor, "was soon carried to Hunneric; the man was apprehended, and questioned about all that had happened, and the recovery of his sight. He gave a faithful account of every circumstance: whereby the Arian bishops were put to the utmost confusion. The reality of the miracle could not be denied, for Felix—the blind man—was known to the whole city."

Again, 5. The time and manner in which this their testimony was published to the world is another convincing proof of their veracity; for they do not publish their accounts of the miracles they relate, as of things that happened long before, or in other parts of the world, but as of facts occurring at the very time, and in the very place where they mention them, and as well known to the people to whom they publish them. Several examples of this we see in those named above; as of St Augustine in his 'City of God,' where, B. 22. cap. 8, he says: "Even at this time miracles are wrought in the name of Jesus, as well by His sacraments as by the prayers and memorials of His saints. The cure of the blind man at Milan was done in the presence of a vast concourse of people, who were there assembled at the bodies of the martyrs Gervase and Protase." A little after, he adds: "There was one miracle wrought among us, so public and so celebrated, that I do not think there is one of all the inhabitants of Hippo who did not see it, or has not been informed of it;" and then he proceeds to relate it. This relation he published in Hippo to the very people before whom he declares that the miracle was performed. Must he not have been insane to do so if what he related had never happened?

In like manner, Theodoret published the life and

wonderful miracles of St Simeon Stylites while the saint was still living, and thousands were alive who had been eyewitnesses of what he related, so that he could not have escaped detection if what he stated had not been literally true. When St Victor, Bishop of Vite, published to the world his history of the African confessors, whose tongues had been cut out by Hunneric, and who yet retained the perfect use of speech, he says: "If any man makes a difficulty in believing this, let him go to Constantinople, and there he may see one of them, Reparatus by name, a sub-deacon, who speaks perfectly, and is highly esteemed by all in the palace of the Emperor Zeno." Could this author have escaped detection had this relation been a fiction? Lastly, the life of St Bernard was written by one of his own disciples, and published soon after his death, while thousands were alive who, had there been any falsehood in the miracles, were able to expose the fraud to the utter confusion of the publishers.

I cannot help adding here two examples similar to the last mentioned, that of St Cyril of Jerusalem, and of St Gregory the Great. The former, in his homily preached to his people "on the paralytic," declares publicly, as a thing well known among them, that the gifts of prophecy, of healing the sick, and of casting out devils, were granted at that time to some of the faithful at Jerusalem; and he there publicly exhorts those on whom these graces were bestowed to be humble, and to repress all thoughts of pride and vanity that might arise in their breasts on that account. But how ridiculous would not this have been had not his hearers well known the truth of what he thus asserted! In like manner, St Gregory the Great writes to St Augustine, the apostle of the English, exhorting him to be humble, and not to allow his mind to be elated by the many miracles God was pleased to work by His hands for the conversion of that people, which would have been highly inconsistent, and would have exposed him to the just censure of the world, if these miracles had never taken place. To these I may add St Chrysostom—though he more properly belongs to the former class—who, in his Discourse 32, tom. 7, mentions to his hearers as a thing public and well known among them, that many had been healed of their diseases by anointing themselves with oil taken from the lamps burning before the relics of the martyrs. It is evident, then, that the manner in which this testimony is given, and the circumstances attending it, are such as to remove every suspicion of imposture, and give the highest value to the attestation.

VII. The nature of the facts attested is another strong evidence of veracity; for these were by no means fit subjects for imposture; but palpable, plain open facts, such as giving sight to the blind, curing the sick, and raising the dead to life. In judging of such cases the learning of a philosopher is not required. In such things the most illiterate person is as capable of discerning the truth as the man of the greatest learning.

VIII. Fourthly, The effects produced by these miracles is another striking proof of their reality. They are chiefly three: 1. "The conversion of heretics." Thus the numbers of Arians converted by the miracles which were wrought by the relics of the martyrs of Milan, and the multitude of Henricians about Thoulouse and other places converted by the miracles of St Bernard, are undeniable proofs of the reality of the miracles by which this was brought about. And this proof is the stronger, because it is well known how obstinate and inveterate these heresies were, and how watchful were their abettors to lay hold of everything against the Catholic Church. Hence we may fairly conclude, that had not these miracles been true, and known beyond all dispute, instead of converting such numbers, they could never have escaped the censure of adversaries so clear-sighted, but would rather have confirmed them in their errors. The same may be said of the miracles of St Dominic, in converting numbers of the Albigenses.

2. "The conversion of sinners" to a life of penance and piety, by means of miracles, is another admirable effect which they have produced, and an undoubted proof of the reality of their existence. Every one knows how difficult it is to change the heart of obdurate sinners, habituated to vice and sensuality; nothing less than the almighty hand of God is able to perform this, especially to do it thoroughly and instantaneously. Miracles are doubtless the most powerful and best adapted external means to convince such sinners of what God requires of them, and of their imminent danger if they continue rebellious to His will; and God Himself, in the case of Pharaoh, and other such examples in Holy Scripture, used them for this very purpose. When, therefore, such conversions, instantaneous and perfect, are publicly known as the consequences of miracles attested to have been wrought for that very end, the effect itself is a convincing proof of the existence of the cause which has produced it. A remarkable instance of this we find in the life of St Bernard, in the conversion of the Duke of Guienne, by the miracles of that holy servant of God, which, with others of a like manner, I omit, for brevity's sake.

3. "The conversion of heathen nations to the Christian faith" is another glorious effect of miracles, and an

incontestable proof of their existence. That heathen nations have in all ages been converted to the faith of Christ, is a fact never called in question: that miracles were a means, proper, adequate, and well adapted to produce this effect, will not be denied: that we might reasonably expect them from a good God on such an important occasion is what the most violent adversaries must admit. Seeing, therefore, that the histories of all those nations do solemnly attest that many miracles were wrought by the saints who converted them, and that their conversion is expressly declared to have been the effect of these miracles, the certainty and notoriety of the effect give convincing proof of the existence of the cause whence it proceeded, and add weight to the testimony by which that existence is attested.

Here we may properly quote the observation of St Augustine, that considering the nature of the Christian religion both as to faith and morals, the opposition it must experience from the corruption of our hearts and our perverse inclinations, especially when these have been confirmed by habit, continued indulgence, and popular prejudices, it seems impossible it should ever gain ground, and be planted in any nation without the help of miracles. Or if at any time this should happen, it would itself be a greater miracle than any of those related; because the conversion of a heathen nation to the faith of Christ without the help of miracles, would be a supernatural effect produced in the hearts of every one converted, by the immediate operation of the power of God, without the use of any external means adequate to the effect produced.

What Dr Campbell beautifully observes of the miracles of the apostles, and of their effects in the conversion of the heathen world, may justly be used here, and is applicable to the same or similar effects in converting heathens, heretics, or sinners in all after-ages. "The very pretext of supporting the doctrine by miracles," says the Doctor, "if a false pretext, would of necessity do unspeakable hurt to the cause. The pretence of miracles will quickly attract the attention of all to whom the new or the disputed doctrine is published. The influence which address and eloquence, appearances of sanctity, and fervours of devotion would otherwise have had, however great, would be superseded by the consideration of what is infinitely more striking and decisive. The miracles, therefore, will first be canvassed, and canvassed with a temper of mind the most unfavourable to conviction." —Dissert., p. 11, § 1. Consequently, if, after such canvassing, the adversaries yield the day, heathens become Christians, heretics rejoin the Catholic faith, and sinners are converted to a penitential and virtuous life, these effects are most convincing proofs that the miracles have stood the test of the strictest scrutiny, and have triumphed over all opposition.

IX. To these remarkable effects of miracles we may add two others, which, though not necessarily produced by them, are such natural consequences as to presuppose the reality of their existence. The first is the erection of monuments in memory of miracles performed. When any public monument actually exists, and when ancient historians living on the spot at the very time of its erection relate what gave occasion to it, these together are an irrefragable proof of the existence of the fact; because, should the historian give a false account, and publish that at the time and in the place where the monument is erected, he could not possibly escape detection. Now many such public monuments are to be found in the Catholic Church, as proofs of the reality of those miracles for which they were erected.

The second is the difficulty to which the adversaries of the Catholic faith have been reduced in order to evade the argument of miracles urged against them, particularly their attributing them to imposture or art magic; for such evasions plainly show that even those very adversaries were convinced of the facts, and therefore found themselves reduced to the above evasions to elude their force. This is no uncommon refuge of the adversaries of the Catholic faith. Osiander, the celebrated father of the Reformation, not being able to doubt the miracles performed by St Bernard, says, "they were Satan's workmanship, for the confirmation of idolatry and false worship."—Epit. Centur., p. 310. Whitaker, in his answer to Bellarmine, acknowledging the existence of the miracles urged against him by that learned cardinal, attributes them to the devil. "The devil," says he, "might preserve the body of Xavier for a short time odoriferous and incorrupt."—Lib. de Eccles., p. 354.

Calvin, in the preface to his Institutions, and the centuriators of Magdeburg, relating miracles in every century of the Church, convinced as they were of the facts, openly impute them to Satan. In like manner the Arians and heathens, as St Ambrose informs us, pretended that the miracles performed by the bodies of Sts Gervase and Protase were wrought by the devil, in order to delude the Christians. Celsus also, and Julian, two inveterate pagan adversaries of Christianity, attributed all the miracles wrought at the establishment of the Christian religion to the same cause; and those enemies of the truth and of true miracles only followed the example of the Pharisees, their fathers and predecessors in this cause, who said of the miracles of Christ Himself, "that He cast out devils through Beelzebub, the prince of the devils," Matt. xii. 24. This evasion is a clear proof that those who resort to it were convinced of the reality of the facts, which they could not deny, as is justly observed by the learned Protestant author of the observations on the conversion of St Paul, p. 101 : "To impute miracles to magic is by no means agreeable to the notions of those who in this age disbelieve Christianity. It will therefore be needless to show the weakness of that supposition; but that supposition itself is no inconsiderable argument of the truth of the facts. Next to the apostles and evangelists, the strongest witnesses of the undeniable force of that truth are Celsus and Julian, and other ancient opponents of the Christian religion;" and we may add Osiander, Whitaker, Calvin, and others, as equally strong witnesses of the miracles of the latter ages, "who were obliged to solve what they could not contradict, by such an irrational and absurd imagination." And, indeed, the absurdity of this is evident from the third and fourth rules of the criterion above laid down, for distinguishing whether miracles be from God or from Satan.

X. Let any man of common sense seriously consider these circumstances attending the testimony given in every age in attestation of miracles, and say, if he thinks it probable, or even morally possible, that such testimony can be false. And, indeed, were it possible for such testimony to deceive us, how could we reasonably believe any one fact that happened before our own days, or of which we have not been eyewitnesses? But we need not argue on this point. The testimony for the continuation of miracles in every age since the apostles, is so full, perfect, and every way well founded, that two of the greatest and most inveterate adversaries that ever have appeared against miracles have been forced to acknowledge it; and for that very reason refuse to trust the issue of the cause upon that ground. These two adversaries are the celebrated Dr Middleton and Mr Hume. "There is not a single point in all history," says the Doctor, "so constantly, explicitly, and unanimously affirmed by them all"—Church historians—"as the continual succession of those"—miraculous—"powers through all ages, from the earliest father who first mentions them, down to the time of the Reformation, which same succession is still farther deduced by persons of the most eminent character for their probity, learning, and dignity in the Romish Church to this very day."—Pref. to Inq.

Such is the character the Doctor gives of the testimony for the existence of miracles in all ages, which surely nothing but the force of truth could have extorted from him. But seeing it would be impossible to deny the continuation of miracles if tried by this rule, he sets out with the determined resolution to reject all miracles after the apostolic age, and never to bring one of them to the test of this examination; because, "If the cause," says he, "must be tried by the unanimous consent of fathers, we shall find as much reason to believe those powers were continued even to the latest ages, as to any other, how early and primitive soever, after the days of the apostles."—Ibid.

As to Mr Hume, he expressly recommends to his readers, "to form a general resolution never to lend any attention to the testimony"—for miracles in favour of religion—"with whatever specious pretext it may be covered." And he assigns this plain reason: "Because," says he, "those who are so silly as to examine the affair by that medium, and seek particular flaws in the testimony, are almost sure to be confounded."—Ess. on Mir., as cited by Dr Campbell, Dissert., p. 60, 61. This is plain dealing, and the most authentic attestation from the mouth of a declared enemy, that the positive testimony for the perpetual continuation of miracles in all the preceding ages of the Church is so well founded, absolute, and complete, that it is impossible to find the slightest flaw in it. Even the clear-sighted David Hume himself, notwithstanding the acuteness of his genius, and the ardent desire of his heart, is forced to confess his inability.

XI. The natural and necessary conclusion from all these observations is, " That the existence of miracles of the second class above mentioned—viz., those attested by judicious historians, or other writers of credit and authority, in every age—is founded on such ample, full, and perfect positive testimony, as exceeds any other historical fact whatsoever, according to Dr Middleton, and that no possible flaw can be found in it, according to Mr Hume; consequently, that no man in his proper senses can call their existence in question, without destroying all historical faith whatsoever, and without acting in direct opposition to one of the essential principles of the human mind, which obliges us to yield our assent to that conviction which a full and unexceptionable testimony necessarily carries along with it in matters of fact, either past or at a distance, as Dr Beattie proves at large in his Essay on Truth."

XII. I shall conclude this subject by the testimonies of two other celebrated Protestants, who, from the force of the continual attestation of miracles in every age, were thoroughly convinced of the reality of their existence down to their own days, and whose authority ought certainly to have great weight with every true child of the Reformation. The first is Luther himself, the great apostle of the Reformation, who, in his book on the Jews, tom. vii., Wittemb., p. 209, says: "Through the course of fifteen hundred years past the Jews have heard that there is the Word of God, have seen the greatest signs and wonders, and have raged against them." And a little after he adds, speaking of the Christian faith: "From God we have learned and received it, as the eternal word and truth of God, confessed and confirmed by miracles and signs during these fifteen hundred years to this present time." Nay, what is still more to our purpose, in his book 'De Purgatione quorundum articulorum,' he even attests miracles wrought in his own time at the shrines of saints, and states it as a thing so public and evident that it can admit of no doubt. "Who can gainsay these things," says he, "which God to this day worketh miraculously at the tombs of the saints? *Ad divorum sepulchra.*"

The other testimony which I shall bring is that of the learned Grotius, whose abilities as a scholar and a judicious critic are justly admired by the world. This great man, upon these words of our Saviour, "These signs shall follow those that believe," declares himself thus: "As the later ages also are full of testimonies of the same thing, I don't know by what reason some are moved to restrict that gift to the first ages only; wherefore, if any one would even now preach Christ in a manner agreeable to Him, to nations that know Him not, I have no doubt but the force of the promise will still remain." I shall make no further observation on these two respectable witnesses than this, that the force of the truth must be great, which obliges persons even against the interest of their own cause to acknowledge it; and that the only reason which moved others afterwards to deny it, was not the love of truth, nor any new light acquired and unknown to those before them, but the miserable necessity of their cause, which, as Dr Middleton fairly acknowledges, forced them into this alternative,—either absolutely to reject the continuation of miracles in the Christian Church, in spite of all the strong and unexceptionable evidence to the contrary, or fairly to give up the Reformation as the work of Satan, and yield the day to the Catholic Church.

XIII. We now proceed to consider the third class of miracles, according to the division given above—that is, such as have undergone the examination of the Church in her processes for the canonisation of saints, and are published to the world as true under the sanction of her authority. And here we shall find such precautions taken for ascertaining the truth of miracles so approved, as render it morally impossible for deceit or fraud, or even mistake, to find admittance.

It is a common calumny against the Church, that her pastors have an interest in promoting the belief of miracles; that therefore they encourage forgeries and impositions; that, having the power in their hand, they prevent all proper examination of such as appear among them; in a word, that they promote imposture in these matters, and discourage all means of detection. The utter groundlessness of this calumny is self-evident; for what person of common-sense can believe that such numbers of pious and learned men in every age should be so lost to every sense of virtue and honesty as to promote impostures of this kind, and that not in a few instances, but in as many as there are miracles received and approved by the Catholic Church, especially if it be added that these very men openly profess as a sacred article of their faith that it is a deadly sin to promote or propagate falsehood in matters of religion, or to propose a false object of veneration to Christian people? Who can persuade himself that in so many ages, in different countries, in such numbers of persons as are here concerned, not one should be found of such common honesty as to disclose the fraud, and to undeceive his fellow-creatures? Whence comes it that of the numbers who have apostatised from the Catholic Church, and have evidently shown that they wanted neither the will nor the means of making such a disclosure, none have ever yet been able to substantiate the charge? The reason is plain, because the accusation is not only false and groundless, but directly opposed to the whole tenor of the Church's conduct in this matter. Far from encouraging imposture, she punishes severely everything of the kind, and uses every means in her power in order to preserve her children from being deceived in things of such importance to their spiritual welfare. This has been her care in every age, and in these later times we find that instead of relaxing, she has increased the strictness of her vigilance.

XIV. The great heroes of Christianity, those blessed martyrs who laid down their lives with heroic constancy in the midst of torments, for the sake of Jesus Christ, were, according to His promises, entitled at their death to immediate admission to His glory. Accordingly, from the unanimous and most authentic records of antiquity, we find the greatest honours paid to them by the Christian world. At their martyrdom, the faithful assembled in crowds to witness their glorious victories; they gathered up their venerable remains with the utmost care; they assembled yearly at their sepulchres to celebrate the day of their triumph; the history of their confession and martyrdom was publicly read for the instruction and encouragement of the faithful, and their acts were communicated to the most distant Churches for comfort and edification. See the letter of the Church of Smyrna to that of Philadelphia, giving an account of the martyrdom of their holy bishop, St Polycarp, and of the behaviour of the faithful upon that occasion.

We find, however, from the same ancient records, that even to have suffered martyrdom was not sufficient to entitle one immediately to these sacred honours; it was required that this should be publicly recognised and acknowledged by the chief pastors of the Church. It was the province of these pastors to judge whether the person was to be esteemed a real martyr or not; whether there were just grounds to believe that he was in possession of eternal bliss, and consequently whether or not the honours given to martyrs were due to him. Even in those early ages this was considered necessary to prevent imposture, and to preserve the multitude from being carried away by appearances; hence came the distinction between approved martyrs, *martyres vindicati*, and those who were not; and to give to these latter the honour due to the former was always thought a crime, and as such was severely punished by the Church. Of this there is a striking example in the famous Lucilla of Carthage, who was so offended at being reprimanded, that she became a great cause and promoter of the Donatist schism.

As to the holy servants of God who died in peace, after spending their days in the rigours of penance, or in the heroic practice of Christian virtues, it was some time after their death before they were admitted to the same honours given to the martyrs. Besides the sanctity of their lives, it was necessary that unquestionable proofs should appear of their being in possession of God in heaven. Miracles wrought by Almighty God, on recourse being had to their prayers, or on applying their sacred relics, or the like, were received as undoubted, and indeed as the only certain proof of their felicity; because, though the sanctity of their lives, if they persevered therein to the end, is the great foundation of their glory in heaven, yet however incontestable the proofs of their sanctity may be, their perseverance cannot be so certainly known, unless Heaven itself speak in their favour by miracles after their death. Hence miracles are always considered a necessary condition in the canonisation of saints, even martyrs, as being the only assured proofs of their having persevered to the end in those holy dispositions which alone could entitle them to heavenly glory.

XV. Now the taking cognisance of miracles for this end has always been the province of the chief pastors of the Church, who have ever looked upon it as a matter requiring mature deliberation and the greatest circumspection. In these later times particularly, the examination has been unanimously referred to the judgment of the Bishops of Rome, who have deemed it proper to redouble their vigilance, and to increase the strictness of the examinations that were wont to be observed in former ages.

Of this we have a remarkable example about the year 1220, in the letter of Honorius III. addressed to the general chapter of the Cistercian order, and the bishop of the place, wherein he narrates: "That many bishops and religious persons, together with the abbot and convent of St Maurice, had some time before given him an account of numbers of miracles wrought by the intercession of their late holy abbot Maurice, and of the constant and general opinion which all that country had of his sanctity, and therefore had entreated him to have him canonised; that in consequence of this application, he had sent a commission to the Bishop of Lyons and the Abbot of St Loup, to make a juridical examination of the miracles, and of the life of the holy abbot, in order to have a just and solid ground for granting the request; that these commissioners had indeed sent him a list of many great miracles, said to be wrought by God through the merits of the holy abbot, and attested upon oath by several witnesses. But it did not appear by the account sent that the commissioners had examined the witnesses severally upon the subjects and circumstances of their attestations with the care and diligence requisite in an affair of such importance, and therefore he could not proceed upon their information, and had ordered the said general chapter and the diocesan bishop to cause the witnesses to be re-examined separately, with the care and diligence which is wont and ought to be used in such matters." Such is the substance of his Holiness's rescript, as narrated in Decret., lib. 2, tit. 20, cap. Venerabili de Testib. et Attestat. From this it is evident, even in the middle ages, when the adversaries of the Catholic Church pretend that so many corruptions, especially with regard to miracles, crept in, how scrupulous the Holy See was in not admitting anything as true, except after the strictest scrutiny, and on the most incontestable evidence.

XVI. After the death of St Francis of Assisium, many miracles were said to be wrought by his intercession, upon which Pope Gregory IX. ordered a strict examination; and in order to proceed with the greater caution, he commissioned certain cardinals, whom he knew to be least favourable, to preside at the scrutiny. Accordingly, the examination was made with the utmost care, and the miracles were found to be so indisputably true, that it was resolved to proceed to his canonisation two years after his death. The same precautions were used by this Pope in examining the miracles wrought by St Anthony of Padua, which were thereupon found to be so certain, great, and numerous, that he was canonised the following year. About the beginning of the fifteenth century, flourished that most wonderful man St Vincent Ferrer, after whose death the strictest inquiry was made as to miracles wrought by his intercession; and from the process of canonisation by Pope Calixtus III. it appears that upwards of eight hundred miracles were proved to have been wrought by him, and this proof was supported by the most convincing testimonies.

XVII. But nothing conveys a better idea of the caution used by the Holy See in these matters, than the following extract from the decree of Pope Nicolas V. for the canonisation of St Bernardin of Sienna, in the year 1450, six years after his death: "In the time of our predecessor Eugenius IV. so many miracles were reported to have been performed by the merits and intercession of St Bernardin, that the most pressing solicitations were made to the Apostolic See to have the reality of those miracles inquired into with proper care, to the end that, after the truth was manifested, due honour might be paid by the Church militant on earth to him who was proved, by the testimony of God, to reign in glory in the Church triumphant in heaven. Our predecessor did what was requisite in a matter of such importance, and, according to the custom of the Apostolic See, intrusted the business to three cardinals of the holy Roman Church, who were empowered to send two venerable bishops, with commission to make the most exact researches in order to discover the truth. And having spent some months in this work, they returned to Rome, and gave a faithful account of what they had found. But our predecessor being taken out of the world before that business was ended, and solicitations being made to us to have it resumed, we resolved to proceed with the utmost care and circumspection. Therefore we appointed three cardinals of the holy Roman Church to send two venerable bishops a second time to inquire into the truth, that so we might proceed with more security after this repeated search."

"Accordingly they sent two bishops, who, on their return, did not only confirm what had been discovered in the time of our predecessor, but also brought attestations of several evident miracles which had been wrought since that time. Nevertheless, we did not allow this second inquiry to suffice, but resolved to make a third, and therefore sent two other venerable bishops, who, after some months, returned with the most convincing proofs that miracles were frequently wrought; and, in particular, they brought an exact narrative of some of the most remarkable."

"After this we sent another bishop to Sienna, who, having stayed there some months, bore witness on his return to the truth and reality of the miracles. We sent the same venerable person also to Aquila, where the saint died, to inquire whether any miracles were wrought there. On his return he confirmed the attestations of others who had been sent before to the same place, and moreover related the most stupendous works, which had been done since the time of the inquiry made by those others; which stupendous works were done not in corners and hidden places, but publicly, and in the sight of the whole multitude. Having received these informations, we caused every particular to be laid open in our consistory, where they were examined. But the matter being of great importance, the determination was delayed till another consistory should be held, that each cardinal might, in the mean time, examine every article more maturely at home. In this second consistory all the votes concurred in this, that the miracles were so many and evident, and the sanctity of the saint's life and the purity of his faith so manifest, that there was reason sufficient to proceed to the canonisation," &c.

XVIII. Let it be remembered that these steps were taken, and this decree published, within the space of six years after the saint's death, and in the country where the events occurred, when all particulars must have been well known, and recent in every one's mind. Let me then ask any man of common-sense, whether he thinks it possible to have used greater caution, or that this investigation could have failed to ascertain the truth of public and well-known facts? or that, had any falsehood been advanced in the decree, it could have escaped detection, considering the time, place, and circumstances in which it was published to the world?

XIX. These examples show how very far it is from being the desire or intention of the pastors of the Church to impose false accounts or forged miracles upon her children; nay, how scrupulously careful they are not to advance or approve anything till by the most mature and repeated examination they have acquired undoubted proofs of the truth.

This appears still more clearly from the regulations of the Council of Trent, and the improvement made in the rigour of the investigation, by which the sovereign Pontiff now regulates his conduct in these researches. The bishops assembled in that Council did not permit the subject of miracles to escape their attention. They were sensible that abuses might creep in among simple people, and that accounts of false or supposititious miracles in particular places, remote from the means of detection, might be circulated and credited, if not properly prevented. Wherefore, following the example of former ages, they framed a decree, by which they not only confirm to the chief pastors of the Church the right of examining new miracles, and of rejecting or approving them as they shall see cause, but also strictly forbid any new miracle to be admitted till it be properly examined and approved by the diocesan bishop.

The words of the decree are as follow: "The holy synod decrees also that no new miracles shall be admitted without the previous examination and approbation of the said bishop, who, when he has arrived at any certainty regarding them, may, with the advice of theologians and other pious persons, do what he shall judge agreeable to truth and piety," Sess. 25, Decr. de Invoc. et Vener. Sanct. This wise regulation effectually discourages all impostures. These can never stand the test of a judicial examination; and without that they can never make great progress in deceiving, nor have any public weight or authority in the Church.

XX. Even though no other precautions than those had been taken for ascertaining the truth of miracles, yet it must be owned that they were amply sufficient to convince any reasonable person of the certainty of the facts so examined and attested. These precautions were repeated examinations by different commissioners, men of known probity and learning, made at different times, of witnesses upon oath, concerning facts of their nature, open, plain, and public, said to have been performed in the presence of multitudes of people of all ranks and stations. These examinations were made at or soon after the time when the facts were said to have happened, when numbers of witnesses were alive, and when everything was fresh in their memories. The process and result of these examinations were weighed with the most mature deliberation by a body of learned and disinterested persons, and, when approved by them, published to the world among the people, and in the place, where the whole had occurred, and where it was impossible that any fraud attempted could escape detection.

All these circumstances are doubtless such means of ascertaining the facts examined and attested, that it seems scarcely possible to add anything in order to give the human mind more assured conviction; and yet we find that the Church, from her desire of rendering these matters absolutely incontestable, and of precluding every possible cavil of her enemies, has, even in these later times, added new precautionary measures, and in her processes for the canonisation of saints uses still greater rigour and severity in the proofs which she demands. The whole series of this process is described at length by one who was thoroughly conversant with it—the late Pope Benedict XIV., in his valuable and elaborate work on the Canonisation of Saints. From it I shall here give a clear and succinct account of what refers to miracles. Whoever considers it with due attention will, I am confident, acknowledge that it is impossible for human prudence to use more effectual means for arriving at the knowledge of the truth; and that if facts so examined and attested could, notwithstanding, be false or forged, we must bid farewell to all faith and credit among men.

XXI. At the death of any holy servant of God, whose virtuous and holy life gives a well-founded hope to those who knew him that his soul has been received into eternal glory, the faithful are not forbidden to have recourse in private to his intercession, or to ask benefits from Almighty God through the help of his prayers. If these favours be not granted, and no sign of his being with God be manifested, this private devotion naturally decays, and in time completely disappears. But if Almighty God shall be pleased to grant the favours asked, and even to work miracles at the invocation of His holy servant; when these, published among the faithful, increase the reputation of his sanctity, and give encouragement to others to have recourse to his intercession, in hopes of receiving like blessings from God through his means,—when this is the case, things are permitted to proceed without any judicial cognisance for some time.

Experience shows how easily the majority of mankind, especially the uneducated, allow themselves to be influenced by anything that strongly affects them. The popular opinion of the sanctity of a person deceased, if followed by a report, whether true or false, of any miracle wrought by his means, cannot fail at first to make a deep impression on the minds of the people. But if the foundation be false, the superstructure will soon fall to the ground. A little time must be given, and some allowance made, for the first transports of devotion. Error cannot long continue to prevail ; and, sooner or later, imposture must be discovered.

But if the reputation of the person's sanctity increases ; if the fame of supernatural events wrought by his intercession continues ; if these things, instead of diminishing, make greater progress, and daily gain more credit in the minds of men,—then, from this constant and increasing public voice in his favour, there arises a well-grounded reason for making more particular inquiry into the nature and truth of the things reported;—if, therefore, the State, a religious order, or any particular persons connected with the deceased, shall think proper to interest themselves in procuring an examination of the case at the supreme tribunal, in order to canonisation, their first application must be to the diocesan bishop, to whom it belongs to take judicial cognisance in the first instance of the popular report in the saint's favour, both as to his life and miracles. This is so indispensable, that the Court of Rome will admit no case to a hearing till this first step be taken, and the acts of this judicial inquiry by the bishop fully proved, with all the formalities prescribed.

These formalities, ten in number, are as follows: 1. To avoid all precipitation (as I observed above), the popular report of the sanctity and miracles of the deceased must have existed for some considerable time before the bishop be allowed to begin his proceedings of inquiry. 2. The bishop must himself preside, if possible, at all the steps of the process; and if he be obliged to substitute any of the inferior clergy, this judge must have a doctor of divinity and a licentiate of canon law for his assistants. 3. He who receives the depositions must countersign every article with the witnesses themselves who subscribe them. 4. Each deponent must be asked for a circumstantial relation of the facts which he attests. It is not allowed to read over to witnesses what may have been deponed by those preceding them, and to cause it to be confirmed by their consent; but each one must be examined by himself apart, and the answers to each interrogatory extended at full length. 5. The notary and the promoter of the case, as well as the witnesses, must be

CONTINUATION OF MIRACLES. 217

sworn to observe profound secrecy with reference to the questions put and the answers given. 6. Information must be sent to the Pope of the whole procedure, and of the judgment of the bishop passed thereupon. 7. A copy of the papers must be made in proper form, authenticated, sealed, and sent to the Congregation of Rites at Rome. 8. The originals are preserved in the archives of the cathedral church of the diocese, in a special chest, sealed, and under different keys, which are deposited with different persons of rank and character. 9. Besides the witnesses presented to the bishop by the promoters of the case, he must also examine as many others as he can find capable of giving any proper information. 10. No extra-judicial acts or attestations are allowed to be inserted among the authentic writings of the process.

Now, who does not see in this procedure the utmost care to prevent imposition, and to arrive at a distinct and certain knowledge of the truth? Remark the particular and separate examination of each witness, the ignorance each one is in of the questions put to the others, and the solemn oath which all take never to disclose the subject of the questions put, or the answers given. In addition to the witnesses presented by the promoters of the case, as many others as can be had are procured, and all care is taken to preserve the papers from improper inspection. What are these but the most careful measures to prevent collusion among the present witnesses or those who may afterwards be examined, and to procure from each the most exact account of what he knows? One would be inclined to think, that a miracle proved by this judgment alone might justly be deemed sufficient to gain belief and credit from any unprejudiced person; and yet these are merely preliminary measures.

XXII. When the diocesan bishop has performed his part, and, from the evidence collected in the above trial, has given his judgment on the miracles examined, an authentic sealed copy of the whole process is forwarded to the Congregation of Rites at Rome, and there it must remain, deposited with the notary of that congregation, for ten years before the seals can be opened or any farther step taken in the case. During this time, however, several things are carefully observed. 1st, If the popular report concerning the virtues and miracles of the saint continues unimpaired and increases, or if it decays and fails. 2dly, If any serious accusation appears against him, any strong suspicion, any doubts as to his conduct. 3dly, If he had composed any writings during his lifetime, these are examined and minutely scrutinised, to prove whether they contain any error, either in faith or morals; and if anything appears against him, the case is dropped and consigned to oblivion.

But if these particulars are favourable, at the expiration of ten years the case is again taken up in the Congregation of Rites, the solicitors for the case demanding of this court that the proceedings of the diocesan bishop may be opened and examined. This is done with all formality; and if, on examining the proceedings, it be found that everything has been performed according to rule, the Pope is applied to for a commission to authorise the congregation to proceed. The case is then removed out of the hands of the diocesan, and every step that follows is taken by the authority of the sovereign Pontiff.

This Congregation of Rites is a tribunal at Rome, composed of certain cardinals who are the chief judges, and of consultors, judges of the second order. The officers of this court are : 1. the promoter of the faith, or solicitor-general, who represents the public, and proposes every difficulty he can devise against the persons whose cases are tried ; 2. the secretary of the congregation ; and, 3. the apostolic protonotary, with several inferior officers, advocates, and notaries, who all take a solemn oath of secrecy with reference to the matters treated before them in cases of canonisation while pending, that nothing may transpire which could give the smallest occasion to the promoters of the case to take undue measures for advancing it. When the case is removed into this court, the first step is the nomination of three commissioners, authorised by the Holy Father to take proper information in the place where the miracles were performed, and where the saint's body is interred. These are generally three local bishops, of whom the Ordinary of the diocese is commonly one,—two form a quorum. Then the solicitors for the case draw up the articles to be examined by the commissioners, and classify under different titles the several facts and miracles which they consider the best founded, and the most proper for proving the sanctity of the deceased, and his glory in heaven. These preparatory writings are revised by the promoter of the faith, who from them forms instructions for his substitute, the vice-promoter, with the commissioners; and these contain all the objections and difficulties which he can devise against the facts and miracles proposed to be examined by the judges.

These papers, together with the commission to the judges, and the form of oath to be taken by the court and witnesses, are sealed and sent to the Ordinary of the place. He convenes all concerned, the commission is opened and read, the oaths are administered, and the proper officers of the court appointed and sworn. A day is then fixed, the witnesses are called, and their depositions taken in some church, chapel, or sacred place, in order to inspire respect, and the greater horror of perjury.

The oath which they take upon the holy Gospels contains two parts: 1. that they will declare the whole truth, without concealing or disguising anything; and, 2. that they will not communicate to any one either the questions put or the answers given. After taking this oath, they are examined as to their quality, age, faith, learning, and then as to the several articles proposed by the solicitor for the case, and on any other subject which the judges think proper. At the end of each session the papers are sealed and locked up till next meeting: and when the whole information has been taken, the papers are authenticated by the names and seals of the judges and principal officers of the court. The originals are deposited in the archives of the diocese; and copies of the whole collated in presence of the judges, and authenticated by their seals and subscriptions, are sent to Rome by an express courier, who is sworn to execute his commission with fidelity.

XXIII. Such is the general procedure of this court. We shall now see in detail the nature of the proof required in order to ascertain the facts examined. The general principle of the Congregation of Rites is, to treat those cases with the same rigour with which criminal cases are tried in civil courts, and to cause the facts to be proved with the same exactness observed in criminal prosecutions. Suspected or inconclusive testimony, which would not be allowed as evidence for condemning a criminal, is rejected in this court as insufficient proof.

In the witnesses the following conditions are absolutely required: 1. There must be at least two or three who speak unanimously to the same fact and its circumstances. Single testimony proves nothing. Contradictory testimonies annul and destroy each other; and such as differ, but not upon essential points, render each other mutually suspected. Those which concur in the same point may serve as a corroboration, but afford no certain proof. This is only allowed when the same facts and circumstances are uniformly attested by at least two or three witnesses. 2. The witnesses must depose what they themselves saw or heard: declarations and testimonies at second hand are never admitted in proof of miracles. 3. The witnesses must be of sufficient age, and have a proper knowledge and discernment to distinguish the nature of the things which they relate; they must be Catholics of known probity, and give an account of the motives for their testimony. 4. All the objections to their testimony which reason and the circumstances can furnish, either from their persons, qualities, or depositions, are proposed and urged by the vice-promoter of the faith. A full hearing is given to them by the court, and they must be answered by the opposite party to the satisfaction of the judges.

XXIV. When the acts and proceedings of the commissioners are sent to Rome, they are strictly examined by the Congregation of Rites, both as to their authenticity and validity—that is, whether every form prescribed by law has been duly observed, and every prudent precaution taken to arrive at the truth; and if the congregation is satisfied on this head, it proceeds to re-examine the whole cause; but fifty years must have elapsed from the death of the saint before these steps can be taken. This delay is ordered, that nothing may be done with precipitation, and to ascertain if any new light appears in the mean time, either for or against the case. At this stage the case is resumed, and when the judicial acts and proceedings of the commissioners have been verified and approved, some of the principal articles of the process are selected to be tried and examined by the congregation itself, in three extraordinary assemblies, held at proper intervals; and with regard to miracles, the question proposed is, "Whether or not a competent number of true miracles has been sufficiently proved in the process made by the commissioners." Still, notwithstanding all the precautions previously used, one may say with truth, that it is only now, in discussing this question, that the trial of the reality of the miracles is made.

For greater precision, the question proposed is divided into two parts, each of which is examined separately. The first is, "Whether the actual existence of the miraculous facts produced in the process have been thoroughly proved before the commissioners? Secondly, Whether these facts be really supernatural and true miracles, the work of God and of good angels?" The discussion of the first of these brings on a review of the whole process, wherein the proceedings of the commissioners, the witnesses, their qualifications, their depositions, and all the circumstances are canvassed; and the promoter of the faith himself urges every objection he can imagine against them. All must be thoroughly solved by the solicitors for the case; and if they fail to satisfy the judges, the miracle is rejected as not proved.

If the facts be indubitable, then the court proceeds to examine the other question, Whether the facts so proved are supernatural and true miracles?

XXV. In examining this point three different classes of miracles are distinguished. Some are of such a stupendous nature as evidently to surpass all created power, and show themselves at once to be the work of the Creator; and these are of the first order. Others less astonishing may, for anything we know, be within the power of those created intellectual beings, whose knowledge and power far exceed ours; and these are of the second order. Others, again, are in substance natural events, which may be produced by the assistance of art—but from the concurrence of circumstances, and the manner in which they are performed, become truly miraculous; and these are of the third order.

Now, when any miracle of the first order is produced, and the fact undoubtedly proved, it needs no further discussion; it carries on the face of it the proofs of its divinity, and shows itself at once to be the immediate work of God;—and such the raising a dead person to life is always considered.

XXVI. In miracles of the second order, which are plainly supernatural—that is, above all the efforts of human power—the question is, to discern whether they be the work of God or the operations of evil spirits. In deciding this, the fact is examined by the rules of the criterion for this purpose. The most important of these we have above described; but some other circumstances are added by this court, and in all make five principal qualities to constitute in their judgment a divine miracle. They are as follows: First, "The reality of the effect." The power of evil spirits is limited, that of God has no bounds; the wonders produced by the devil are at best but vain appearances, which absorb the attention or deceive the senses—but a true miracle produces a real effect. Secondly, "The duration:" effects of enchantment are only momentary; those of true miracles are permanent. Thirdly, "The utility:" God Almighty does not employ His power in vain. Frivolous events and changes, which merely produce fear or wonder, are unworthy the attention of a reasonable man, much less do they deserve that the Divine Wisdom should make use of a particular order of His providence to produce them. Still less can it be supposed that Almighty God will act in a miraculous manner to exhibit things unbecoming, ridiculous, or favourable to any unjust or wicked design. Fourthly, "The means used:" prayer, invocation of the holy name of God, of the blessed Trinity, and of the saints, are the means of obtaining true miracles from God; false wonders are produced by having recourse to the devil, by superstitious spells, shameful artifices, or extravagant actions. Fifthly, "The principal object:" Almighty God can have no other ultimate end in all He does than His own glory and our real happiness. The confirmation or the advancement of piety and Christian justice, and the sanctification of souls, are the only supreme motives ultimately worthy of His goodness and infinite wisdom. Miracles of the second order must be attended with all these qualities before they can be admitted in this court as divine, and the absence of any one of them would effectually discredit the case for ever.

XXVII. Miracles of the third order, as cures of diseases, are examined in the strictest manner; and it must necessarily be proved, to the conviction of the judges, that they were attended with all those circumstances which evidently show that the operation was divine. The circumstances indispensably required are: First, That the disease be considerable, dangerous, inveterate, and such as commonly resists the power of known medicines, or at least that a cure by their means would be long and difficult. Secondly, That the disease have not come to a crisis, after which it is natural to expect a mitigation of the symptoms and a cure. Thirdly, That no ordinary natural remedies have been applied, or that such time have elapsed that they could have no influence in the cure. Fourthly, That the cure be sudden and instantaneous; that the violent pains or imminent danger cease at once, instead of diminishing gradually, as we see in the operations of nature. Fifthly, That the cure be perfect and complete. Sixthly, That the health recovered be permanent, and not followed by a speedy relapse.

XXVIII. The concurrence of all these conditions and circumstances must be proved with the utmost clearness, before the miraculous character of the facts can be admitted; and in this investigation there is the greatest rigour used. The promoter of the faith raises every possible objection; and is allowed to call in the assistance of theologians, physicians, natural philosophers, mathematicians, and others skilled in the respective matters relating to the miracle under examination. To these the case is submitted, and if they can satisfactorily account for the effect by natural means, or if they can offer any well-founded objection against the miraculous nature of the fact, which the others cannot solve, the miracle is forthwith rejected. In order, however, that all justice may be done, the solicitors for the case also are allowed to call in to their assistance persons learned in the several sciences, to answer the difficulties proposed by the promoter of the faith, and, if possible, to obviate his objections.

XXIX. Such are the proceedings of Rome, in ascertaining the existence and continuation of miracles in these later ages; and by this rigorous process have been tried, approved, and published to the world, numbers of miracles performed by Almighty God, at the intercession of his saints, down to the very day in which we live. Let, then, the most determined enemies of miracles attentively consider this short sketch of these proceedings, and ask their own hearts if the scrupulous care and rigorous investigation employed by this court does not merit their highest praise, rather than their censure? Let them say if they could devise means better calculated to prevent error and detect imposture than those used by this tribunal?

The most sacred things in religion, solemn oaths, and the fear of the greatest ecclesiastical censures, are employed to elicit the exact truth; and the most careful precautions that human prudence can suggest, are taken to satisfy the judges of the capacity, the morals, and disinterestedness of the witnesses. The judges proceed by slow steps, with full deliberation, and the same matters are examined again and again at distant intervals, in order to avoid any mistake from haste, or error from enthusiastic zeal. And when we consider the proceedings of the Ordinary, and the scrutiny to which they are subjected at Rome, the re-examination by the apostolical commissioners, and the revision of their proceedings with the same severity; the objections made by the promoter of the faith, and the questions raised by physicians and other learned persons, we shall be forced to acknowledge that a miraculous fact, which has undergone this rigorous trial, and comes to us invested with the approbation of

CONTINUATION OF MIRACLES.

this tribunal, is attended with evidence so convincing that any man must be devoid of common-sense and reason who denies it. Seeing, then, that even in these times many miracles have passed through this fiery ordeal, and have been published to the world with the full sanction of this court, the conclusion is obvious. The positive proof for the continuation of miracles is strong and convincing beyond dispute. The miraculous powers have not, even to this day, been withdrawn from the Catholic Church. Miracles still continue, from time to time, to be wrought in her communion. Hitherto the promises of Christ in this respect have had no limitation, and they will continue to be fulfilled to the end of ages.

APPENDIX

ON

THE CATHOLIC DOCTRINE OF TRANSUBSTANTIATION

NOTE.

As the circumstances which produced the following pages were somewhat remarkable, a succinct account of them may not be unacceptable to the reader. In the summer of 1775, two worthy Edinburgh citizens, non-juring Episcopalians, having had religious doubts excited in their minds, turned their attention to examine the faith of their forefathers. Desiring to obtain reliable information, they addressed themselves to Dr Hay; while, at the same time, they communicated the result of their interviews with him to their own clergyman, the Rev. Mr (afterwards Bishop) Abernethy Drummond. This excited the zeal, and called forth all the controversial energies of that gentleman. He not only discussed various points verbally, but he drew up in writing a series of difficulties and objections to Catholic doctrine. In particular, he took great credit to himself for what he considered his unanswerable argument against transubstantiation, and, in the fulness of his confidence, he called upon Dr Hay, and challenged him to put in print all that he could say in defence of it, promising to prepare and publish a reply. Dr Hay, in consequence, wrote his Appendix, to explain the doctrine itself, and to expose the sophistry of the arguments used against it.

Mr Abernethy Drummond did indeed publish his promised reply; but, whatever weight it may have had with the public generally, it had evidently no effect upon the two members of his congregation with whom the controversy had originated, for they were both received into the Catholic Church by Dr Hay.

EDITOR.

St Mary's, Edinburgh,
  June 2, 1873.

APPENDIX,

BY WAY OF DIALOGUE:

IN WHICH THE AUTHORITY OF MIRACLES, IN PROOF OF DOCTRINE, IS FURTHER EXAMINED AND ILLUSTRATED BY A PARTICULAR EXAMPLE, THAT OF TRANSUBSTANTIATION, WHICH, AS IT INVOLVES MANY DIFFICULTIES BOTH FROM SENSE AND REASON, SEEMS TO BE THE MOST PROPER FOR SUCH EXAMINATION.

Orthodoxus.   Philaretes.

Orth. GOOD morning, Philaretes. Why so early a visit from you to-day? I hope all is well.

Phil. All is well, thank God; but I have come to ask your opinion of a recent discussion between your friend Eusebius and Benevolus, concerning transubstantiation; have you heard of it?

Orth. I have; and think Benevolus must have been in great excitement when he expressed himself in such an unguarded manner, if what is reported of him be correct.

Phil. You mean, I suppose, when he said that he would not believe transubstantiation though Eusebius should work a miracle, even though he should raise a man from the dead to prove it.

Orth. I do.

Phil. Well, sir, he not only said so in the heat of discussion, but he has since repeated the same after reflection; nay, he has affirmed it under his hand, in some letters that have passed between him and Eusebius. Indeed, so confident is he of being in the right, that he affirms he is able to defend that proposition before a general council, and that he feels as certain that Eusebius is in the wrong in objecting to it, as he is certain that the Word of God is true.

Orth. Boldly said, indeed; but, pray, does he pretend to bring any proof for that assertion? Does he allege anything from the Word of God in defence of it?

Phil. He does, I assure you. I have jotted down his arguments, and have come here this morning to have your opinion on the subject, as I wish thoroughly to understand it.

Orth. You are always welcome, and never more so than when you come on such business; for it affords me great pleasure to give you all the assistance in my power, especially on the important subject of religion.

Phil. I am much obliged by your kindness, which I have already experienced, and of which I shall always preserve a grateful remembrance. And now, let me know first what you think of the above proposition itself, and then I shall state the arguments brought by Benevolus in defence of it.

Orth. Very little knowledge of theology is required to see that the proposition is highly blamable and deserving of censure; and I am not surprised that several well meaning Christians are pained by it. The very sound of it is offensive to pious ears; and no wonder —for it involves a supposition nearly bordering upon blasphemy, if it be not really such.

Phil. That it sounds harshly, I admit, but to me it

does not appear to contain anything positively blasphemous. I shall be glad, therefore, if you will give me your reasons for passing upon it so severe a censure.

Orth. I will do so to your satisfaction. In the first place, you must observe that God alone is master of life and death; and no created being, whatever be its natural powers, can of itself either give life to man, or restore it after God has deprived him of it. To give life, or to restore it after death, is a work proper to the almighty power of the Creator.* If, therefore, Eusebius or any other, as an instrument in the hand of God, should raise a man from death in proof of transubstantiation, and yet Benevolus should refuse to believe that doctrine, this refusal would necessarily imply that transubstantiation is a falsehood, notwithstanding the attestation given to it; and as none but God can perform such a miracle, it implies that Almighty God works a miracle proper to Himself alone, in favour of falsehood, which is evidently blasphemous.

Phil. I see well the force of your remark; but may it not be alleged that, though God Himself can no more work miracles in support of falsehood than He can lie or deceive, yet He may permit the devil or wicked men to work miracles for evil ends? And if so, may it not be supposed that a miracle wrought in proof of transubstantiation is the work of Satan and not of God, which at once frees Benevolus's proposition from all shadow of blasphemy?

Orth. Properly speaking, the devil can perform no miracle whatever; the lying signs and wonders within the reach of his power being very different from a miracle in the Christian acceptation of the word; much

---

* See Chap. X. on the Criterion, where this is proved at length.

less can Satan perform even any of those lying wonders, in circumstances where such would unavoidably be mistaken for the work of the Most High;* and in this I daresay Benevolus himself will agree with me. But allowing that Almighty God should permit evil spirits to perform wonders within the sphere of their natural strength, this could never free the above proposition from the charge of blasphemy, unless you can at the same time prove that to raise a dead man to life is within the natural power of Satan; for this is the example which Benevolus himself makes use of in his assertion.

Phil. And why may it not be said that the devil can raise the dead?

Orth. Whoever attempts to prove this will find that he has undertaken a very difficult task. First, Because there are the strongest arguments from the Word of God to prove that to raise the dead is an operation proper to God alone. Secondly, Because though deists and other infidels have long laboured to show that such a power resides in Satan, they have never yet been able to establish it. Thirdly, Because of the fatal consequences that would necessarily follow if this point could be made good.

Phil. Pray, what consequence would follow?

Orth. Nothing less than the undermining the very foundations of Christianity. Observe—the Christian religion glories in being attested by miracles, which only the Almighty could perform, and which, therefore, incontestably prove its divine origin. Among these raising the dead to life has always been considered a miracle of the first order, and the proper work of God Himself. If, therefore, you can show that this does not exceed

---

* See this proved above, Chap. X. on the Criterion.

the natural power of Satan, you deprive religion of its chief support, and cast a doubt on all the miracles ever wrought in its favour. For, if it be within the natural power of the devil to perform so great a miracle as the raising of a dead man to life, what security have we that he may not perform all the others also? And what an important triumph would this be to deism and infidelity? Let Benevolus, therefore, chose which side he pleases, he will never be able to extricate himself from this dilemma: "Either his proposition must stand convicted of blasphemy, or the Christian religion must fall in its vindication."

Phil. What you say is very strong indeed, nor do I see what answer can be made I therefore entirely give up the point as to the proposition itself, and only wish to know what reply you would make to such arguments as may be used in defence of it.

Orth. Have a little patience; we must not leave the proposition so soon. What I have said is not the only reason for condemning it. It is equally censurable on another ground, which holds good, even on the supposition that to raise the dead is a work within the natural power of Satan. I suppose Benevolus does not imagine that, if Eusebius should raise one from the dead in proof of transubstantiation, he would make use of enchantments, or call upon the devil for assistance. Eusebius, though a Papist, is a Christian, who believes in one God, and in Jesus Christ His Son. If he believes transubstantiation to be a true doctrine, he does so only because he is persuaded that it was revealed by God; and, if he ever should attempt to raise one from the dead in proof of it, he would do so only by invoking the Almighty God for that purpose.

Phil. All this will be readily granted; but what then?

Orth. Let us suppose that Eusebius does so; that he calls upon God to perform this miracle, and that the miracle called for is actually performed: with what reason can Benevolus refuse to believe the doctrine thus attested? It is impossible to give a shadow of reason for his incredulity, but on a supposition which leads to, or rather plainly includes, another blasphemy; namely, that Almighty God, when invoked by teachers of false doctrine, but who pretend to be sent by Him—for such Benevolus must believe Eusebius to be in the present case—and when called upon to work a miracle in testimony of their false doctrine, though He will not Himself perform the miracle, may yet permit the devil to do so? Would not God, in this case, concur as effectually to bear witness to a falsehood, as if He Himself had wrought the miracle? Does not a king as effectually confirm and approve any commission, to which he allows his seal to be affixed by his minister, as if he had sealed it with his own hand? Miracles are the broad seal of heaven; and the devils, as well as other creatures, are but God's all agents, in whatever way He pleases to employ them.

When, therefore, Almighty God is directly called upon to perform a miracle, whether He Himself does it, or permits the devil, the weight of the attestation given by it to men is evidently the same; and in either case, where the doctrine proposed is untrue, He equally concurs to attest a falsehood. If to assert this be not blasphemy, I know not what is. Yet even this is not all. There is still another objection to this supposition; for if it could be shown that God, in the above circumstances, could permit the devil to perform the miracle required, then also, as in the former case, we must bid farewell to Christianity.

When we see wicked men, who openly oppose God

and His truth, seeking by enchantments, and by calling upon the devil, to work signs and wonders, in confirmation of their errors, we easily understand that Almighty God, for His own wise ends, may permit the devil to use his natural strength, and do things miraculous in the eyes of the beholders. This was the case with the magicians of Pharaoh, and the false prophets mentioned Deut. xiii., and will be the case with Antichrist at the end of the world; but all examples of this kind carry their mark upon their forehead, showing that such teachers are not from God, even though signs and wonders be performed. But if a person, asserting that he is divinely commissioned, calls upon God to work a miracle in confirmation of what he teaches, and if this miracle actually be performed, especially if it be one of the highest order, and above the natural power of creatures, it must give undoubted conviction of the truth both of his mission and his doctrine.

Upon this ground the world was converted to Christianity. Its preachers professed that they were commissioned by God; they called upon Him to work miracles to attest the truth of what they preached, and accordingly in His name the miracles were performed. This was sufficient; mankind, from the natural feeling of their hearts, were convinced that, in those circumstances, Almighty God could not have permitted wicked spirits to perform such miracles had the teachers been impostors, or their doctrine false; and therefore, without hesitation, they embraced Christianity as truth revealed by their Creator. But if, in such circumstances, Almighty God could allow the devil to perform miracles to attest falsehood, then we could have no certainty in believing the first teachers of Christianity, as their miracles might have been performed by Satan, and their doctrines have been merely a delusion. See to what a shocking conclusion Benevolus's proposition necessarily leads us!

Phil. I must own, I had no idea that it involved such consequences; and yet, from what you say, I see no means of defending it from them. For my own part, I am thoroughly convinced of its dreadful tendency; nor should I insist more upon the subject; but, as I may have occasion to converse with others, I should wish to know what can be said to the arguments by which they may pretend to support it.

Orth. Let us us hear, then, what these arguments are. I may venture to say beforehand that they are not to the purpose; nay, that you yourself can be at no loss, after what has been said, to see their weakness and inconclusiveness.

Phil. I shall not say what intrinsic weight they may really have; but I cannot help thinking that they have a considerable degree of plausibility. I shall propose them in Benevolus's own words: "Though you should work a miracle, even raise a person from the dead in attestation of transubstantiation, I should not be convinced by it, but would believe that Almighty God had permitted it as a trial of my faith and steadfastness in the truth, and not as a proof of the doctrine; and I have good reason to say so—1st, because it is plain, both from the Old and New Testament, from the magicians of Egypt, the false prophets mentioned Deut. xiii., and from Antichrist, that miracles may be wrought seemingly in attestation of false doctrine, though really they are only permitted to try people's faith; and, 2dly, because transubstantiation is incapable of being proved by miracle." In these words you see that two reasons are included in defence of the proposition, "That God may permit wicked spirits to work miracles for their own ends, though

His design in permitting them is only to try our faith; and that transubstantiation is incapable of being proved by any miracle."

Orth. The first of these has already been answered; but that you may still more clearly see its weakness, I shall make another observation. There are, you know, two kinds of miracles, that may be wrought in confirmation of doctrine; some that do not exceed the natural power of spiritual beings, whether good or bad, and are termed relative miracles; others which are above the reach of all created power, that can be performed only by God Himself, and are therefore called absolute miracles.* A relative miracle, known as such, can never of itself give thorough conviction of the truth of any doctrine, unless it be otherwise proved to be the work of God, or of good angels commissioned by Him; but a miracle of the second kind must produce absolute conviction that the person, at whose desire it is performed, is sent by God, and that "the word of the Lord in his mouth is true," 1 Kings, xvii.†

Now the examples cited by Benevolus from the Scriptures are all of the first kind, merely relative; they show, indeed, that God may, and sometimes does, permit the devil, by his agents, to do extraordinary things within the compass of his own natural strength, seemingly in proof of falsehood, though permitted by God only to try people's faith, or for some other good end; but what is that to the point? The raising of a dead man to life is above the utmost power of Satan, a miracle proper to God alone, and therefore the most unanswerable proof of any doctrine in confirmation of which it is performed. Allowing,

---

* See above, Chap. I. on the different kinds of miracles.
† See above, Chap. IX. on the authority of miracles.

then, that the devil is sometimes permitted to do signs and wonders within the reach of his own power, in support of false doctrine, will this ever excuse Benevolus for refusing to believe a doctrine, which he supposes confirmed by a miracle proper to God himself, and which none but His almighty power can perform?

For my part, I see nothing to which such incredulity can better be compared than to that of Pharaoh; for though Moses wrought before that prince such miracles as compelled even his own magicians to confess, "That the finger of God was there, yet Pharaoh's heart was hardened, and he hearkened not unto them," Exod. viii. 19. It is also extremely unfortunate for Benevolus that our blessed Saviour Himself brings this very case of "refusing to believe though one should rise from the dead," as an instance of the most obstinate and consummate infidelity, Luke, xvi. 31. Nor do I see how Benevolus's proposition can escape the same condemnation; at least I think it manifest that this first argument, which you have brought, cannot justify it.

Phil. I must indeed acknowledge that I do not see how it can; and its fallacy is evident from the distinction between relative and absolute miracles, to which I did not at first advert. But what do you say to the second reason alleged, that "transubstantiation is incapable of being proved by any miracle?"

Orth. If this be really true, and can be clearly proved, then the dispute is at an end, and victory must be with Benevolus. I suppose he has summed up all that can be said in proof of this assertion, as I know it is a favourite topic of his; let us hear, then, what he says for this purpose.

Phil. I assure you he says a great deal, and perhaps more to the point than you imagine. I will state his arguments in his own words: "I say transubstantiation is incapable of being proved by a miracle, and that for two reasons: First, because there is the same evidence against that doctrine that there can be for the truth of any miracle—I mean the testimony of the human senses; for, if I believe my senses, I cannot believe transubstantiation; and if I disbelieve my senses, I could not believe the truth of your miracle. Secondly, Transubstantiation is incapable of being proved by a miracle, because it involves many contradictions." He proceeds then to show some of the many contradictions which flow from this tenet, and which make it absolutely impossible that any miracle can prove it to be true; for what is in itself founded on contradiction, and therefore an impossibility, can never be proved a truth, by any evidence whatever.

Orth. I imagined that he would take his stand there. These are the common arguments used against transubstantiation, and have been again and again fully answered by those who hold that doctrine. I should not wish, however, to occupy your time by repeating here what others have said; but as all the arguments against transubstantiation are founded on either a real or pretended ignorance of what its defenders believe and teach, I shall lay before you a clear explanation of the doctrine itself, from which you will immediately see how little to the point are all the objections brought against it.

Phil. You will afford me particular pleasure; for, to say the truth, I have not a clear idea of it myself; and in many discussions I have thought that the disputants did not seem to understand each other, or even to have a distinct idea of what they themselves would argue for.

Orth. That is too frequently the case in controversies on religion. Each one thinks himself master of the subject, though in reality his knowledge of it be extremely superficial; generally he forms false and unjust ideas of the tenets of his adversaries, and, in combating them, he only combats the phantoms of his own imagination. Hence there is no end to disputes, and to improper, nay, impious expressions, among which, I fear, Benevolus's proposition will find a distinguished place. This, in a great measure, I have shown already, but it will be more evident as we proceed in our examination.

Phil. I believe your observation is just, and I am persuaded that many religious discussions would soon terminate, if the parties, before they begin to argue, would fix the precise point in question, and lay down a clear explanation of their respective tenets. This I long to hear done with regard to transubstantiation.

Orth. All the arguments of reason urged against this doctrine are drawn from philosophy; and you see that the two arguments used by Benevolus are entirely of this kind. The supporters of transubstantiation, then, are only called upon to reconcile it with sound philosophy, and if they do all objections vanish.

In philosophy we must distinguish what is founded on evident facts and experience from what is merely theoretical, and invented to explain the phenomena of nature. The former is steady and uniform, and must be the same, in all times, to every attentive inquirer; the other is fluctuating and uncertain, and has changed in almost every age. Objections have been made against transubstantiation, from the principles adopted by the different systems of philosophy, and have, with equal ease, been solved from the same assumed principles. It is needless, however, to repeat here what has been urged from systems now exploded. I shall confine myself, therefore, to what is now regarded as the most certain and rational system, and, from its principles, I shall explain to you the Catholic teaching concerning transubstantiation.

Phil. I suppose you mean the philosophy of the mind and of common-sense, which Dr Reid, in his Inquiry, and Dr Beattie, in his Essay on Truth, have so clearly explained, and so solidly established.

Orth. I do; and from the language of nature, explained by these learned gentlemen, I lay down the following observations, which will serve as so many principles in our present inquiry.

First, The different qualities which we observe in bodies, by means of our senses—their colour, smell, taste, and the like—are not in these bodies themselves what they are in our mind. In us they are sensations, feelings, or perceptions excited in our mind, by the mediate or immediate action of external objects upon the organs of our senses. Thus, the feeling which we have of colour, is not in the coloured body, but is excited by the rays of light reflected in a certain manner from that body, which, striking on our eyes, excite in the mind that sensation which we call colour; and, according to the different proportions in which the rays of light are reflected to our eyes, the sensations of different colours are excited. In like manner, when we taste sugar, the sweetness is not in the sugar, but is a perception or feeling excited in our mind by the particles of sugar acting upon our organ of taste when applied to it. The same observation holds true in all the sensible qualities which we perceive in bodies; and may be explained by a familiar example. When the point of a needle is pressed upon any part of our body, we experience that uneasy sensation which we call pain; now it is evident this pain is not in the needle, but is a feeling of our mind caused by the needle. So when we smell a rose, the agreeable odour which we experience is not in the rose, but is a sensation excited in our mind by the perfume of the rose applied to our organ of smell.

Secondly, In examining objects we must carefully distinguish three things; first, the feelings or sensations excited in our minds by the actions of those objects upon our organs of sense; secondly, the particular qualities or dispositions of the objects themselves, by which they excite such feelings; and thirdly, the material part or substance of the objects, in which the particular qualities or dispositions reside.

Thirdly, A little attention to what passes in our minds will convince us that we are totally ignorant of the material part or substance of all surrounding objects; that we are no less ignorant of the nature of the particular qualities or dispositions of bodies, by which they act upon our organs, and excite certain feelings and sensations in our mind; and that all our natural knowledge of bodies is confined to their sensible qualities alone, as perceived by us. From these we argue that there are bodily objects really existing without us, and independent of us; that they have in themselves certain qualities or arrangements of their component parts, calculated to excite various sensations in us, when applied to the organs of our senses; that these qualities are different in different objects, which excite various sensations, according to their respective qualities; that these qualities may be changed in the same object, so that it shall cease to excite the sensations in us which it formerly did, and excite others which it did not raise before, &c.

Fourthly, As it is experience alone that shows us the connection between the several bodies around us, and the corresponding sensations which they excite in our minds; and as this connection is constant, we naturally conclude that these bodies are the causes of the sensations which we feel, and being ignorant of the manner in which they produce these effects, "without inquiring farther," as Dr Reid justly observes, "we attribute to the cause some vague and indistinct notion of power or virtue to produce the effect. In many cases the purposes of life do not make it necessary to give distinct names to the cause and the effect; and hence it happens, that being closely connected in the imagination, though very unlike to each other, one name serves for both, which occasions an ambiguity in many terms in all languages. Thus magnetism signifies both the power or virtue in the loadstone to attract the iron as a cause, and the motion in the iron towards the loadstone as an effect. Heat signifies both a sensation of our mind, and a quality or state of bodies apt to excite that sensation in us. The names of all smells, tastes, sounds, as well as heat and cold, have a like ambiguity in all languages, though, in common language, they are rarely used to signify the sensations, but generally the external qualities indicated by the sensations."

Fifthly, In like manner, this general term, the sensible qualities of bodies, is ambiguous: it signifies both that particular aptitude, power, or virtue in bodies to excite certain sensations in our mind, when applied to our organs of sense; and also these very sensations themselves. In the former sense it signifies a thing of which we have no idea, and are totally ignorant in what it consists; in the latter, it signifies a thing with which we are thoroughly acquainted.

Sixthly, As we are totally ignorant of the nature of sensible qualities residing in the objects around us, so we are equally ignorant of the reason why they excite their corresponding sensations in our mind. We can see no reason why the rays of light variously reflected to our eyes, should excite in us the sensations of various colours, nor why the motion of the air should excite the idea of sound, or the fire heat, or sugar sweetness, or the like. By experience we know that it is so, but why or how it is so, of this we know nothing. This we must resolve into the will of the Creator, Who has so ordered, and Who doubtless might have ordered otherwise had He so pleased.

Seventhly, Besides the sensations which external bodies excite in our mind, by our organs of sense, as the immediate objects of these organs, we also find from experience, that they produce many other sensible effects, both upon our bodies and upon each other, when applied to action. Thus ipecacuan, besides the ideas of its colour, taste, and smell, which it excites in our mind by the organs of our senses, when taken into the stomach, also produces sickness; opium allays pain, and causes sleep; wine intoxicates; and so of other things. These effects of different bodies we know by experience; but we are totally ignorant why they produce them, or what particular quality or disposition it is in each, which produces the effect proper to it. But as experience teaches us that they constantly do produce these effects, in the same circumstances, we naturally attribute to each body a quality, power, or virtue proper to itself, bestowed upon it by the Creator; and all such powers of bodies may be included under the general name of sensible qualities, because they manifest themselves to our senses by the effects which they produce.

Eighthly, If we inquire in what all these sensible qualities of bodies consist, or what is that particular disposition of each body, by which it produces the effects proper to it, we must acknowledge our total ignorance, and confess that we know nothing. If we suppose the original matter, which composes the substance of bodies, to be the same in all, and that it acts mechanically, which seems to be the most generally received opinion, then we can conceive no other way of accounting for the different qualities of different bodies, than by the figure, motion, and combination of the particles of matter in the structure of each.

It is true, indeed, that a difference in these things alters the sensible qualities of bodies; witness the various and opposite qualities of quicksilver, according to the various changes wrought in the structure of its component parts by fire; and it seems to be the approved opinion of philosophers, that all the vast variety of productions from the earth is owing only to the different modifications of the same nutritive juice, according to the different plants by which it is imbibed. But whether this be really the case, and holds good in all varieties of creatures—or if there be, in fact, different kinds of primitive matter, of which bodies are composed, and to which their various qualities are owing, we know not. Whether these qualities of bodies arise from the mechanical structure of their parts; or if they be the immediate effect of the divine will, impressed upon different compositions of the same original matter, by way of a law, we are entirely ignorant.

Phil. What you have said seems perfectly clear, and the substance of it may, I think, be thus summed up in a few words: the sensible effects which various bodies produce, either in ourselves, or in each other, are objects of knowledge, of which we are absolutely certain, from the testimony of our senses. From these sensible effects we justly argue the existence of the bodies which produce them; and we also infer that those bodies have in themselves certain qualities by which they are capable of producing these effects. But with regard to the matter or substance of the bodies in which those qualities reside, its nature and structure, or the nature of the qualities themselves by which the effects are produced, this is entirely hidden from our eyes. All this I easily understand, as it is extremely clear; but I do not perceive what connection it has with transubstantiation.

Orth. That we shall now see, after taking a view of our manner of reasoning concerning the substance of bodies. Let us suppose, then, according to the general opinion of the learned, that the elementary matter, or *materia prima*, of all bodies, is the same throughout the whole creation; and that the vast diversity of material objects arises only from different forms in their composition and structure. This original matter is the common substance of all bodies; its particular structure in various bodies constitutes their essential diversity, or their different natures; and it is by their sensible qualities, as perceived by us, that we distinguish one substance from another. Hence, for instance, what we properly understand by the substance of iron, is the elementary matter formed in such a manner as to excite in our minds that collection of sensible qualities which we perceive in iron. What we understand by the substance of bread, is a portion of the same elementary matter, so formed as to excite in our mind that other collection of sensible qualities which we perceive in bread; and so of all others.

Now it is reasonable to suppose that the Author of Nature acts uniformly in the ordinary course of nature, and that when effects are the same, the causes also producing them are the same. When, therefore, we find the same collection of sensible qualities in different bodies, we conclude that their substance is the same; and, on the contrary, when we find the sensible qualities in one body different from those in another, we conclude that their substances are different, although, in reality, we know nothing whatever of the nature of the one substance or of the other, nor in what their difference consists. Thus, in examining a piece of iron and a piece of wood, we find the collection of sensible qualities in the one very different from those in the other; and therefore we distinguish them as different substances, and give them different names. But when we examine two pieces of iron, or two pieces of wood, by themselves, we find the sensible qualities of both the same; and therefore we conclude that their substance also is the same, and we apply to them the same name.

The sensible qualities of bodies are the immediate and sole objects of our senses, and with regard to them our senses are the sole and absolute judges, from whose ultimate sentence there is no appeal. In like manner, whatever changes occur in these qualities fall immediately under the cognisance of the particular senses, to which it belongs to give us proper and certain information of such changes. From such information we argue that if any change be produced in the qualities, there must also be a corresponding change in the nature of the body itself, by which these effects are produced, although we are ignorant wherein this change in the cause consists. But where our senses inform us of no change in the qualities, we conclude that there is no change in the body from which these effects proceed.

Now, though this manner of reasoning be most just, and may be safely depended upon in all the ordinary occurrences of life, at least where we have no positive reason to doubt it; yet we see no impossibility in supposing that Almighty God may cause two very different substances so to act upon us as to affect our senses in the very same way, and thereby exhibit to us the same sensible qualities. Nay, we are so far from seeing any impossibility in this, that we know from revelation it has often been the case.

The substance of a human being, composed of a soul and body, is confessedly very different from that of an angel, which is purely spiritual; and yet it is certain, from the Word of God, that angels have often assumed the sensible qualities of living men,—that is, have appeared as such to the sight of those who beheld them—have spoken and conversed in their hearing—have taken hold of them, and wrestled with them—have walked, sat down, ate, drank, and exhibited themselves to the senses of those who beheld them, in the same way that a man would.

It cannot be called in question that there is an infinite distance between the bodily substance of a dove, composed of flesh and blood, and the incomprehensible substance of the Divinity; and yet we know that, when our blessed Saviour was baptised in the Jordan, the Holy Ghost, the third Person of the adorable Trinity, was pleased to exhibit Himself to those present, under the outward appearance of a dove, affecting their sight in the same way that a dove would have done, had it been hovering over our Saviour at the time. In these and other similar cases related in Scripture, it is plain that the above way of arguing, from the sameness of the sensible effects, to the sameness or similarity of the cause producing them, would not hold. This may be farther illustrated even in natural things; for how often do we see cooks, apothecaries, and vintners, compounding dishes, drugs, and various wines, representing so exactly what they are not, that the nicest judge, upon the strictest examination, could not distinguish them from what they represent? In these cases, also, were we to conclude, from the sameness of the sensible qualities, that the substances of the things are really what the qualities represent, we should be deceived as in the former cases. Yet in neither would the senses be deceived; for the sensations excited in our minds by their means, correspond perfectly to the action of these external objects; and from the sensations we conclude with absolute certainty the existence of the external objects, and infer that they have a power or quality of so acting upon our senses, as to excite these sensations in our mind; but with absolute certainty we can go no farther.

But to come to the point, if we apply the above observations to bread and wine, we find that they have a number of sensible qualities—that is, a certain colour, taste, smell, &c., proper to themselves—and when examined by our senses, they excite in our minds the sensations to which we apply these names, and which we call the sensible qualities, forms, species, or appearances of bread and wine. These we know by our senses—with these we are conversant by experience; but of the substance of bread and wine, in which these qualities reside, or wherein that particular structure, virtue, or power consists, which excites these perceptions in our mind, we know nothing. This is not in the least perceptible to us.

Now, what Catholics teach concerning transubstantiation is precisely this: " 1. That the change made is only in the material substance of the bread and wine, which is wholly imperceptible to us; that this substance of the bread and wine is entirely taken away by the power of

God, and ceases to be any longer there; and that the substance of the body and blood of Christ, which is equally imperceptible to our senses, is substituted in its place, and now exists where bread and wine existed before. 2. That there is no change made in any of the sensible qualities of the bread and wine; these remain exactly as they were; for Jesus Christ, now present instead of the bread and wine, exhibits Himself to us under the same appearances which the bread and wine had before the change."

Phil. You astonish me! Is this really the doctrine of Catholics? This is plain and intelligible; but, to hear Benevolus and others on this subject, you would think it such a mass of absurdity, that even those who believed it could not give any intelligible account of what they mean.

Orth. That may well be; perhaps those gentlemen have never taken the trouble to inform themselves of the real belief of Catholics; or they may have read what Catholic authors write upon this subject with the eye of prejudice and prepossession, and perhaps some of them find it convenient to cast all the obscurity they can upon Catholic doctrine. But, be that as it may, what I have said is the precise doctrine of the Catholic Church, as is manifest from her own words in the Council of Trent, where she speaks thus: "If any one shall deny that in the sacrament of the blessed Eucharist are contained truly, really, and substantially the body and blood, along with the soul and divinity of our Lord Jesus Christ, and therefore whole Christ, but shall say that he is there only in sign, figure, or power, let him be Anathema," Sess. 13. Can. 1. "If any man shall say that in the blessed sacrament of the Eucharist, the substance of the bread and wine remains along with the body and blood of our Lord

Jesus Christ, and shall deny that wonderful and singular conversion of the whole substance of the bread into the body, and of the whole substance of the wine into the blood, the appearances of bread and wine only remaining, which conversion the Catholic Church most fitly calls transubstantiation, let him be Anathema," Sess. 13. Can. 2.

In these two canons three things are declared: that the body and blood of Jesus Christ are truly present in the Eucharist after consecration, where they were not before; that the substance of the bread and wine, which was there before, is there no longer; and that nothing remains of what was bread and wine but only the appearances;—and hence the Council concludes that this, being a change of the substances, is fitly called transubstantiation, which you see is the very doctrine I laid down above almost in the same terms: for if what was there before be not there now, and what was not there before be now present, then it follows that the change of the one into the other must consist in destroying or taking away the one, and substituting the other in its place.

Phil. I cannot say that it yet seems to me quite clear. On the contrary, the words of the Council rather increase my difficulty; for as it says that the whole substance of the bread and wine is changed into the body and blood of Christ, this would seem to imply that the elementary matter of the bread and wine passes into the body and blood of Christ, and goes to compose its substance; and therefore that the material part of the bread and wine is not destroyed nor taken away, but still remains and composes the very body and blood of Christ, somewhat in the same way that the elementary matter of food is changed into the substance of our body, goes to compose it, and to repair its daily waste.

Orth. Nothing is more foreign to the sense of the Council, and to the belief of the whole Catholic Church, than what you here advance; nay, a little attention will convince you that it is evidently repugnant to common-sense to say that the elementary matter of the bread and wine passes into the body and blood of Jesus Christ, and goes to compose its substance; because the body of Christ is already perfect and entire, incapable of increase or diminution, and has a real existence before consecration. Now, to say that two bodily substances, distinct, existing separately, and wholly independent of each other, should become identical, is evidently inconsistent. You may, if you please, say that the material substance of the bread is united to the body of Christ, is added to it, is compenetrated with it, or the like; in these suppositions, considered in themselves, we do not see any impossibility, though they are very different from what Catholics teach;—but to say that it becomes His identical body, the same which existed before consecration, at the right hand of the Father, is a palpable absurdity.

When we say that the food we take is changed into the substance of our body, we mean that the material particles of the food, changing the form which they had, and acquiring a new form, by the action of our organs, but still unchanged in themselves, go to supply the place of the material particles of our body, which are daily consumed and cast off by the usual secretions; or, being added to what was there before, serve to increase our bulk and stature; but to suppose that either of these, or any such change, could happen to the glorious body of Jesus Christ, would be ridiculous.

Besides, Catholics believe that it is the self-same body of Christ which is at the right hand of the Father in heaven, that is present in the Eucharist. Now, if the material substance of bread be supposed to remain, and to enter into the composition of the body of Christ in the Eucharist, either by incorporation, or compenetration, or in whatever other way you can imagine, it will no longer be the self-same glorious body which is at the right hand of the Father, but one very different—a new compound, made up of the pre-existing body of Christ, already perfect and entire, and this additional matter of bread, which now enters into its composition; which it is ridiculous to suppose, and which is directly contrary to the express belief of Catholics.

If, therefore, you suppose that the material substance of the bread and wine be not entirely destroyed, and does not wholly cease to exist there after consecration, you must say that it remains along with the body and blood of Christ; and this is the very thing which the Council condemns and anathematises in the above-cited canon. It is plain, therefore, that by the conversion of the whole substance of the bread and wine into the body and blood of Christ, the Council means nothing else than that the substance of the bread and wine is, by the almighty power of God, instantaneously taken away—ceases to be there; and that the body and blood of Christ are, by the same almighty power, and in the same instant of time, placed in its stead—the presence of this latter, by virtue of the words of consecration, necessarily implying the absence of the former.

This is still clearer from the Catechism of this Council, composed and published by its order, for the use of those who have the charge of souls. In the Second Part upon the Eucharist, explaining the effects of consecration, it says: " The Catholic Church firmly believes, and openly professes, that in this sacrament the words of consecration accomplish three things: first, that the true and real body of Christ, the same that was born of the Virgin, and is now seated at the right hand of the Father in heaven, is rendered present in this sacrament; the second, that no part of the substance of the elements remains in it; the third, that the accidents, which are perceived by our senses, are still there, in a wonderful and inexplicable manner without a subject; because (it immediately adds) the substance of the bread and wine is so changed into the very body and blood of our Lord, that the substance of the bread and wine entirely ceases to be."* A little after, the second of these effects is more fully considered, and both reason and authority are brought to prove that no part of the substance of the bread and wine remains after consecration. And in No. XCII. it is declared that this wonderful change is performed without any change in Christ, "because He is neither generated, nor changed, nor increases, but remains whole in His own substance;" *Neque enim Christus aut generatur, aut mutatur, aut augescit, sed in sua substantia totus permanet.*

From these passages the explanation I have given of the doctrine of the Council is clear and evident; for if Jesus Christ, the same Who is at the right hand of the Father in heaven, be after consecration present in this sacrament, where He was not before; if He suffers no alteration in Himself—is neither generated, nor changed, nor increases, but remains whole in His own substance; if no part of the substance of the bread and wine remains, but entirely ceases any longer to be, —it necessarily follows that the change of substance declared by the Council can mean nothing else than

* Cum panis et vini substantia in ipsum Domini corpus et sanguinem ita mutetur, ut panis et vini substantia *omnino* esse desinat.

that the substance of the bread and wine ceases to exist, and that the substance of the body and blood of Christ succeeds in its place.

Phil. I am now thoroughly satisfied as to the sense of the Council, which you have made perfectly plain; nay, the above declaration, that in this sacrament Christ is neither changed nor increases, but remains whole in His own substance, necessarily implies the explanation you have given; for it is impossible that this could be true, if the material substance of the bread should be supposed, in any imaginable way, to be any longer there; but, pray, is this the way it is explained by the divines of the Catholic Church?

Orth. By all without exception. Nay, according to their principles, it is impossible that they should differ on any of the three points above mentioned, because these are taught, not as school opinions, but as dogmas of faith, truths revealed by God, declared by His Church to be so, and essentially included in the words of the institution. You see how the Catechism of the Council above cited expressly declares that " the Catholic Church firmly believes, and openly professes, that the words of consecration accomplish three things," &c. Other divines speak in the same manner: I shall name a few of the most celebrated for your further satisfaction.

I begin with the learned Cardinal Bellarmine, whose authority is above exception in delivering the true doctrine of the Church, and whose controversial works are justly esteemed a standard on those subjects. The third book of his treatise on the Eucharist relates entirely to the real presence and transubstantiation. In the eleventh and following chapters he refutes various errors, and rejects as heretical the opinion of Durandus, who taught the very thing which you propose, that the elementary matter of the bread remains in the Eucharist after consecration, and becomes the matter of the body of Christ; which is an evident proof how widely different such an opinion is from the faith of Catholics.

In the eighteenth chapter he explains the doctrine of the Church in opposition to all these errors, and does it by showing what is meant when we say that one thing is changed into another. For this, he says, these three conditions are required; first, that the thing changed cease to exist—for it is unintelligible to say that one thing is changed into another, unless that which is changed ceases to be what it was before; secondly, that something succeed in the place of that which now ceases to be, otherwise it would not be a conversion, but a corruption or an annihilation; thirdly, that there be a mutual connection or dependence between the destruction of the one and the succession of the other, so that the one necessarily implies the other.*

* This third condition is particularly to be observed. Every change, of whatever kind it be, whether of the thing itself or of its mode or quality, necessarily supposes the absence of one thing, mode, or quality, and the presence of another; and this is essential to the nature of every change. But there is not in every change a mutual dependence between the presence of the one and the absence of the other; so that the one necessarily follows or presupposes the other in one and the same action. A man truly changes his coat when he puts off one and puts on another; but he does that by two separate actions, done at different times, and quite independent of one another. In cases of this kind we cannot say there is a change of one thing into another, as we cannot say this man changes the coat he puts off into the one he puts on. To verify this expression it is requisite that the change be made at the same instant and by the same action, so that the presence of the one term must necessarily imply the absence of the other; as when we say, light is changed into darkness, heat into cold, and the like: wherein the very same moment that darkness and cold appear, light and heat cease; and the presence of the one necessarily implies the absence of the other.

Now, as transubstantiation is a change, not of the accidents or appearances of the bread and wine, which are admitted to remain unchanged, but of the whole material substance of the bread and wine into the substance of the body and blood of Christ, according to these conditions, by this change nothing can be understood but that the substance of the bread and wine ceases to exist, and that it is replaced by the body and blood of Christ. This, his Eminence observes, is a perfect "conversion of the one substance into the other;" because the body and blood of Christ, being now present in virtue of the words of consecration, the verification of these sacred words necessarily excludes the presence of the substance of the bread and wine; which, by the almighty power of God, ceases to be where it was before, at the same instant, and by the same action by which the body and blood of Christ exist there. He further observes, that this singular conversion differs in two points from all other changes that we know, whether natural or supernatural. First, because in other changes it is probable that the elementary matter remains, *in utroque termino*, both after and before the change;* but in transubstantiation, *certum est*, says he,

---

* I find, however, several who are of opinion that in some, at least, of the supernatural changes related in the Scriptures, such as the turning of Moses' rod into a serpent, there was a total change both of the material substance of the rod and of its form, there being an instantaneous destruction of the one, and production of the other; and this opinion is followed above, under the Criterion, where this example, among others, is brought as an instance of a miracle proper to the almighty power of God alone. The truth seems to be, that without a revelation it is impossible certainly to know whether the material substance be destroyed in these supernatural conversions, or is only transformed as to its structure and composition; though the turning a dry rod into a living creature doubt-

materiam primam non manere; "it is certain that the elementary matter does not remain." Secondly, in other conversions, either all or some of the sensible qualities are changed, but, in transubstantiation, all the sensible qualities remain as they were before, the material substance alone being changed. This is the explanation given of this mystery by the celebrated cardinal; and in the remaining chapters he repeats and inculcates the same, both in his proofs and in his answers to objections.

In all the natural conversions of one thing into another, the change is made only in the form or sensible qualities of the object, while the material substance remains unchanged. In transubstantiation the very reverse takes place. The change is made in the material substance, while the form or sensible qualities remain

less requires much more than such a change of structure. If the orginal elementary matter be of different kinds in different creatures, then a change of one creature into another must imply a change of the elementary matter itself; if this be homogeneal throughout the whole creation, then it seems sufficient, at least for all natural changes of one thing into another, that there be a change of form and structure only. Instantaneous changes of either kind evidently show the finger of God, especially when anything inanimate is changed into a living creature, which implies a new creation of life; and hence what the magicians of Egypt did could not be a real change of their rods into serpents, as we know it was the work not of God but of the devil, to whom such a power cannot belong. It may be accounted for by fascination, or we may conceive that some of the evil spirits by their great agility removed the rods so quickly as to be imperceptible to those present, whilst others, with equal celerity, substituted real serpents in their place; nor can this seem anyway improbable, as we see among ourselves many similar and surprising examples done by jugglers from their great dexterity and sleight of hand. But this was no more changing rods into serpents, than it is changing one coat into another when we put off one and put on another. See the preceding note.

perfectly the same; and as in other conversions the change consists in this, that the former sensible qualities are destroyed, and at the same instant other sensible qualities are introduced in their place, the material substance remaining common to both; so in transubstantiation the change consists precisely in this, that the substance of bread is destroyed, and at the same instant the body of Christ succeeds in its place, whilst the sensible qualities remain the same in both.

The next authority I bring forward is that of Tournely, a celebrated French theologian of this century, who, in his lectures upon the Eucharist, after refuting various errors regarding transubstantiation, thus explains the sense of the Church concerning it: "The substance of bread and wine does not cease by a mere suspension of the divine preservation, but by a positive action—consecration—by which the body of Christ becomes present, the substance of bread and wine receding."*

In the judicious exposition of Pope Pius's Creed, published at Paris in the year 1768, with the epitome of the general controversies of the two learned bishops and brothers, Adrian and Peter of Wallemburg, the article of the real presence and transubstantiation is thus declared: "We believe, according to the truth of the words of Christ, Who says, 'This is my body,' that in the blessed Eucharist His body is present by transubstantiation. For as Christ, after He took bread, verily pronounced what He offered, under the outward appearances, to be His body—and as His words could not mean the substance of bread and wine, as is evident, nor even His own natural body, if the substance of the bread and wine remained under their

---

* Quâ (consecratione) perfecta corpus Christi sit presens, recedente panis et vini substantiâ.—Tournely, *De Euchar.*

proper accidents—it necessarily follows that the substance of the bread ceases to be, and the substance of His body alone remains under these accidents."*

To these celebrated authors I shall add a more recent one, Monsieur de Reval, in his Philosophical Catechism against the Deists, published at Liege and Brussels in the year 1773. He begins the article on the Eucharist by this question,—"To deny the possibility of the real presence, is it not to deny the power of God?" To which he gives this plain answer,—"It is an absolute denial of it, for it is refusing to God the power of destroying a piece of bread, and of concealing a human body under its appearances."† These distinct testimonies of such celebrated and standard authors, among innumerable others, are more than sufficient to show you what is the true sense of Catholic divines on this subject.

Phil. They are so, indeed; nor can the matter, in my opinion, admit of the smallest doubt. But, pray, is not this way of understanding the expression, conversion, or change of one thing into another, contrary to the common acceptation of it among mankind?

Orth. Very far from it: on the contrary, a little attention will convince you that this is the common and universally received meaning of it. Indeed, no example can be shown where the object changed is ever supposed to pass into, or compose that into which it is changed; but in every case we are persuaded that the object

---

* Necessario fieri debuit ut substantia panis desineret et sola substantia corporis sub illis accidentibus remaneret.

† C'est la nier absolument, puisque c'est refuser à Dieu le pouvoir de détruire un morceau de pain, et de cacher un corps humain sous ces apparences.

changed ceases any longer to exist, and that another comes in its place, but in such manner that the presence of the one always implies the absence of the other. Thus, when we say that light is turned into darkness, does it ever enter into our mind that the light remains after the change, and enters into the composition of darkness? Never. What we mean is, that the light ceases to exist, and the darkness comes in its place, but in such manner that the presence of the darkness necessarily implies the absence of the light. When we say heat is turned into cold, we never think that the heat remains after the change, and goes to compose the cold; but the plain meaning is, that the heat entirely ceases, and is banished by its opposite, cold, supervening in its stead. In like manner, when we say that a sinner is changed into a saint, do we ever imagine that his former impiety and guilt remain after his conversion, and enter into the composition of his sanctity? By no means; we understand, by that expression, that his impiety and guilt are taken away by the grace of God, which succeeds in their stead.

Examples of this kind are innumerable; but, to make the matter still clearer, I shall consider the expression a little more minutely when applied to compound objects. In these it commonly happens that the precise thing changed is only a part of the compound, but as the change of one part alters the condition of the whole, we say, in common language, that the object itself is changed.

In bodies we may consider two parts, in which a change may be effected—the material substance of which a body is composed, and the sensible qualities, by which we distinguish it from other bodies. In all the natural conversions of one body into another, with which we are acquainted, nothing more is required than that a change take place in the sensible qualities, whilst the material substance remains the same. This is enough to enable us to say that the body is changed. Thus we say that quicksilver, by one chemical operation, is changed into sweet mercury, by another into red precipitate, by another into turbith mineral—all which differ from each other in their sensible qualities, and in the effects which they produce. Yet these changes take place only in the structure and composition of the component particles of the quicksilver, while the material substance itself remains the same in all its various preparations, and may, by a counter-operation, be brought back to the form of quicksilver again. Still, though the material substance remains, we justly say that the compound object itself, the quicksilver, is changed into these its different forms.

In like manner, when we say the food we take is changed into our flesh and blood, we do not mean that the material substance is changed in its nature, but only that the structure which it had in the composition of food, and the sensible qualities resulting from that structure, are altered by the action of our organs; so that the elementary matter which was in the food is now composed in the form of flesh and blood, and exhibits their sensible qualities. So, also, we say that the nutritive juice of the earth is changed into all the vast variety of plants composing the vegetable world; but the meaning of this expression is, that the particles of matter in the nutritive juice, being imbibed by the different plants, change their form, and structure, and sensible qualities, into another form, and qualities different from the former, according to the nature of the plant which absorbs them, the original matter being still the same in the juice and in the plant.

Now, if we examine all these changes of forms or sensible qualities, we perceive that they consist precisely in this, that the form and sensible qualities which the elementary matter had in the quicksilver, in the food, and in the nutritive juice, are destroyed; and, at the same time, another form and other sensible qualities are substituted in their place, while the material substance, which receives this new form, remains unchanged, the common subject both of the form destroyed and of that received.

In transubstantiation no change is made in the appearance or sensible qualities of the bread and wine, these remaining exactly as they were before; the change takes place in the material substance alone. As, therefore, the change of these qualities in the former cases implies nothing more than the destruction or extinction of one form or set of sensible qualities, and the substituting of others in their place; so in transubstantiation the change of substances can imply no more than the destruction or extinction of one substance, and the putting another in its place. And as the above and other such natural changes are properly called transformations, because they are changes of the form or sensible qualities, the same substances remaining; so this other is properly called transubstantiation, because it is a change of the substance, whilst the forms or sensible qualities continue as they were.

Phil. Sir, I am now thoroughly satisfied with what you say, and think I have a clear and distinct idea of the Catholic doctrine of transubstantiation, far different indeed from what I ever had before. But permit me to ask you one other question. As Catholics hold that the material substance of the bread is no longer there, what do they say becomes of it? In what manner does it cease to be?

Orth. The answer to this question will show you a very important maxim, by which Catholics are regulated in matters of religion. Whatever articles they hold as truths revealed by God, to these they adhere with invariable attachment. Concerning such points there are no different opinions; they are not regarded as matters of opinion, but as absolute truths, declared by the infinite veracity of God, Who reveals them. Hence they are taught and believed in the same way, throughout the whole world, by all the members of the Church, who, being convinced of their truth, make firm and open profession of them. Of this kind are the three points above mentioned concerning transubstantiation—namely, that Jesus Christ, God and man, Who died on the cross, and is now glorious at the right hand of the Father in heaven, is truly, really, and substantially present in the blessed Eucharist. That no part of the material substance of the bread and wine remains there, but is wholly changed into the substance of the body and blood of Christ, and that Jesus Christ presents Himself to us, in this holy mystery, under the outward appearance of bread and wine, which remains, in every respect, the same as before consecration. These, therefore, they believe and profess at all times, and in all circumstances.

But besides points of faith or revealed truths, there are many other things that may be investigated concerning religious matters, which have not been revealed by God. With regard to these, Catholic theologians form such judgments and opinions as appear to them the most reasonable; and they are at perfect liberty to adopt whatever opinion they please concerning such questions, provided it does not contradict any revealed truth. But on these matters the Church herself forms no opinion. Of this kind are the questions you have just proposed. If you ask the Catholic Church what becomes of the substance of the bread and wine? how it is destroyed? in what manner it ceases to be? she will answer you, that she knows nothing of the matter; and for this plain reason, that God Almighty has not been pleased to reveal it to her. The subject is too abstruse for human eyes to penetrate; it is absolutely impossible to know it unless God speak to disclose it; and since He has not done so, she rests contented in her ignorance. Her theologians say, indeed, that we may conceive the substance of the bread and wine to be taken away by annihilation, destruction, or dissolution; by simple removal, or in numberless other ways, easy to almighty power, though inconceivable to us; but all that can be said upon this is conjecture, and mere human opinion. Of this nothing can be determined with certainty, because the subject-matter is beyond the sphere of our knowledge, and we have no data on which to found any reasoning whatever.

Phil. Sir, this gives me particular satisfaction, and conveys a more exalted idea of the Catholic religion than anything I had hitherto imagined. I see the main point with Catholics is to preserve inviolate the sacred truths which God has revealed, or, as St Jude expresses it, "To contend earnestly for the faith which has been once delivered to the saints." This with them is a fixed point, from which they never vary; but they give themselves little concern in inquiring why or how these things are so. Regarding these it is impossible that the mind of man, by its own strength, should ever arrive at any certain knowledge in this mortal state; and therefore inquiries of this kind form no part of their creed, but are considered, as they truly are, more as matters of curiosity than of practical utility.

Orth. And matters of dangerous curiosity, too, as the experience of many can attest. Wherefore, leaving that, I shall now show you some obvious consequences which follow from the above explanation of transubstantiation, that will throw additional light on this subject, and invalidate some of the principal objections of Benevolus and others against it.

1. It is evident, from what we have seen, that transubstantiation is not impossible to Almighty God: we see nothing inconsistent or contradictory in what is taught respecting it. It cannot be called in question that Almighty God, when He pleases, is able to change the material substance of one body into another, by removing or destroying the one in an instant, and substituting the other in its place. We see many examples in the sacred Scriptures of sensible changes of this kind wrought instantaneously by the divine power, as of a rod being turned into a serpent, water into blood, and water into wine; and surely, if the Creator could give being and existence to what was not, He can with equal ease change the being and existence of what is. Again, from the examples we have seen above, both in natural and supernatural things, of different objects being exhibited to our senses under sensible qualities not their own, it is evidently not only not impossible, but perfectly easy for Jesus Christ to exhibit Himself to us under whatever sensible qualities He pleases; consequently it is not impossible for Him to assume those of bread and wine; and therefore there is no impossibility whatever in the doctrine of transubstantiation, as believed and taught by the Catholic Church.

2. It is manifest that this doctrine of transubstantia-

tion being possible, if we suppose it true, may justly become an object of divine faith. To understand this, you must recall to mind that faith is the belief of a truth revealed by God, merely because He has revealed it; I say merely, because, if either our senses or our reason convince us of the truth of any subject of revelation, our belief is no longer purely divine faith, but rather knowledge.

St Paul tells us that faith "cometh by hearing, and hearing by the word of God," Rom. x. 17; and that it is "the evidence of things not seen," Heb. xi. 1—that is, the conviction and firm belief which we have of things that do not appear to us from any other source of knowledge than from divine revelation alone; and our blessed Saviour declares that the whole merit of faith consists in believing merely because God speaks, though we neither see nor understand. "Because thou hast seen me, Thomas, thou hast believed; blessed are they who have not seen and yet have believed," John, xx. Hence, properly speaking, only supernatural truths, which do not fall under our senses, and cannot be discovered by reason, are the immediate and proper objects of revelation and of divine faith.

The change wrought in transubstantiation is entirely of this kind; it does not fall under the cognisance of our senses, the substances in which it is effected being altogether imperceptible to us. If, therefore, we suppose the doctrine of transubstantiation true, it is impossible that either our senses or our reason should ever discover it, nor could we ever come to the knowledge of it but by revelation from God; but if He should declare it to us, it immediately becomes a proper object of faith, as much as any other supernatural truth in the Christian religion.

3. It is no less evident, that if transubstantiation be so

revealed, its revelation, and consequently its reality and truth, may be proved by miracles, as well as any other article of Christian faith. It is a truth which does not fall under the examination of our senses, and cannot possibly be known by reason; it is a fact entirely depending upon the free-will of God. Hence, then, it is evident that our senses and our reason are by no means judges of it, nor in any way concerned in it. All that is required to convince us of its reality is to know with certainty that God declares it. But what greater assurance can we have that God reveals any truth to man, than a miracle proper to Himself, and wrought in his name? Such a miracle, therefore, wrought in proof of transubstantiation, must be the most convincing evidence that God declares it, and consequently that it is true.

4. You will clearly perceive, then, the utter fallacy of the first argument used by Benevolus against believing in transubstantiation, though attested by a miracle. His words, as you have said, are these: "Because there is the same evidence against that doctrine that there can be for the truth of any miracle—I mean the testimony of the human senses; and so one cannot rationally believe the one without disbelieving the other: for if I believe my senses, I cannot believe transubstantiation; and if I disbelieve my senses, I could not believe the truth of your miracle." Is it not evident that Benevolus knows nothing of the Catholic doctrine of transubstantiation when he argues in this manner?

Phil. I must own it is impossible to excuse him; for it is plain, from what you say, that the change wrought in transubstantiation is totally imperceptible to our senses—that they have no part in the belief or disbelief of it, and can give no evidence either for or against it; whereas the change wrought by a miracle performed in attestation of any doctrine, must be a sensible change, necessarily falling under the cognisance of our senses, and subjected to their examination. It is absurd, therefore, to pretend that there is the same evidence against transubstantiation that we have for the truth of any miracle; and I think it clear as noon-day, that the very reverse of what Benevolus asserts is certainly true; "for I may rationally believe transubstantiation without disbelieving my senses, and may be certain from my senses of the reality of a miracle, without injuring them in the smallest degree by believing transubstantiation."

Orth. I see you thoroughly comprehend what I have said, and the conclusion which you draw is most just; for surely no man of common-sense, who understands the real Catholic doctrine of transubstantiation, would ever expose himself by bringing such an argument against it as Benevolus does. The only excuse I can offer for Benevolus and Dr Tillotson, from whom he takes it, is, that both are ignorant of the true Catholic doctrine. This will be shown still further from the last consequence of the above explanation.

5. It is clear that our senses are in no way deceived in our belief of this mystery. Before the change, our senses represented to us the appearances of bread and wine, because they were really there, and therefore our senses were not then deceived; but of the nature of the substance of bread and wine, which exhibited these appearances, they told us nothing—that was quite imperceptible to them. Arguing from the uniformity of the works of the Creator, we concluded, indeed, from the appearances, that the substance of bread and wine was there; but this was a judgment of our reason, not the information of our senses. On the other hand, after

consecration our senses represent to us the same appearances of bread and wine, and for the same reason, because these appearances are there still; consequently our senses are no more deceived now than in the former case; for in both cases what they represent is strictly conformable to truth. But as to the substance of the body and blood of Christ, which, after consecration, is presented to us under these appearances, our senses can tell us no more respecting it than, before consecration, they could tell us of the substance of bread and wine.

If, after consecration, we had nothing else to guide our reason than we had before, our judgment in both cases would be the same—namely, that as the appearances of bread and wine continue, so the same substances exist. We are convinced, however, that God Almighty has declared, that by consecration, the substance of bread and wine is no longer there, but that it is changed into the body and blood of Jesus Christ; and as we confess this change to be perfectly possible to Him, we readily yield the judgment of reason, and firmly believe that what God declares is true. Yet in this it is evident that our senses are as far from being deceived now as they were before consecration; for then they told us what was really there—the appearances of bread and wine —and now they tell us that they perceive the same: and, indeed, the same appearances are there still.

Observe, if our faith told us that the sacred host was red, and our eyes saw it white—that it was bitter, and our taste felt it sweet, &c.—then, indeed, our faith and our senses would be opposed to each other, and if our faith was true, our senses must be deceived. But as the case stands, our faith and our senses go hand in hand in everything in which the senses are concerned; and,

APPENDIX.

therefore, though our faith be most true, yet our senses are by no means deceived. It follows, therefore, that we may rationally believe transubstantiation without disbelieving our senses, and this overthrows the whole foundation upon which the argument of Benevolus stands.

Phil. What you say, in my opinion, admits of no reply; for it is evident that the object of our faith in believing transubstantiation, and the object of our senses when a miracle is wrought before us, are entirely of different kinds. The former is an act of the omnipotence of God, produced in a subject, which is altogether imperceptible to us, where no visible effect appears, nor any change is made in the sensible qualities. The latter is a sensible effect produced by the same almighty power, but in the sensible qualities of the objects around us. The former can be known only by the sense of hearing, informed by the Word of God; the latter can be known by the senses of sight and touch, —is the proper object of these senses, and naturally falls under their examination. It is as unreasonable, then, to deny transubstantiation, which can be known only by hearing, because my sight and touch do not inform me of it, as it would be to deny that sugar is sweet, because I do not see the sweet taste with my eyes.

Orth. Your remark is just, and equally applicable to all supernatural revealed truths; they are all above reason; they fall not under the examination of our other senses, and can be known by hearing only, as St Paul expressly declares; and therefore it is altogether unphilosophical to argue against them either from sense or reason. If they be revealed by God, that is sufficient, and ought to silence every objection; and if the proofs of their revelation be the same as the proofs for the other truths of Christianity, no apparent contradiction can be urged as an argument against any one of them without sapping the foundation of all the others.

This observation leads us to the second argument alleged by Benevolus against the belief of transubstantiation, though attested by miracle, because he thinks this doctrine involves many contradictions. This argument is not new any more than the former; it has been often urged against Catholics, and as often refuted; but as you said that Benevolus mentions some contradictions, which he attributes to transubstantiation, I shall be glad to hear what seem to him the most weighty.

Phil. I shall show you that in his own words :* " Our blessed Saviour," says he, " having consecrated the holy Eucharist before His death, when His natural body was unglorified, and in the same state with that of other men, if transubstantiation be true, the one body of Christ behoved to be endued with opposite qualities at the same time—that is, with the qualities of ordinary flesh and blood, in His living body with which He spoke and acted, and with the qualities of a glorified body, in the blessed sacrament which He had just then consecrated. Or, in other words, our Saviour's one body was mortal, perishing, and corruptible flesh and blood, in His natural person; and was an immortal, incorruptible, impassible, and spiritual body, in the Holy Eucharist lying before Him. Now, as mortal and immortal, corruptible and incorruptible, passible and impassible, are qualities diametrically opposed, it is as impossible they can be properties of one and the same body, at the same time, as it is impossible for a thing to be and not to be at the same time; consequently the doctrine of transubstantiation

---

* The discussion between Eusebius and Benevolus is a fact, which occurred not ten years ago.

must be false." This is his great argument, in which he seems to place particular confidence as altogether unanswerable.

Orth. I am surprised he did not add other two of the same kind and no less specious : namely, that if this doctrine be true, the body of Christ must be in thousands of places at the same time,—and the whole living body of a man must be contained in the small space of a consecrated host—yea, in every visible particle of it; both of which seem no less impossible than the other.

Phil. I know that these objections also are brought against this doctrine, and I have seen some letters of Benevolus, in which he condemns the assertion that a body can be in different places at once as the greatest absurdity; but I suppose he thought the former so unanswerable that he required no other argument against Eusebius. I shall be glad, however, to hear what can be said to all the three, which I take to be the principal points alleged from reason against this doctrine.

Orth. They are so; and I shall now endeavour to satisfy you thoroughly regarding them. But first, I must observe that none of these apparent contradictions brought against transubstantiation are more opposed to the light of reason than is our belief respecting the mysteries of the Trinity and incarnation. That there should be three persons in the Godhead; that these should be really distinct, so that we can with truth affirm of the one what we cannot say of the others; and yet that all three should be but one and the self-same God,—are mysteries that humble human reason, and directly contradict all its lights.

Again, that this divine, increated, self-existent nature should be intimately united with the created, finite, and mortal nature of man; that both these natures should exist in one and the same Person; and that in consequence of this union God should truly suffer and die,—is so opposed to all the ideas of human reason, that it was a scandal to the Jews, and a stumbling-block to the Gentiles, and is to this day a matter of ridicule to freethinkers and deists. Now Benevolus believes these truths, notwithstanding the difficulties which they seem to involve; nor does he think them of any weight against the revelation of these mysteries in the holy Scriptures; yet the doctrine of transubstantiation is much more clearly revealed in Scripture than the Trinity or the incarnation. How unreasonable, then, is it to believe them, and yet refuse to believe the other!

Phil. What you say would be unanswerable, if the contradictions in both cases were only apparent; but Benevolus affirms the contrary, and says that they are widely different; his words are these: "The argument which I have charged home against transubstantiation is, that it involves the plainest and most self-evident contradictions; but with respect to the Holy Trinity, our ignorance is an effectual bar against the possibility of proving it an absurdity, and therefore no parallel can be fairly drawn between the Trinity and unity of God and transubstantiation." That is, as I apprehend, the contradictions contained in transubstantiation are self-evident and real; those in the Trinity only apparent, owing to our ignorance of the intermediate links by which the whole chain is connected.

Orth. That is certainly his meaning; but do you not observe one great objection to this bold assertion? If a contradiction be self-evident, and therefore real, it must certainly appear so at once to every man of commonsense. And yet there have been, and are at the present day, thousands and thousands of men, eminent for their good sense, their learning, and their piety, who do not see the smallest contradiction in transubstantiation, but who firmly believe it as a divine truth. Either, then, we must say that all these are devoid of reason who cannot perceive the plainest and most self-evident contradiction, or we must conclude that those pretended contradictions are neither so plain nor so self-evident as Benevolus affirms with such presumptuous assurance.

Phil. For my own part, I agree entirely with this last part of your conclusion; but Benevolus is so deeply prepossessed with his own idea that he makes no difficulty in declaring, that whoever believes transubstantiation should be sent to the physicians instead of being reasoned with.

Orth. At that I am not surprised; for there are such ardent spirits in the world. Truth, however, when opposed by such, will in reality suffer little, because their ardour generally carries them beyond the mark, which always ends in the triumph of truth, and in their own confusion. But, pray, does he add nothing farther to show the disparity he appeals to?

Phil. Yes, he says a great deal to explain and illustrate it. "An absurdity," he says, "is an opposition between two known ideas or things; and therefore, when we have no knowledge of the nature of the things of which we speak, it is impossible to prove any contradiction between them, even though it should exist. To explain myself, as I have a distinct idea of a human body, and as I also know what it is to be liable to death and corruption, and what it is to be exempt from them, I can say with certainty, that one and the same body cannot be mortal and immortal, corruptible and incorruptible, at the same time, because these are opposite modes of existence. But as I have no idea of what the divine nature is, nor any idea of a divine person, I cannot perceive any opposition or contradiction between the subsistence of three divine persons in one and the same divine nature.

"Were the nature of God the same with the nature of man, and a divine person like a human person, the doctrine of the Trinity would indeed be as absurd, and therefore as incredible, as transubstantiation; but as these natures and persons are infinitely different, therefore no argument can be formed from the one to the other, and consequently the doctrine of the Holy Trinity, however incomprehensible to human reason, yet cannot be shown to be contradictory to it. That the nature of God should be incomprehensible to human reason need not excite wonder. It not only may, but must be so; because a finite nature can never comprehend an infinite. But, though the doctrine of the Holy Trinity be thus above reason, and, as such, may justly be enjoined by revelation as matter of belief—because nothing is more reasonable than to believe upon the testimony of God what is above our reason—yet transubstantiation, which is not properly speaking above, but plainly contrary to reason, cannot be revealed by God, and therefore ought not to be believed." This is the whole of his reasoning, as delivered by himself, in his letters to Eusebius.

Orth. In this long citation from Benevolus, and in the former one, to which this is a sequel, there are several expressions which, I fear, will not stand the test of sound theology; but this I overlook as not strictly connected with our present subject, and shall willingly give him all the praise he deserves for several just principles and solid truths which he has here laid down, and in which I agree with him. They are as follow: 1. That an absurdity is an opposition between two known ideas or things. 2. That when we have no knowledge of the nature of the things of which we speak, it is impossible to prove any contradiction between them. 3. That we may be certain of the truth of a proposition, though we have no knowledge of the nature of the things or terms which compose it, as in the case of the Holy Trinity. 4. That a proposition is said to be above reason when it is true in itself, but when we do not see the connection between its terms, from our ignorance of their nature and properties. 5. That a proposition is against or contrary to reason, when we have a clear and distinct idea of the nature and properties of its terms, and see plainly the opposition or contradiction between them.

Upon these solid grounds Benevolus justly defends the mystery of the blessed Trinity from all imputation of absurdity or contradiction. Contradiction can never be proved against that mystery, for this plain reason, that we have no idea of the divine nature, or of what a divine person is; nor indeed, in our present state, can we possibly form a clear and comprehensive idea of them or their properties. Upon the same ground he pretends to prove that transubstantiation involves a manifest contradiction, which, according to the above principles, necessarily supposes a clear and distinct knowledge of the nature and properties of its object. His whole assertion, then, depends upon the correctness of this supposition, and I am willing to rest the issue of the cause upon it.

Phil. This is very fair indeed; but, pray, have we not a clear and distinct knowledge of a human body? and was not the humanity of Jesus Christ like unto us in all things, sin only excepted?

Orth. Our knowledge of the nature of the human body, and indeed of all other bodies, is exceedingly imperfect. Our knowledge of the nature of the humanity of Jesus Christ is much more so, and still more ignorant are we of the objects of the doctrine of transubstantiation. Call to mind the explanation of that mystery given above from the Council of Trent, that "the substance of the bread and wine are changed into the substance of the body and blood of Jesus Christ, the outward appearances of bread and wine remaining unchanged." Now, has Benevolus a clear and distinct knowledge of the substance of bread and wine? does he clearly see what is possible or impossible to be done with it by the almighty power of the Creator? Has he a clear and distinct knowledge of the substance of the body and blood of Jesus Christ? Does he know everything of which it is capable or incapable? Does he comprehend fully the nature and properties of the humanity of Jesus Christ? of that sacred humanity which is hypostatically united with the divine nature in one person? Does he clearly understand all that was possible or impossible for this human nature so united with the divinity to do, even in its mortal state? Does he see all that it is capable or incapable of doing, now that it is glorified at the right hand of the Father? And yet all this is requisite to be known, and to be known as clearly as we know what two are, and what ten are, before we could prudently pronounce that transubstantiation involves a plain and self-evident contradiction.

It is clear, then, that the objects of transubstantiation are far above the reach of our understanding, being the internal substance of bread and wine, which is wholly imperceptible to us, and the glorified body of Jesus Christ, intimately and incomprehensibly united in one person with the divinity. These, in our present mortal state, we can never in the least degree comprehend nor understand; consequently, according to Benevolus's own principles, it is impossible to prove a contradiction in what is affirmed regarding them. Transubstantiation, therefore, for anything we know, may be true—and if true (to use Benevolus's own words), though incomprehensible to human reason, yet cannot be shown to be contrary to it. It is above reason, and, as such, may justly be enjoined by revelation as a matter of belief, because nothing is more reasonable than to believe upon the testimony of God what is above our reason.

Thus you see that upon the very principles adopted by Benevolus, the mystery of the Trinity and of transubstantiation, and indeed all supernatural truths proposed to our belief by revelation, must stand or fall together. Their objects are concealed from our eyes. We have an exceedingly imperfect knowledge of their nature and properties. Without revelation we never could have formed the least idea of them; and therefore, any objections raised against them, from reason or the senses, must either affect all revealed truths or none, for they all rest upon the same foundation.

Phil. From this clear reasoning I perceive where Benevolus's mistake lies, and the only excuse I can plead for him is, what you have mentioned—namely, that he has never understood the Catholic doctrine of transubstantiation, otherwise he would not expose himself, by arguing so violently against it, as if he had a distinct idea of that doctrine, which he certainly has not, and without which, the whole train of his reasoning concludes unanswerably against himself.

But what I cannot account for is this, that though, in his whole reasoning, he manifestly assumes that he has a thorough knowledge of the properties of a glorified body, yet, in one of his letters to Eusebius, he fairly owns that he knows nothing whatever of the matter. His words are these: "You ask me whether the same body cannot, by the power of God, be in different places at the same time? to which I answer, that if you mean a glorified body, I cannot tell, because I know no more of the properties of a glorified body than I do of a spirit." Now, after this plain confession of his ignorance, wherein he certainly speaks the truth, how can he declaim so violently against transubstantiation, as involving manifest contradictions; when, according to his own principles, he cannot prove any contradiction in it, without having a thorough knowledge of all the properties of a glorified body? Is this acting like a theologian, a philosopher, or even like a man?

Orth. This, my dear sir, need not surprise you; it is only one instance, among many, of the self-contradictions into which every one must necessarily fall who is engaged in defending error. Truth is ever consistent, and its beauty never appears in a stronger light than when contrasted with the inconsistencies and contradictions of the self-sufficient adversaries who oppose it.

Phil. Your observation is just. But now, suppose the above pretended contradictions were urged against you, I should be glad to know what answer you would give to each.

Orth. In the first place, I say, I am not obliged to give an answer to any of them till you first prove their reality, which, from your ignorance of the things themselves, you never can, just as Benevolus would answer to the pretended contradictions in the mystery of the Trinity or incarnation. In the second place, I should observe, that the contradictions urged against transubstantiation, have even less weight against it than those regarding the Trinity have against that mystery. Those which deists urge against the Trinity appear in the mystery itself, in the very terms in which it is proposed; whereas it is not even asserted that the doctrine of transubstantiation, as above explained, contains in itself a shadow of contradiction or impossibility—and I might defy Benevolus himself to point out any such in it.

All the contradictions or impossibilities supposed to be involved in transubstantiation, are pretended to be found only in its consequences. If it be true, say they, then it will follow that the same body of Jesus Christ must be in many different places at one and the same time; that the same one body of Christ may have opposite qualities; that the whole body of a man must be contained in the small space of a host,—and so on. But these are brought forward only as consequences of the doctrine, whilst the doctrine itself stands free of all contradiction—whereas the contradictions alleged against the Holy Trinity attack the very mystery itself; as it is apparently impossible, say they who deny it, that three persons really distinct among themselves, and of each of whom we can affirm what we cannot say of the others, should yet be but one and the self-same individual divine being. If, therefore, our ignorance of the nature of the objects in the blessed Trinity invalidates these apparent contradictions, and exonerates us from any obligation of even attempting to explain them, though they affect the very existence of the mystery itself; how much more must our ignorance of the nature of the objects, in the mystery of transubstantiation, destroy the apparent weight of any contradiction brought against it, and excuse us from the obligation of explaining or endeavouring to reconcile them, considering that they attack not the mystery itself, but affect only the consequences supposed to flow from it?— But, in the third place, from what I have said above, you will find no difficulty in giving an answer even to each of those supposed contradictions.

Phil. I should be glad to see what could be said to each of them.

Orth. That I will now show you, and begin with examining whether it be possible for one and the same body to be in different places at the same time. This, though readily acknowledged by several learned Protestants, is held by Benevolus and others as an absolute impossibility. But I fear it would not be easy for them to show any clear contradiction in it, because of our limited and imperfect knowledge both of body and place.

The miracle of feeding five thousand men, besides women and children, with five barley loaves and two small fishes, affords so strong an argument to prove that the power of God can make even natural bodies exist in different places at the same time, that I might defy Benevolus to give any satisfactory answer to it: but upon that I shall lay no stress. The question is not of a natural body, but respecting the body of Jesus Christ; that body which even before His death, while in a mortal state, as well as now, was intimately united with the divinity, was even then capable of assuming the qualities of a glorified body, as was done at the transfiguration, and is now totally and unchangeably in a glorified state at the right hand of His Father. Now, if transubstantiation be true, it will evidently follow, not that a natural body may be in different places at once, but that this glorious body of Jesus Christ may be, nay, must be, in numberless places at one and the same time. But who shall dare affirm this to be impossible? Does Benevolus, or any mortal man, comprehend the qualities and perfections of that glorified body, which is incomprehensibly united to the divine nature in one Person? Shall finite man dare to pronounce what is possible or impossible for the glorified body of a God, made man? Shall the creature take upon him to explain what the body of his Creator is capable or incapable of doing! We must therefore acknowledge here, as Benevolus does, with regard to the Holy Trinity, that our ignorance of the nature and qualities of a glorified body, especially of that united in one person with the divinity, is an effectual bar against disproving its existence in different places at the same time, and therefore no parallel can be drawn between it and a natural body.

This being the case, the second pretended contradiction said to flow from transubstantiation, that the same one body of Jesus Christ would have opposite qualities at the same time, at once falls to the ground. For if the body of Jesus Christ can be in different places at one and the same time, what contradiction can there be in His exhibiting Himself to us with certain qualities in one place, and with others in another? Observe that these qualities are extrinsic to the essence of the body; they do not affect or alter its nature. It was the self-same Holy Ghost that appeared at the Jordan under the form of a dove, and to the apostles under the form of fiery tongues; and surely no man can doubt that He could have taken both these appearances, had He pleased, at the same time.

It is the self-same Jesus Christ Who sat at table in a human form with His apostles, and was at the same time, in the blessed sacrament, under the form of bread. The outward appearances under which He exhibited Himself to His apostles in two different places at once, made no difference in His nature. He was perfectly the same in both, and hence the force of this argument, in which

Benevolus so much exults, vanishes. It is clear that the fallacy couched under it arises from supposing that the different qualities of which he speaks, change the nature of our Saviour's body; and that they would be in it not only at the same time, but also in the same place,—both of which suppositions are false.

As to the other pretended impossibility, that the whole body of a man should be contained under the small space of a host, and in all its visible particles, it disappears at once upon the same principles. Our Saviour Himself assures us, that at the resurrection even our bodies shall become like the angels of God, putting on the properties and qualities of spirits. Now one quality of spirits is to be unconfined to any magnitude in themselves, and much less in the appearance which they assume to our eyes. The angels that appeared of old to the servants of God were the same, whether they assumed the form of a man of large or small stature; and shall it be called in question that Jesus Christ, God and man, can appear to us under any form or magnitude He pleases? Our ignorance of the qualities of His glorious body puts an effectual bar to the possibility of proving any absurdity in His doing so.

Phil. What you say admits, in my opinion, of no reply; and to me it seems evident that no contradiction can be proved in transubstantiation, for the same reason that it is impossible to prove any such in the mystery of the Trinity, or indeed in any of the sacred mysteries of the Christian religion. Our imperfect knowledge, or rather our total ignorance, of the objects of these mysteries, precludes us from judging of what is possible or impossible in them, because they are all above our reason. What we know of them we could never have imagined, had not God revealed it to us; and His revelation gives us the utmost certainty of what He announces concerning them. On that ground, therefore, we rationally believe, though we neither see nor understand them.

Orth. Your observation is just; and the natural consequence is, that as there cannot be a more convincing proof that God reveals any doctrine, than a miracle proper to God wrought in attestation of it, so the doctrine of transubstantiation is as capable of being proved a revealed truth by such a miracle wrought for that end, as is any other mystery whatever of the Christian religion. The incredulity of Benevolus, therefore, is without excuse, and his celebrated proposition is not only blasphemous in itself, but all he says in defence of it is totally destitute of reason, and can proceed only from an unpardonable ignorance of the real doctrine which he undertakes to condemn.

Phil. Sir, I am much obliged to you for all the trouble you have taken, and shall endeavour to improve by your instructions.

Orth. You are exceedingly welcome. Adieu.

THE END.

PRINTED BY WILLIAM BLACKWOOD AND SONS, EDINBURGH.

CATALOGUE

OF

WILLIAM BLACKWOOD & SONS'

PUBLICATIONS

45 GEORGE STREET, EDINBURGH
and
37 PATERNOSTER ROW
LONDON

CATALOGUE.

The History of Europe,

FROM THE COMMENCEMENT OF THE FRENCH REVOLUTION IN 1789 TO THE BATTLE OF WATERLOO. By Sir Archibald Alison, Bart., D.C.L. Library Edition, 14 Vols. demy 8vo, with Portraits and a copious Index, £10, 10s.

On Large Paper, 14 vols., £14, 14s.

Crown 8vo Edition, 20 vols., £6.

People's Edition, 12 vols., closely printed in double columns, £2, 8s.; and Index Volume, 3s.

"An extraordinary work, which has earned for itself a lasting place in the literature of the country, and within a few years found innumerable readers in every part of the globe. There is no book extant that treats so well of the period to the illustration of which Mr Alison's labours have been devoted. It exhibits great knowledge, patient research, indefatigable industry, and vast power."—*Times*.

"There is much in Mr Alison's History of the French Revolution against which we intend to record our decided protest; and there are some parts of it which we shall feel compelled to notice with strong disapprobation. We therefore hasten to preface our less favourable remarks by freely acknowledging that the present work is, upon the whole, a valuable addition to European literature, that it is evidently compiled with the utmost care, and that its narration, so far as we can judge, is not perverted by the slightest partiality."—*Edinburgh Review*.

"Alison's *History of Europe*, and the States connected with it, is one of the most important works which literature has produced. Years have elapsed since any historical work has created such an epoch as that of Alison: his sources of information and authorities are of the richest and most comprehensive description. Though his opinions are on the Conservative side, he allows every party to speak for itself, and unfolds with a master's hand how far institutions make nations great, and mighty, and prosperous."—*Preface to the German Translation*.

Continuation of the History of Europe,

FROM THE FALL OF NAPOLEON TO THE ACCESSION OF LOUIS NAPOLEON. By Sir Archibald Alison, Bart., D.C.L. Uniform with the Library Edition of the foregoing, 9 vols., £6, 7s. 6d.

PEOPLE'S EDITION, 8 vols. crown 8vo, 34s.

Atlas to Alison's History of Europe;

Containing 109 Maps and Plans of Countries, Battles, Sieges, and Sea-Fights. Constructed by A. Keith Johnston, F.R.S.E. With Vocabulary of Military and Marine Terms. Library Edition, £3, 3s.; People's Edition, £1, 11s. 6d.

Epitome of Alison's History of Europe.
Sixteenth Edition, 7s. 6d., bound.

Atlas to Epitome of History of Europe.
4to, 7s.

Life of John Duke of Marlborough.
With some Account of his Contemporaries, and of the War of the Succession. By **Sir Archibald Alison, Bart., D.C.L.** Third Edition, 2 vols. 8vo. Portraits and Maps, 30s.

Essays: Historical, Political, and Miscellaneous.
By **Sir Archibald Alison, Bart., D.C.L.** 3 vols. demy 8vo, 45s.

Lives of Lord Castlereagh and Sir Charles
Stewart, SECOND AND THIRD MARQUESSES OF LONDONDERRY. From the Original Papers of the Family, and other sources, embracing a full Account of the Campaign of 1813 and 1814 in Germany and France, and of the Congresses of Vienna, Laybach, and Verona. By **Sir Archibald Alison, Bart., D.C.L.** 3 vols. 8vo, £2, 2s.

Principles of the Criminal Law of Scotland.
By **Sir Archibald Alison, Bart., D.C.L.** 8vo, 18s.

Practice of the Criminal Law of Scotland.
By **Sir Archibald Alison, Bart., D.C.L.** 8vo, cloth boards, 18s.

The Principles of Population,
AND THEIR CONNECTION WITH HUMAN HAPPINESS. By **Sir Archibald Alison, Bart., D.C.L.** 2 vols. 8vo, 30s.

Outlines of Human Physiology.
By William Pulteney Alison, M.D., Professor of the Institutes of Medicine in the University of Edinburgh, &c. &c. 8vo, 12s.

Outlines of Pathology and Practice of Medicine.
By William Pulteney Alison, M.D. 8vo, 18s.

On the Management of the Poor in Scotland,
AND ITS EFFECTS ON THE HEALTH OF THE GREAT TOWNS. By **William Pulteney Alison, M.D.** Crown 8vo, 5s. 6d.

Angler's Diary,
For Recording the Quantity of Fish Killed, &c. 8vo, bound in green leather, 4s.

Poetical Works of Thomas Aird.

Fourth Edition, Fcap. 8vo, 6s.

"Mr Aird is a poet of a very high class, and in that class he occupies no mean or middling place. His imagination is lofty, his invention fertile, his sentiments heroic, and his language generally clear and forcible."—*Scotsman.*

The Old Bachelor in the Old Scottish Village.

By **Thomas Aird**. Fcap. 8vo, 4s.

"The book is full of a quiet sustained humour, genuine pathos, simple unaffected poetry, and displays not only fine imaginative power, but a hearty sympathy with nature in all her aspects, and with the simple tastes and pleasures of rustic life. A more delightful book we cannot imagine."—*Manchester Advertiser.*

Ancient Classics for English Readers.

Edited by the **Rev. W. Lucas Collins, M.A.**

The Volumes already published are:—

HOMER'S ILIAD. By Rev. W. L. Collins, M.A.
HOMER'S ODYSSEY. By the Same.
HERODOTUS. By G. C. Swayne, M.A.
CÆSAR. By Anthony Trollope.
VIRGIL. By Rev. W. L. Collins, M.A.
HORACE. By Theodore Martin.
ÆSCHYLUS. By R. S. Copleston, B.A.
XENOPHON. By Sir Alex. Grant, Bart.
CICERO. By Rev. W. L. Collins, M.A.
SOPHOCLES. By C. W. Collins, M.A.
PLINY. By Rev. A. Church, M.A., and Rev. W. J. Brodribb, M.A.
EURIPIDES. By W. B. Donne, M.A.
JUVENAL. By E. Walford, M.A.
ARISTOPHANES. By the Editor.
HESIOD. By Rev. James Davies, M.A.

A Volume of this Series is published Quarterly, 2s. 6d.

Interludes.

By **Alfred Austin**, Author of 'The Season,' 'The Golden Age,' &c. Fcap. 8vo, 5s.

"Enough has been written and quoted to show that Mr Austin is not a mere rhymster, spinning lines without beauty and devoid even of sense. He is hot, impulsive, generous, and thoroughly poetical. He has something to say, and he says it in words that dwell in the mind. He has songs to sing, and he sings them with a sweetness and melody that are rarely found."—*Scotsman.*

Lays of the Scottish Cavaliers, and other Poems.

By **W. Edmondstoune Aytoun, D.C.L.**, Professor of Rhetoric and Belles-Lettres in the University of Edinburgh. Twenty-second Edition. Fcap. 8vo, 7s. 6d.

"Mr Aytoun's 'Lays' are truly beautiful, and are perfect poems of their class, pregnant with fire, with patriotic ardour, with loyal zeal, with exquisite pathos, with noble passion. Who can hear the opening lines descriptive of Edinburgh after the great battle of Flodden, and not feel that the minstrel's soul has caught the genuine inspiration?"—*Morning Post.*

"Professor Aytoun's 'Lays of the Scottish Cavaliers'—a volume of verse which shows that Scotland has yet a poet. Full of the true fire, it now stirs and swells like a trumpet-note—now sinks in cadences sad and wild as the wail of a Highland dirge."—*Quarterly Review.*

Aytoun's Lays of the Scottish Cavaliers.

An Illustrated Edition. From designs by **Sir J. Noel Paton** and **W. H. Paton, R.S.A.** Engraved by John Thomson, W. J. Linton, W. Thomas, Whymper, Cooper, Green, Dalziels, Evans, &c. In small Quarto, printed on Toned Paper, bound in gilt cloth, 21s.

"The artists have excelled themselves in the engravings which they have furnished. Seizing the spirit of Mr Aytoun's 'Ballads' as perhaps none but Scotchmen could have seized it, they have thrown their whole strength into the work with a heartiness which others would do well to imitate. Whoever there may be that does not know these 'Lays' we recommend at once to make their acquaintance in this edition, wherein author and artist illustrate each other as kindred spirits should."—*Standard.*

Bothwell: A Poem.

By **W. Edmondstoune Aytoun, D.C.L.** Third Edition. Fcap. 8vo, 7s. 6d.

"A noble poem, healthy in tone and purely English in language, and closely linked to the historical traditions of his native country."—*John Bull.*

"Professor Aytoun has produced a fine poem and an able argument, and 'Bothwell' will assuredly take its stand among the classics of Scottish Literature."—*The Press.*

The Ballads of Scotland.

Edited by **Professor Aytoun.** Fourth Edition. 2 vols., fcap. 8vo, 12s.

"No country can boast of a richer collection of Ballads than Scotland, and no Editor for these Ballads could be found more accomplished than Professor Aytoun. He has sent forth two beautiful volumes which range with Percy's 'Reliques'—which, for completeness and accuracy, leave little to be desired—which must henceforth be considered as the standard edition of the Scottish Ballads, and which we commend as a model to any among ourselves who may think of doing like service to the English Ballads."—*The Times.*

Norman Sinclair.

By **W. Edmondstoune Aytoun, D.C.L.** 3 vols. post 8vo, 31s. 6d.

Firmilian, or the Student of Badajos.

A SPASMODIC TRAGEDY. By **T. Percy Jones** (Professor Aytoun). In small 8vo, 5s.

"Humour of a kind most rare at all times, and especially in the present day, runs through every page; and passages of true poetry and delicious versification prevent the continual play of sarcasm from becoming tedious."—*Literary Gazette.*

Memoir of William E. Aytoun, D.C.L.

Author of 'Lays of the Scottish Cavaliers,' &c. By **Theodore Martin.** With Portrait. Post 8vo, 12s.

"This biography is quite a model in its way, and a delightful relief after much that has been done of late years in a similar line. Good taste, right feeling, and a generous but seldom excessive appreciation of the subject, mark the work."—*Manchester Guardian.*

Blackwood's Magazine,

FROM COMMENCEMENT IN 1817 TO DECEMBER 1872. Nos. 1 to 686, forming 112 Volumes. £30.

Index to Blackwood's Magazine.

The First 50 Volumes. Octavo, 15s.

Tales from "Blackwood."

Twelve Volumes. Sewed, 12s. Bound in cloth, 18s. The Volumes are sold separately, 1s. and 1s. 6d., and may be had of most Booksellers, in Six Volumes, handsomely half-bound in red morocco, 28s. 12 Volumes in 6, half Roxburghe, 21s. 12 Volumes, half-calf, richly gilt, 30s.

CONTENTS.

VOL. I. The Glenmutchkin Railway.—Vanderdecken's Message Home.—The Floating Beacon.—Colonna the Painter.—Napoleon.—A Legend of Gibraltar.—The Iron Shroud.

VOL. II. Lazaro's Legacy.—A Story without a Tail.—Faustus and Queen Elizabeth.—How I became a Yeoman.—Devereux Hall.—The Metempsychosis.—College Theatricals.

VOL. III. A Reading Party in the Long Vacation.—Father Tom and the Pope. —La Petite Madelaine.—Bob Burke's Duel with Ensign Brady.—The Headsman: A Tale of Doom.—The Wearyful Woman.

VOL. IV. How I Stood for the Dreepdaily Burghs.—First and Last.—The Duke's Dilemma: A Chronicle of Niesenstein.—The Old Gentleman's Teetotum.—"Woe to us when we lose the Watery Wall."—My College Friends: Charles Russell, the Gentleman Commoner.—The Magic Lay of the One-Horse-Chay.

VOL. V. Adventures in Texas.—How we got Possession of the Tuileries.—Captain Paton's Lament.—The Village Doctor.—A Singular Letter from Southern Africa.

VOL. VI. My Friend the Dutchman.—My College Friends—No. II.: Horace Leicester.—The Emerald Studs.—My College Friends—No. III.: Mr W. Wellington Hurst.—Christine: A Dutch Story.—The Man in the Bell.

VOL. VII. My English Acquaintance.—The Murderer's Last Night.—Narration of Certain Uncommon Things that did formerly happen to Me, Herbert Willis, B.D.—The Wags.—The Wet Wooing: A Narrative of '98.—Ben-na-Groich.

VOL. VIII. The Surveyor's Tale. By Professor Ayton.—The Forrest-Race Romance.—Di Vasari: A Tale of Florence.—Sigismund Fatello.—The Boxes.

VOL. IX. Rosaura: A Tale of Madrid.—Adventure in the North-West Territory.—Harry Bolton's Curacy.—The Florida Pirate.—The Pandour and His Princess.—The Beauty Draught.

VOL. X. Antonio di Carara.—The Fatal Repast.—The Vision of Cagliostro.— The First and Last Kiss.—The Smuggler's Leap.—The Haunted and the Haunters.—The Duellists.

VOL. XI. The Natolian Story-Teller.—The First and Last Crime.—John Rintoul.—Major Moss.—The Premier and his Wife.

VOL. XII. Tickler among the Thieves!—The Bridegroom of Barna.—The Involuntary Experimentalist.—Lebrun's Lawsuit.—The Snowing-up of Strath-Lugas.—A Few Words on Social Philosophy.

Blackwood's Standard Novels.

Uniform in size and legibly printed. Each Novel complete in one Volume.

Florin Series, Illustrated Boards.

Tom Cringle's Log. By Michael Scott.
Cruise of the Midge. By the Author of 'Tom Cringle's Log.'
Cyril Thornton. By Captain Hamilton.
Annals of the Parish. By John Galt.
The Provost, and other Tales. By John Galt.
Sir Andrew Wylie. By John Galt.
The Entail. By John Galt.
Reginald Dalton. By J. G. Lockhart.
Pen Owen. By Dean Hook.
Adam Blair. By J. G. Lockhart.
Lady Lee's Widowhood. By Col. Hamley.
Salem Chapel. By Mrs Oliphant.
The Perpetual Curate. By Mrs Oliphant.
Miss Marjoribanks. By Mrs Oliphant.

Or in Cloth Boards, 2s. 6d.

Shilling Series, Illustrated Cover.

The Rector and the Doctor's Family. By Mrs Oliphant.
The Life of Mansie Waugh. By D. M. Moir.
Peninsular Scenes and Sketches. By F. Hardman.
Sir Frizzle Pumpkin, Nights at Mess, &c.
The Subaltern.
Life in the Far West. By G. F. Ruxton.
Valerius: A Roman Story. By J. G. Lockhart.

Or in Cloth Boards, 1s. 6d.

OTHER WORKS IN PREPARATION.

Blackwood's Maps of the Counties of Scotland.

In Cloth Case for the Pocket, 1s. each.
The same strongly bound in leather, in one vol. post 8vo, 10s. 6d.

The Maid of Sker.

By **R. D. Blackmore**, Author of 'Lorna Doone,' &c. Originally published in 'Blackwood's Magazine.' New Edition. Crown 8vo, 6s.

"His descriptions are wonderfully vivid and natural, although he loves to paint nature in her most extravagant freaks. His pages are brightened everywhere with quiet humour; the quaint dry turns of thought remind you occasionally of Fielding."—*Times.*

"A work which reads in some parts like the famous autobiographies of Defoe, and in others contains descriptions of natural beauty worthy of Kingsley, and nautical adventures not inferior to the best things in Marryat."—*Athenæum.*

"But let fact or fiction begin or end where they will, the book is exceeding able, and strikingly original."—*Saturday Review.*

"Mr Blackmore's book is in our opinion a genuine success, one of the few good novels that have been written for many years, and one which will live."—*Spectator.*

Lilias Lee, and other Poems.
By **James Ballantine**, Author of 'The Gaberlunzie's Wallet,' &c. Fcap. 8vo, 5s.

Battle of Dorking. Reminiscences of a Volunteer:
From 'Blackwood's Magazine.' Second Hundredth Thousand, 6d.

Belief—What is it?
Or, The Nature of Faith as Determined by the Facts of Human Nature and Sacred History. 8vo, 7s.

Tables for Travellers.
Adapted to the Pocket or Sextant-Case. Compiled by **Admiral Bethune**, **C.B.**, **F.R.A.S.**, and **F.R.G.S.** Cloth, 3s. 6d.

The Boscobel Tracts.
RELATING TO THE ESCAPE OF CHARLES THE SECOND AFTER THE BATTLE OF WORCESTER, AND HIS SUBSEQUENT ADVENTURES. Edited by **J. Hughes**, Esq., A.M. A NEW EDITION, with additional Notes and Illustrations, including Communications from the **Rev. R. H. Barham**, Author of the 'Ingoldsby Legends.' In Octavo, with Engravings, 16s.

" 'The Boscobel Tracts' is a very curious book, and about as good an example of single subject historical collections as may be found. Originally undertaken, or at least completed, at the suggestion of the late Bishop Copplestone, in 1827, it was carried out with a degree of judgment and taste not always found in works of a similar character."—*Spectator.*

Memoirs of the Life and Times of **Henry Lord**
Brougham. Written by **Himself**. 3 vols. octavo, £2, 8s. The Volumes are sold separately, 16s. each.

The Forester:
A Practical Treatise on the Planting, Rearing, and General Management of Forest-trees. By **James Brown**, Wood-Surveyor and Nurseryman, Stirling. Fourth Edition. Royal 8vo, with Engravings, £1, 11s. 6d.

In preparing the present Edition, the Author has carefully re-written the book, and added nearly one hundred new sections upon important subjects, which were necessary to bring it up to the advanced state of the times, and to make it in all respects worthy of continuing in public favour, as a complete directory in all matters connected with the improved state of Aboriculture at the present day.

" What we have often stated in these columns we now repeat, that the book before us is the most useful guide to good arboriculture in the English language."—*Review of Third Edition in Gardeners' Chronicle by Dr Lindley.*

" Beyond all doubt this is the best work on the subject of forestry extant."—*Journal of Horticulture.*

The Book of Ballads.

Edited by **Bon Gaultier**. Eleventh Edition, with numerous Illustrations by Doyle, Leech, and Crowquill. Gilt edges, post octavo, 8s. 6d.

Family Records of the Bruces and the Cumyns.

With an Historical Introduction and Appendix from authentic Public and Private Documents. By **M. E. Cumming Bruce**. Quarto, cloth, £2, 10s. Large-Paper Edition, medium quarto, cloth, £3, 10s.

Jessie Cameron: A Highland Story.

By the **Lady Rachel Butler**. Second Edition. Small octavo, with a Frontispiece, 2s. 6d.

Handy Book of Meteorology.

By **Alexander Buchan, M.A., F.R.S.E.**, Secretary of the Scottish Meteorological Society, &c. A New Edition, being the Third. [*In the press.*]

In this Edition the Charts of the Distribution of Atmospheric Pressure and of Terrestrial Temperature will be revised; the Relations of Temperature to Atmospheric Pressure and Winds will, with the aid of Illustrative Charts, be more fully discussed, and the principle will be applied in explanation of unusually Hot and Cold Seasons, as well as Seasons of excessive Drought or excessive Rainfall; Charts will be given showing the Distribution of Rain over the Continents of the Globe, and its connection with the distribution of atmospheric pressure and temperature, and with prevailing winds, will be pointed out; the Prevailing Winds over the Globe will be represented on Charts; and otherwise the book will be revised throughout.

Introductory Text-Book of Meteorology.

By **Alexander Buchan, M.A., F.R.S.E.**, Author of 'Handy Book of Meteorology,' &c. Crown 8vo, with 8 Coloured Charts and other Engravings, pp. 218. 4s. 6d.

"A handy compendium of Meteorology by one of the most competent authorities on this branch of science."—*Petermann's Geographische Mittheilungen.*

"We can recommend it as a handy, clear, and scientific introduction to the theory of Meteorology, written by a man who has evidently mastered his subject."—*Lancet.*

"An exceedingly useful volume."—*Athenæum.*

Memoir of the Political Life of the Right Honourable Edmund Burke,

with Extracts from his Writings. By the **Rev. George Croly, D.D.** 2 vols. post 8vo, 18s.

Handbook of the Mechanical Arts

Concerned in the Construction and Arrangement of Dwelling-Houses and other Buildings; with Practical Hints on Road-making and the Enclosing of Land. By **Robert Scott Burn**, Engineer. Second edition, crown 8vo, 6s. 6d.

Practical Ventilation,

As applied to Public, Domestic, and Agricultural Structures; with Remarks on Heating, Construction of Fire-Places, Cure of Smoky Chimneys, and an Appendix on the Ventilation of Ships, Steamboats, and Railway Carriages. By **Robert Scott Burn**, Engineer. Crown 8vo, 6s.

The History of Scotland:

From Agricola's Invasion to the Extinction of the last Jacobite Insurrection. By **John Hill Burton**, Historiographer-Royal for Scotland. New and Enlarged Edition, in 8 vols. crown 8vo. *To be published monthly.*

The Book-Hunter.

By **John Hill Burton**. In crown 8vo. Second Edition, 7s. 6d.

"A book pleasant to look at and pleasant to read—pleasant from its rich store of anecdote, its geniality, and its humour, even to persons who care little for the subjects of which it treats, but beyond measure delightful to those who are in any degree members of the above-mentioned fraternity."—*Saturday Review.*

The Scot Abroad,

AND THE ANCIENT LEAGUE WITH FRANCE. By **John Hill Burton**. 2 vols. crown 8vo, in Roxburghe binding, 15s.

"No amount of selections, detached at random, can give an adequate idea of the varied and copious results of reading which are stored up in the compact and pithy pages of 'The Scot Abroad.'"—*Saturday Review.*

"A charming book."—*Spectator.*

The Cairngorm Mountains.

By **John Hill Burton**. In Crown 8vo, 3s. 6d.

"One of the most complete as well as most lively and intelligent bits of reading that the lover of works of travel has seen for many a day."—*Saturday Review.*

Sermons.

By **John Caird, D.D.**, Professor of Divinity in the University of Glasgow. Thirteenth Thousand. Fcap. 8vo, 5s.

"They are noble sermons; and we are not sure but that, with the cultivated reader, they will gain rather than lose by being read, not heard. There is a thoughtfulness and depth about them which can hardly be appreciated, unless when they are studied at leisure; and there are so many sentences so felicitously expressed that we should grudge being hurried away from them by a rapid speaker, without being allowed to enjoy them a second time."—*Fraser's Magazine.*

Religion in Common Life:

A Sermon preached in Crathie Church, October 14, 1855, before Her Majesty the Queen and Prince Albert. By **John Caird, D.D.** Published by Her Majesty's Command. Bound in cloth, 8d. Cheap Edition, 3d.

Autobiography of the Rev. Dr Alexander Carlyle,

Minister of Inveresk. Containing Memorials of the Men and Events of his Time. Edited by **John Hill Burton**. In 8vo. Third Edition, with Portrait, 14s.

"This book contains by far the most vivid picture of Scottish life and manners that has been given to the public since the days of Sir Walter Scott. In bestowing upon it this high praise, we make no exception, not even in favour of Lord Cockburn's *Memorials*—the book which resembles it most, and which ranks next to it in interest."—*Edinburgh Review.*

"A more delightful and graphic picture of the everyday life of our ancestors it has never been our good fortune to meet with."—*National Review.*

A Treasury of the English and German Languages.

Compiled from the best Authors and Lexicographers in both Languages. Adapted to the Use of Schools, Students, Travellers, and Men of Business; and forming a Companion to all German-English Dictionaries. By **Joseph Cauvin, LL.D. & Ph.D.**, of the University of Göttingen, &c. Crown 8vo, 7s. 6d., bound in cloth.

"An excellent English-German Dictionary, which supplies a real want."—*Saturday Review.*

"The difficulty of translating English into German may be greatly alleviated by the use of this copious and excellent English-German Dictionary, which specifies the different senses of each English word, and gives suitable German equivalents. It also supplies an abundance of idiomatic phraseology, with many passages from Shakespeare and other authors aptly rendered in German. Compared with other dictionaries, it has decidedly the advantage."—*Athenæum.*

Captain Clutterbuck's Champagne.

A WEST INDIAN REMINISCENCE. Post 8vo, 12s.

"We can conscientiously commend 'Captain Clutterbuck's Champagne' to all who like a really original story with no nonsense in it."—*Press.*

The Punjab and Delhi in 1857:

BEING A NARRATIVE OF THE MEASURES BY WHICH THE PUNJAB WAS SAVED AND DELHI RECOVERED DURING THE INDIAN MUTINY. By the **Rev. J. Cave-Brown**, Chaplain of the Punjab Movable Column. With Plans of the Chief Stations and of the different Engagements, and Portraits of Sir J. Lawrence, Bart., Sir H. Edwardes, Sir R. Montgomery, and Brig.-Gen. J. Nicholson. 2 vols. post 8vo, 21s.

"This is a work which will well repay the trouble of perusal. Written by one who was himself present at many of the scenes he narrates, and who has had free access to the papers of Sir J. Lawrence, Sir R. Montgomery, and Sir H. Edwardes, it comes with all the weight of official authority, and all the vividness of personal narrative."—*Press.*

Coquet-Dale Fishing Songs.

Now first collected by a North-Country Angler, with the Music of the **Airs**. 8vo, 5s.

Sporting Days.

By **John Colquhoun**, Author of 'The Moor and the Loch,' &c. Crown 8vo, 5s.

Rocks and Rivers;

Or, Highland Wanderings over Crag and Correi, "Flood and Fell." By **John Colquhoun**, Author of 'Sporting Days.' 8vo, 6s. 6d.

Salmon-Casts and Stray Shots.

Being Fly-leaves from the Note-Book of **John Colquhoun**, Esq., Author of 'The Moor and the Loch,' &c. Second Edition, fcap. 8vo, 5s.

The Coming Race.

Sixth Edition, crown 8vo, 6s.

"Language, literature, and the arts, all touched on with admirable verisimilitude, are impressed into the service of his thesis; and often, in reading of the delights of this underground Utopia, have we sighed for the refreshing tranquillity of that lamp-lit land."—*Athenæum.*

"Its kindly satire, its gentle moralisings, its healthy humour, and its extensive knowledge well applied, combine to separate it from the mass of ephemeral publications, and give evidence of literary skill very rarely to be met with in books written for the circulating libraries."—*Examiner.*

"The book is well written, and ingeniously worked out."—*Saturday Review.*

Venus and Psyche,

WITH OTHER POEMS. By **Richard Crawley**. Fcap. 8vo, 5s.

"Mr Crawley writes verses through which there runs an abundant vein of genuine poetry. . . . Much, very much, of Mr Crawley's poetry is perfectly original—the creation of his own fancy—which is eminently near akin to the vision and the faculty divine, and is equally powerful in painting scenes of terror and tenderness. His minor poems are most of them beautiful, and some of them exquisite pieces of piercing satire."—*Evening Standard.*

The Genesis of the Church.

By the **Right Rev. Henry Cotterill, D.D.**, Bishop of Edinburgh. Demy 8vo, 16s.

"The book is strikingly original, and this originality is one of its great charms—the views of an able and cultivated man whom long study has made fully master of his subject."—*Scottish Guardian.*

"In Dr Cotterill's volume a book of great ability has been presented to the world."—*Edinburgh Courant.*

"His book breathes the spirit and is stamped with the character of the present age. It requires, and will amply repay, the most careful and attentive reading; and it is likely to carry conviction to many a mind which has been merely repelled by the ordinary quoting of texts or appeals to Church History to prove the existence of the three Orders, and the necessity of the apostolical succession."—*Literary Churchman.*

Chronicles of Carlingford.

Salem Chapel. 2s. in boards, or 2s. 6d. in cloth.
The Rector, and the Doctor's Family. 1s. in boards, or 1s. 6d. in cloth.
The Perpetual Curate. 2s. in boards, or 2s. 6d. in cloth.
Miss Marjoribanks. 2s. in boards, or 2s. 6d. in cloth.

Cornelius O'Dowd upon Men and Women,

AND OTHER THINGS IN GENERAL. 3 vols. crown 8vo, 10s. 6d. each.

"The flashes of the author's wit must not blind us to the ripeness of his wisdom, nor the general playfulness of his O'Dowderies allow us to forget the ample evidence that underneath them lurks one of the most earnest and observant spirits of the present time."—*Daily Review.*

The Fatherhood of God:

Considered in its General and Special Aspects, and particularly in relation to the Atonement; with a Review of Recent Speculations on the Subject. By **Thomas J. Crawford, D.D.** Third Edition, revised and enlarged, with a Reply to the Strictures of Dr Candlish. 9s.

"The plan of this work is comprehensive and yet definite. It embodies much original thought, and the author's habits of searching inquiry and careful arrangement stand him in good stead. Whatever difference of opinion there may be on sundry topics, it would be idle to question the great ability shown by the learned Professor. As the subjects treated of have been and are so much discussed, it will be satisfactory to many to receive a book which expounds so fully, and maintains so forcibly, and on a Scriptural basis, the views of one so well qualified to speak."—*Journal of Sacred Literature.*

The Doctrine of Holy Scripture respecting the

Atonement. By **Thomas J. Crawford, D.D.**, Professor of Divinity in the University of Edinburgh. 8vo, 12s.

"This addition to the latest contributions to the elucidation of the doctrine of the atonement must inevitably take a high rank among them. It collates and analyses the teachings, not only of the apostles, but of all Scriptural authors on the subject. The work is done in a critical, thorough, exhaustive manner, and gives us an exhaustive thesaurus of Scriptural doctrine on the subject."—*Princeton Review.*

Sketches of the South and West;

Or, Ten Months' Residence in the United States. By **Henry Deedes.** Fcap. 8vo, 5s.

Descartes

On the Method of Rightly Conducting the Reason, and Seeking Truth in the Sciences, and his Meditations, and Selections from his Principles of Philosophy. In One vol. post 8vo, 4s. 6d.

Japan;

Being a Sketch of the History, Government, and Officers of the Empire. By **Walter Dickson**. 8vo, 15s.

"The entire work is not only pleasant and instructive reading, but one that ought to be read and re-read by all who wish to attain anything like a coherent idea of the real condition of Japan. Its value can hardly be overestimated."—*London and China Express.*

"Mr Dixon's work gives a general account of the History of Christianity in Japan more accurately than any preceding writer in the English language. . . . . His work is the most valuable one that has yet appeared."—*Quarterly Review.*

A Family Tour round the Coasts of Spain and

Portugal DURING THE WINTER OF 1860-61. By **Lady Dunbar** of Northfield. Post 8vo, 5s.

The Divine Footsteps in Human History.

8vo, 10s. 6d.

Seats and Saddles, Bits and Bitting,

AND THE PREVENTION AND CURE OF RESTIVENESS IN HORSES. By **Francis Dwyer**. A New and Enlarged Edition. Crown 8vo, with Engravings, 7s. 6d.

"Of Major Dwyer's book we can speak with much approbation. To those who are fond of the science of horsemanship, and who will give themselves time for some study of it, we know no work that comprehends so much good matter in so small a space."—*Baily's Monthly Magazine.*

Essays.

By the **Rev. John Eagles, A.M.**, Oxon. Originally published in 'Blackwood's Magazine.' Post 8vo, 10s. 6d.

CONTENTS:—Church Music, and other Parochials.—Medical attendance, and other Parochials.—A few Hours at Hampton Court.—Grandfathers and Grandchildren.—Sitting for a Portrait.—Are there not Great Boasters among us?—Temperance and Teetotal Societies.—Thackeray's Lectures: Swift.—The Crystal Palace.—Civilisation: the Census.—The Beggar's Legacy.

The Sketcher.

By the **Rev. John Eagles, A.M.** Originally published in 'Blackwood's Magazine.' 8vo, 10s. 6d.

"This volume, called by the appropriate name of 'The Sketcher,' is one that ought to be found in the studio of every English landscape-painter. . . . . More instructive and suggestive readings for young artists, especially landscape-painters, can scarcely be found."—*The Globe.*

Sonnets.

By the **Rev. John Eagles, A.M.** Crown 8vo, 5s.

Works of George Eliot. Library Edition.

Adam Bede. 2 vols., fcap. 8vo, 12s.
The Mill on the Floss. 2 vols., fcap. 8vo, 12s.
Scenes of Clerical Life. 2 vols., fcap. 8vo, 12s.
Silas Marner. Fcap. 8vo, 6s.
Felix Holt. 2 vols., fcap. 8vo, 12s.

Works of George Eliot. Cheap Edition.

Adam Bede. 3s. 6d.
The Mill on the Floss. 3s. 6d.
Scenes of Clerical Life. 3s.
Silas Marner. 2s. 6d.
Felix Holt. 3s. 6d.

Middlemarch: A Study of English Provincial Life.

By **George Eliot.** In Eight Books, 5s. each.

1. Miss Brooke.
2. Old and Young.
3. Waiting for Death.
4. Three Love Problems.
5. The Dead Hand.
6. The Widow and the Wife.
7. Two Temptations.
8. Sunset and Sunrise.

The SAME complete in 4 vols. crown 8vo, bound in cloth, 42s.

The Spanish Gypsy.

By **George Eliot.** Fourth Edition, crown 8vo, 7s. 6d.

"It is emphatically a great poem, great in conception, great in execution."—*Blackwood's Magazine.*

"She is a great writer, and in the 'Spanish Gypsy' she has achieved a great work."—*Times.*

"It is impossible, indeed, to speak too highly of the intellectual conception at the basis of the poem, and the finish and power with which it is worked out and adorned."—*Spectator.*

Wise, Witty, and Tender Sayings,

In Prose and Verse. Selected from the Works of George Eliot. By **Alexander Main.** Handsomely printed on Toned Paper, bound in gilt cloth, 5s.

"But undoubtedly George Eliot is the only woman of our time whose writings would be remembered for their humour alone, or whose sayings, just now collected into a volume by themselves, are at all likely, like Shakespeare's sayings, to pass into the substance of the language."—*Spectator.*

"This little volume, which is everything that could be desired in the way of get-up, brings George Eliot's weightier thoughts and reflections, which lie scattered throughout her books, conveniently near; and busy readers may easily repair the results of inevitable haste by frequently devoting to it a spare half-hour. It is a book to have beside one, to be often taken up and laid aside again; for every page supplies food for meditation, and something, too, that is well calculated to be helpful in the conduct of life."—*Nonconformist.*

A Memoir of John Elder,

Engineer and Shipbuilder. By **W. J. Macquorn Rankine**, with Portrait. Crown 8vo. 2s. 6d.

The Education (Scotland) Act, 1872.

With Introduction, Explanatory Notes, and Index. By **Alexander Craig Sellar**, Advocate, Secretary to the Lord Advocate of Scotland. Price 6s. Another Edition—the Text only—price 6d.

Essays on Social Subjects.

Originally published in the 'Saturday Review.' A New Edition. First and Second Series. 2 vols., crown 8vo, 6s. each.

"Two remarkable volumes of occasional papers, far above the average of such miscellanies. They are the production of a keen and kindly observer of men and manners, and they display a subtle analysis of character, as well as a breadth of observation, which are remarkable. With much of occasional force, these Essays have sufficient solidity to make a book; and while they recall the wit of Montaigne and the playfulness of Addison, they are animated by a better moral tone, and cover a larger range of experience."—*Christian Remembrancer.*

Euchologion; or, Book of Prayers:

Being Forms of Worship issued by the Church Service Society. A New and Enlarged Edition, 6s. 6d.

"We know of no book which could be recommended as likely to be of greater use to the clergyman, especially to the young and inexperienced, than this second edition of 'Euchologion.'"—*Scotsman.*

The Crown and its Advisers;

Or, Queen, Ministers, Lords, and Commons. By **Alexander Charles Ewald, F.S.A.** Crown 8vo, 5s.

"We may congratulate Mr Ewald on the possession of a popular style and a clear method. . . . His observations on everything connected with the usages of Parliament are sound, and calculated to be very useful to the class of persons he is addressing. . . . A commendable attempt to explain in simple and popular language the machinery of the English Government."—*Pall Mall Gazette.*

"May be regarded in some respects as a Constitutional Manual."—*Standard.*

Institutes of Metaphysic:

The Theory of Knowing and Being. By **James F. Ferrier, A.B. Oxon.**, Professor of Moral Philosophy and Political Economy, St Andrews. Second Edition. Crown 8vo, 10s. 6d.

Lectures on the Early Greek Philosophy,

AND OTHER PHILOSOPHIC REMAINS OF PROFESSOR FERRIER OF ST ANDREWS. Edited by **Sir Alexander Grant** and **Professor Lushington**. 2 vols. post 8vo, 24s.

"These lectures, in so far as they treat of Greek philosophy down to Plato, have been carefully elaborated, and are of much value—of higher value, indeed, than any writings on the same subject in the English language; and in point of clearness, depth, and resolute search after truth, and tenacious hold of it when found, we doubt if they are surpassed in any language. . . . For our part, we do not know any philosophical writings so fascinating to a young student of philosophy as these early pages."—*Scotsman.*

Field-Map, Lothians Hunt;

with List of the Meets and Distances from General Post-Office, Edinburgh, and from the nearest Railway Stations. Bound in leather, 5s.

History of Greece under Foreign Domination.

By **George Finlay, LL.D.**, Athens. 7 vols. 8vo—viz. :

Greece under the Romans. B.C. 146 to A.D. 717. A Historical View of the Condition of the Greek Nation from its Conquest by the Romans until the Extinction of the Roman Power in the East. Second Edition, 16s.

History of the Byzantine Empire. A.D. 716 to 1204; and of the Greek Empire of Nicæa and Constantinople, A.D. 1204 to 1453. 2 vols. £1, 7s. 6d.

Mediæval Greece and Trebizond. The History of Greece, from its Conquest by the Crusaders to its Conquest by the Turks, A.D. 1204 to 1566; and the History of the Empire of Trebizond, A.D. 1204 to 1461. 12s.

Greece under Othoman and Venetian Domination. A.D. 1453 to 1821. 10s. 6d.

History of the Greek Revolution. 2 vols. 8vo, £1, 4s.

"His book is worthy to take its place among the remarkable works on Greek history which form one of the chief glories of English scholarship. The history of Greece is but half told without it."—*London Guardian.*

"His work is therefore learned and profound. It throws a flood of light upon an important though obscure portion of Grecian history. . . . In the essential requisites of fidelity, accuracy, and learning, Mr Finlay bears a favourable comparison with any historical writer of our day."—*North American Review.*

Flowers from Fatherland in English Soil.

Translations from the German by **John Pitcairn Trotter**; **A. Mercer Adams, M.D.**; and **George Coltman, M.A.** Crown 8vo, 6s.

"A volume of translations that may be heartily recommended for their rare excellence."—*London Quarterly Review.*

"This is a very elegant volume of poems. The translations are good in most cases, spirited often, and readable always. And it is as gratifying as it is astonishing to mark the ease and elegance with which some of Heine's perfect gems are placed in their English setting."—*Illustrated London News.*

The Campaign of Garibaldi in the Two Sicilies:

A Personal Narrative. By **Charles Stuart Forbes**, Commander, R.N. Post 8vo, with Portraits, 12s.

"A volume which contains the best sketch hitherto published of the campaign which put an end to Bourbon rule in the Two Sicilies. It is accompanied with plans of the chief battles; and its honest unexaggerated record contrasts very favourably with the strained and showy account of the Garibaldians just published by M. Dumas."—*Examiner.*

Geological and Palæontological Map of the British

Islands, including Tables of the Fossils of the different Epochs, &c. &c., from the Sketches and Notes of Professor **Edward Forbes**. With Illustrative and Explanatory Letterpress. 21s.

Earl's Dene. A Novel.
By R. E. Francillon. 3 vols. post 8vo, 31s. 6d.

A Dictionary of the Gaelic Language,
Comprising an ample Vocabulary of Gaelic Words, and Vocabularies of Latin and English Words, with their Translation into Gaelic, to which is prefixed a Compendium of Gaelic Grammar. Compiled and published under the Direction of the Highland Society of Scotland. 2 vols. quarto, cloth, £5, 5s.

The Novels of John Galt.
Annals of the Parish.
The Provost.
Sir Andrew Wylie.
The Entail, or the Lairds of Grippy.
4 vols. fcap. 8vo, 2s. each.

The Gardener:
A MAGAZINE OF HORTICULTURE AND FLORICULTURE. Edited by David Thomson, Author of 'A Practical Treatise on the Culture of the Pine-Apple,' 'The Handy Book of the Flower-Garden,' &c.; Assisted by a Staff of the best practical Writers. Published Monthly, 6d.

Publications of the General Assembly of the Church of Scotland.
1.—**Family Prayers.**
Authorised by the General Assembly of the Church of Scotland. A New Edition, crown 8vo, in large type. 4s. 6d.
ANOTHER EDITION, crown 8vo. 2s.

2.—**Prayers for Social and Family Worship.**
For the Use of Soldiers, Sailors, Colonists, and Sojourners in India, and other persons, at home and abroad, who are deprived of the ordinary services of a Christian Ministry. Second Edition, crown 8vo, 4s. Cheap Edition, 1s. 6d.

3.—**The Scottish Hymnal.**
HYMNS FOR PUBLIC WORSHIP, Published for Use in Churches by Authority of the General Assembly.

VARIOUS SIZES—VIZ.:

1. Large type, cloth, red edges, 1s. 6d.; French morocco, 2s. 6d.; calf, 6s.
2. Bourgeois type, cloth, red edges, 1s.; French morocco, 2s.
3. Minion type, limp cloth, 6d.; French morocco, 1s. 6d.
4. School Edition, in paper cover, 2d.
    No. 1, bound with the Psalms and Paraphrases, cloth, 3s.; French morocco, 4s. 6d.; calf, 7s. 6d.
    No. 2, bound with the Psalms and Paraphrases, cloth, 2s.; French morocco, 3s.

4.—**The Scottish Hymnal, with Music.**
Selected by the Committees on Hymns and on Psalmody. The harmonies arranged by W. H. Monk, cloth, 1s. 6d.; French morocco, 3s. 6d. The same in the Tonic Sol-fa Notation, 1s. 6d. and 3s. 6d.

The Principles and Practice of the Law of Trusts

and Trustees in Scotland, with Notes and Illustrations from the Law of England. By **Charles Forsyth, Esq.**, Advocate and Barrister-at-Law. 8vo, 18s.

Idylls and Lyrics.

By **William Forsyth**, Author of 'Kelavane,' &c. Crown 8vo, 5s.

"This is a little volume of unpretending but genuine poetry."—*Standard*.

"Good poetry is not so common a commodity nowadays that it should be passed over without special mark. When found, it should be brought to light that it may be admired. It is for this reason that special attention is here called to a little volume of 'Idylls and Lyrics,' by Mr William Forsyth. . . . Mr Forsyth is a poet. There is genuine music in almost every line he writes. He sees what most men fail to see; he hears what most men fail to hear; and he writes with a felicity of style that few men can equal. In all this volume there is scarcely a page which does not teem with beauties—all the more beautiful that while they want not in vigour and in fineness of perception, they are simple and clear to every reader."—*Scotsman*.

Introductory Addresses

Delivered at the Opening of the **University of Glasgow**, Session 1870-71. With a Prefatory Notice of the new Buildings by **Professor Allan Thomson, M.D.**; and Photograph of the University. Small 4to, 4s. 6d.; small Paper Edition without Photograph, 2s. 6d.

The Subaltern.

By **G. R. Gleig, M.A.**, Chaplain-General of Her Majesty's Forces. Originally published in 'Blackwood's Magazine.' Library Edition. Revised and Corrected, with a New Preface. Crown 8vo, 7s. 6d.

"Originally published in 'Blackwood's Magazine' in 1825, it was at once received with favour, and the present generation of readers will no doubt endorse the verdict of their fathers, and find pleasure in reading Mr Gleig's faithful and picturesque account of his boyish campaign. The volume, though as interesting as any novel, is in all respects the actual record of its author's own experience, and it is in fact the day-to-day journal of a young officer who embarked at Dover with his battalion in 1813, joined Lord Wellington's army a few days before the storming of San Sebastian, just as the French, under Soult, were being driven back through the Pyrenees on to their own soil, and had his share of the fighting on the Bidassoa. . . . We must not omit to notice the new preface which gives an additional interest to the present issue of 'The Subaltern,' and which recounts the present-day aspect of the tract of country where were fought the last battles of the Peninsular War. There is something touching in the old clergyman thus going over the ground he trod sixty years ago as a young soldier, full of military ardour, and recognising the cities and the soil on which were acted the glorious and unforgotten scenes in which he bore a hero's part."—*The Times*.

On the Influence exerted by the Mind over the

Body, IN THE PRODUCTION AND REMOVAL OF MORBID AND ANOMALOUS CONDITIONS OF THE ANIMAL ECONOMY. By **John Glen, M.A.** Crown 8vo, 2s. 6d.

Goethe's Faust.

Translated into English Verse by **Theodore Martin**. Second Edition, post 8vo, 6s.

Cheap Edition, fcap., 3s. 6d.

"The best translation of 'Faust' in verse we have yet had in England."—*Spectator.*

"Mr Theodore Martin's translation is unquestionably the best in the language, and will give to English readers a fair idea of the greatest of modern poems."—*Press.*

Poems and Ballads of Goethe.

Translated by **Professor Ayton** and **Theodore Martin**. Second Edition, fcap. 8vo, 6s.

"There is no doubt that these are the best translations of Goethe's marvellously-cut gems which have yet been published."—*The Times.*

A Walk across Africa;

Or, Domestic Scenes from my Nile Journal. By **James Augustus Grant**, Captain H.M. Bengal Army, Fellow and Gold Medallist of the Royal Geographical Society. 8vo, with Map, 15s.

"Captain Grant's frank, manly, unadorned narrative."—*Daily News.*

"Captain Grant's book will be doubly interesting to those who have read Captain Speke's. He gives, as his special contribution to the story of their three years' walk across Africa, descriptions of birds, beasts, trees, and plants, and all that concerns them, and of domestic scenes throughout the various regions. The book is written in a pleasant, quiet, gentlemanly style, and is characterised by a modest tone. . . . The whole work is delightful reading."—*Globe.*

Memoirs and Adventures of Sir William Kirkaldy

of *Grange*, Governor of the Castle of Edinburgh for Mary Queen of Scots. By **James Grant**. Post 8vo, 10s. 6d.

"It is seldom, indeed, that we find history so written, in a style at once vigorous, perspicuous, and picturesque. The author's heart is thoroughly with his subject."—*Blackwood's Magazine.*

Memoirs and Adventures of Sir John Hepburn,

Marshal of France under Louis XIII., &c. By **James Grant**. Post 8vo, 8s.

Memorials of the Castle of Edinburgh.

By **James Grant**. A New Edition. In crown 8vo, with 12 Engravings, 3s. 6d.

"Of the different books of this nature that have fallen in our way, we do not remember one that has equalled Mr Grant's 'Memorials of the Castle of Edinburgh.'"—*Spectator.*

Symbolism;

OR, MIND, MATTER, AND LANGUAGE AS THE NECESSARY ELEMENTS OF THINKING AND REASONING. By **James Haig, M.A.** Crown 8vo, 12s.

"The book is in reality a popular exposition of philosophy and philosophical systems expressed in the clearest language. . . . The author occasionally displays considerable originality and ingenuity in his investigations. . . . He seems to suggest that philosophy and theology should go hand in hand. . . . Here we must take leave of this sturdy thinker with some admiration of his bold ideas and careful research. . . . The general reader will gather with little trouble from his pages some of the flowers of philosophical literature."—*Examiner.*

Wenderholme:

A STORY OF LANCASHIRE AND YORKSHIRE LIFE. By **Philip Gilbert Hamerton,** Author of 'A Painter's Camp,' &c. 3 vols. post 8vo, £1, 11s. 6d.

Lectures on Metaphysics.

By **Sir William Hamilton, Bart.,** Professor of Logic and Metaphysics in the University of Edinburgh. Edited by the **Rev. H. L. Mansel, B.D., LL.D.,** Dean of St Paul's; and **John Veitch, M.A.,** Professor of Logic and Rhetoric, Glasgow. Fifth Edition. 2 vols. 8vo, 24s.

Lectures on Logic.

By **Sir William Hamilton, Bart.** Edited by **Professors Mansel** and **Veitch.** Second Edition. In 2 vols., 24s.

Discussions on Philosophy and Literature,

EDUCATION, AND UNIVERSITY REFORM. By **Sir William Hamilton, Bart.** Third Edition. 8vo, 21s.

Memoir of Sir William Hamilton, Bart.,

Professor of Logic and Metaphysics in the University of Edinburgh. By **Professor Veitch** of the University of Glasgow. 8vo, with Portrait, 18s.

"No better piece of philosophical biography has hitherto been produced in this country."—*North British Review.*

"Professor Veitch has succeeded in blending the domestic with the intellectual life of Sir W. Hamilton in one graphic picture, as biographers rarely do succeed."—*Saturday Review.*

"Hamilton's was a heroic life, and Professor Veitch has told it affectionately, truly, and well."—*Pall Mall Gazette.*

Annals of the Peninsular Campaigns.

By **Captain Thomas Hamilton.** A New Edition Edited by **F. Hardman,** 8vo, 16s. Atlas of Maps to illustrate the Campaigns, 12s.

Men and Manners in America.

By **Captain Thomas Hamilton**. With Portrait of the Author. Fcap., 7s. 6d.

The Operations of War Explained and Illustrated.

By **Edward Bruce Hamley**, Colonel in the Royal Artillery, Companion of the Bath, Commandant of the Staff College, &c. 3d Edition, 4to, with numerous Illustrations, 28s.

"Colonel Hamley's treatise on the 'Operations of War' is, we do not hesitate to say, the best that has been written in the English language."—*The Times.*

"On all matters relating to the practice of the profession it forms the most perfect book of reference that has been published."—*United Service Magazine.*

The Story of the Campaign of Sebastopol.

Written in the Camp. By **Col. E. Bruce Hamley**. With Illustrations drawn in Camp by the Author. 8vo, 21s.

"We strongly recommend this 'Story of the Campaign' to all who would gain a just comprehension of this tremendous struggle. Of this we are perfectly sure, it is a book unlikely to be ever superseded. Its truth is of that simple and startling character which is sure of an immortal existence; nor is it paying the gallant Author too high a compliment to class this masterpiece of military history with the most precious of those classic records which have been bequeathed to us by the great writers of antiquity who took part in the wars they have described."—*The Press.*

Wellington's Career;

A Military and Political Summary. By **Col. E. Bruce Hamley**. Crown 8vo, 2s.

Lady Lee's Widowhood.

By **Col. E. Bruce Hamley**. Crown 8vo, 2s. 6d.

"A quiet humour, an easy, graceful style, a deep, thorough, confident knowledge of human nature in its better and more degrading aspects, a delicate and exquisite appreciation of womanly character, an admirable faculty of description, and great tact, are the qualities that command the reader's interest and respect from beginning to end of 'Lady Lee's Widowhood.'"—*The Times.*

Our Poor Relations.

A Philozoic Essay. By **Col. E. Bruce Hamley**. With Illustrations, chiefly by Ernest Griset. Crown 8vo, cloth gilt, 3s. 6d.

"This is a charming little book, such as may be read through in half an hour; nor would it be easy to spend half an hour more pleasantly, or indeed to more profit. Slowly, very slowly indeed, but still by a sure progress, we are struggling out of the merely selfish and masterful view of the relations between ourselves and the lower animals; and Colonel Hamley's Essay, with its wide, kindly sympathies and delicate fancy, will help it on."—*Spectator.*

The Position on the Alma.

In Seven Sketches from the Field on the Day after the Battle. By **Col. E. Bruce Hamley.** Cloth, 5s.

A New Sea and an Old Land;

Being Papers suggested by a Visit to Egypt at the end of 1869. By **General W. G. Hamley.** 8vo, with coloured Illustrations, 10s. 6d.

"Such are the contrasts the book deals with, handling them in a style that is not only pleasant but picturesque; and those who care to have ancient Egypt made easy will attain their object with the smallest possible expenditure of temper and trouble by placing themselves under his guidance."—*Saturday Review.*

Handy Book of Laws

CHIEFLY AFFECTING SCOTLAND. Abridged and plainly stated for general use. By an **Ex-Sheriff-Substitute.** Sewed, 6d.

The Handy Horse-Book;

Or, Practical Instructions in Riding, Driving, and the General Care and Management of Horses. By "**Magenta.**" A New Edition, with 6 Engravings, 4s. 6d.

"As cavalry officer, hunting horseman, coach-proprietor, whip, and steeple-chase-rider, the author has had long and various experience in the management of horses, and he now gives us the cream of his information."—*Athenæum.*

"He propounds no theories, but embodies in simple untechnical language what he has learned practically."—*Sporting Gazette.*

A Glossary of Navigation.

Containing the Definitions and Propositions of the Science, Explanation of Terms, and Description of Instruments. By the **Rev. J. B. Harbord, M.A.**, Assistant Director of Education, Admiralty. Crown 8vo. Illustrated with Diagrams, 6s.

Definitions and Diagrams in Astronomy and Navigation.

By the **Rev. J. B. Harbord, M.A.** 1s. 6d.

Short Sermons for Hospitals and Sick Seamen.

By the **Rev. J. B. Harbord, M.A.** Fcap. 8vo, cloth, 4s. 6d.

Scenes and Adventures in Central America.

Edited by **Frederick Hardman.** Crown 8vo, 6s.

Poems. By the Lady Flora Hastings.

Edited by Her Sister, the late Marchioness of Bute. Second Edition, with a Portrait. Fcap., 7s. 6d.

Works of D. R. Hay, F.R.S.E.

A Nomenclature of Colours applicable to the Arts and Natural Sciences, to Manufactures, and other purposes of General Utility. 228 examples of Colours, Hues, Tints, and Shades. 8vo, £3, 3s.

The Laws of Harmonious Colouring. Adapted to Interior Decorations; with Observations on the Practice of House-Painting. Post 8vo, 6s. 6d.

The Geometric Beauty of the Human Figure Defined. To which is prefixed a System of Æsthetic Proportion. Applicable to Architecture and the other Formative Arts. 16 Plates. Royal 4to, 30s.

The Harmonic Law of Nature applied to Architectural Design. 8 Plates. Royal 8vo, boards, 2s. 6d.

The Orthographic Beauty of the Parthenon referred to a Law of Nature. 12 Plates. Royal 8vo, sewed, 5s.

The Natural Principles of Beauty, as developed in the Human Figure. 5 Plates. Royal 8vo, sewed, 5s.

The Science of Beauty, as developed in Nature, and applied in Art. 23 Plates. Royal 8vo, cloth, 10s. 6d.

The Natural Principles and Analogy of the Harmony of Form. 18 Plates and numerous Woodcuts. 4to, 15s.

Proportion, or the Geometric Principle of Beauty analysed. 17 Plates and 38 Woodcuts. 4to, 25s.

Original Geometrical Diaper Designs. Accompanied by an Attempt to develop and elucidate the true Principles of Ornamental Design, as applied to the Decorative Arts. 57 Plates and numerous Woodcuts. Oblong folio, 42s.

The Principles of Beauty in Colouring Systematised. 14 Coloured Diagrams. 2d Edition. 8vo, 15s.

First Principles of Symmetrical Beauty. 100 Plates. Post 8vo, 6s.

On the Science of those Proportions by which the Human Head and Countenance, as represented in ancient Greek Art, are distinguished from those of ordinary Nature. 25 Plates. Royal 4to, 36s.

The Works of the Right Rev. Bishop Hay,

of Edinburgh. Together with a Memoir of the Author, and Portrait engraved from the Painting at the College of Blairs. Edited under the supervision of the **Right Rev. Bishop Strain.** A New Edition, in 5 vols. Crown 8vo, 21s.

"Able and original work."—*London Scotsman.*

"There is a good deal of original thought in this work. . . . There is hardly a chapter which does not contain something that may be termed suggestive."—*John Bull.*

Bishop Hay on Miracles.

The Scripture Doctrine of Miracles Displayed, in which they are impartially examined and explained, according to the Light of Revelation and the Principles of Sound Reason. By the **Right Rev. Dr George Hay,** Bishop of Edinburgh. 2 vols. crown 8vo, 10s. 6d.

The Poems of Felicia Hemans.

Complete in One Volume, Royal 8vo, with Portrait by Finden, Cheap Edition, 5s. Another Edition, with Memoir by her Sister, Seven Volumes, fcap., 35s. Another Edition, in Six Volumes, cloth, gilt edges, 15s. The same 6 vols. bound in 3, 12s. 6d., or cloth, extra gilt edges, 15s.

The following Works of Mrs Hemans are sold separately, bound in cloth, gilt edges, 4s. each :—

RECORDS OF WOMAN.
FOREST SANCTUARY.
SONGS OF THE AFFECTIONS.

DRAMATIC WORKS.
TALES AND HISTORIC SCENES.
MORAL AND RELIGIOUS POEMS.

Select Poems of Mrs Hemans.

In One Vol., fcap. 8vo. 3s

Memoir of Mrs Hemans.

By her **Sister.** With a Portrait, fcap. 8vo, 5s.

The Practice in the Several Judicatories of the

Church of Scotland. By **Alexander Hill, D.D.** Sixth Edition, Revised and Enlarged. Fcap. 8vo, 4s.

A Book about Roses,

HOW TO GROW AND SHOW THEM. By **S. Reynolds Hole,** Author of 'A Little Tour in Ireland.' Fourth Edition, Enlarged. Crown 8vo, 7s. 6d.

"It is the production of a man who boasts of thirty 'all England' cups, whose Roses are always looked for anxiously at flower-shows, who took the lion's share in originating the first Rose-show *pur et simple*, whose assistance as judge or *amicus curiæ* is always courted at such exhibitions. Such a man 'ought to have something to say worth hearing to those who love the Rose,' and he *has* said it."—*Gardeners' Chronicle.*

"We cordially recommend the book to every amateur who wishes to grow Roses as at once the pleasantest and the best yet written on the subject."—*The Field.*

"A very captivating book, containing a great deal of valuable information about the Rose and its culture, given in a style which cannot fail to please."—*Journal of Horticulture.*

The Six of Spades:

A Book about the Garden and the Gardener. By the **Rev. S. Reynolds Hole,** Author of 'A Book About Roses,' &c. Crown 8vo, 5s.

Homer's Odyssey and Iliad.

Translated into English Verse in the Spenserian Stanza. By **P. S. Worsley, M.A.**, Fellow of Corpus Christi College, Oxford; and **John Conington, M.A.**, Corpus Professor of Latin in the University of Oxford. 4 vols. crown 8vo, 39s.

"If the translator has produced a work which, having caught the spirit of the poem, can delight those to whom the original is a sealed book, he can desire no higher praise; and this praise belongs justly to Mr Worsley. . . . He has placed in the hands of English readers a poem which deserves to outlive the present generation."—*Edinburgh Review.*

"We assign it, without hesitation, the first place among existing English translations."—*Westminster Review.*

The Odes and Epodes of Horace,

A Metrical Translation into English, with Latin Text, Introduction, and Commentaries. By **Lord Lytton**. Crown 8vo, 14s.

Mary Queen of Scots

AND HER ACCUSERS. By **John Hosack**, Barrister-at-Law. This work contains the 'Book of Articles' produced against Queen Mary at Westminster, which has never hitherto been printed. A New and Enlarged Edition, with a Photograph from the Bust on the Tomb in Westminster Abbey. 8vo, cloth, 15s.

"A careful study of Mr Hosack's book will show that he has explicitly or implicitly answered every one of the fifteen arguments in the famous Note L. of Hume's History of this reign."—*Quarterly Review.*

"Whatever surmises may be formed about Mary's knowledge or assent, there can now be no doubt that the murder was contrived, not by Mary, but by her accusers."—*Scotsman.*

"He has confuted those who, by brilliant writing and a judicious selection of evidence, paint the Queen of Scots as an incarnate fiend, and who are dramatic poets rather than historians."—*The Times.*

A Treatise on the Conflict of Laws of England

and Scotland. By **John Hosack**, of the Middle Temple, Barrister-at-Law. 8vo, 10s. 6d.

Decisions of the Court of Session, 1781-1822.

Collected by **David Hume, Esq.**, Professor of the Law of Scotland in the University of Edinburgh. 4to, boards, £3, 3s.

Ballads from the German.

By **Henry Inglis**. Fcap. 8vo, 5s.

Marican, and other Poems.

By **Henry** Inglis. 8vo, 8s.

The Law of Creeds in Scotland.

A Treatise on the Legal Relation of Churches in Scotland, Established and not Established, to their Doctrinal Confessions. By **A. T. Innes.** 8vo, cloth, 15s.

Historical Record of the 79th Regiment of Foot,

Or Cameron Highlanders. By **Captain Robert Jameson,** H.P. Depot Battalion, late Quartermaster 79th Highlanders. Crown 8vo, 7s. 6d.

The Mother's Legacie to her Unborne Childe.

By **Mrs Elizabeth Joceline.** Edited by the **Very Rev. Principal Lee.** Cloth, gilt edges, 32mo, 4s. 6d. Also in morocco antique, 8s. 6d.

"This beautiful and touching Legacie."—*Athenæum.*

"A delightful monument of the piety and high feeling of a truly noble mother."—*Morning Advertiser.*

The Scots Musical Museum.

Consisting of upwards of Six Hundred Songs, with proper Basses for the Pianoforte. Originally published by **James Johnson**; and now accompanied with Copious Notes and Illustrations of the Lyric Poetry and Music of Scotland, by the late **William Stenhouse**; with additional Notes and Illustrations, by **David Laing** and **C. K. Sharp.** 4 vols. 8vo, Roxburghe binding, £2, 12s. 6d.

The Royal Atlas of Modern Geography.

In a Series of entirely Original and Authentic Maps. By **A. Keith Johnston,** F.R.S.E., F.R.G.S., Author of the 'Physical Atlas,' &c. With a complete Index of easy reference to each Map, comprising nearly 150,000 Places contained in this Atlas. Imperial Folio, half-bound in russia or morocco, £5, 15s. 6d.; or with General Index in a separate volume, 8vo, both half-bound morocco, £6, 10s. Each Plate may be had separately with its Index, 3s. Dedicated by special permission to Her Majesty.

"Of the many noble atlases prepared by Mr Johnston and published by Messrs Blackwood and Sons, this Royal Atlas will be the most useful to the public, and will deserve to be the most popular."—*Athenæum.*

"We know no series of maps which we can more warmly recommend. The accuracy, wherever we have attempted to put it to the test, is really astonishing."—*Saturday Review.*

"The culmination of all attempts to depict the face of the world appears in the Royal Atlas, than which it is impossible to conceive anything more perfect."—*Morning Herald.*

"This is, beyond question, the most splendid and luxurious, as well as the most useful and complete, of all existing atlases."—*Guardian.*

"An almost daily reference to, and comparison of, it with others, since the publication of the first part some two years ago until now, enables us to say, without the slightest hesitation, that this is by far the most complete and authentic atlas that has yet been issued."—*Scotsman.*

The Handy Royal Atlas.

45 Maps clearly printed and carefully coloured, with General Index. By **A. Keith Johnston, F.R.S.E., F.R.G.S.**, &c. Imp. 4to, £2, 12s. 6d., half-bound morocco.

This work has been constructed for the purpose of placing in the hands of the public a useful and thoroughly accurate ATLAS of Maps of Modern Geography, in a convenient form, and at a moderate price. It is based on the 'ROYAL ATLAS,' by the same Author; and, in so far as the scale permits, it comprises many of the excellences which its prototype is acknowledged to possess. The aim has been to make the book strictly what its name implies, a HANDY ATLAS—a valuable substitute for the 'Royal,' where that is too bulky or too expensive to find a place, a needful auxiliary to the junior branches of families, and a *vade mecum* to the tutor and the pupil-teacher.

"This is Mr Keith Johnston's admirable Royal Atlas diminished in bulk and scale, so as to be, perhaps, fairly entitled to the name of "Handy," but still not so much diminished but what it constitutes an accurate and useful general Atlas for ordinary households."—*Spectator.*

"The 'Handy Atlas' is thoroughly deserving of its name. Not only does it contain the latest information, but its size and arrangement render it perfect as a book of reference."—*Standard.*

Keith Johnston's School Atlases.

Atlas of General and Descriptive Geography. A New and Enlarged Edition, suited to the best Text-Books; with Geographical information brought up to the time of publication. 26 Maps, clearly and uniformly printed in colours, with Index. Imperial 8vo, half-bound, 12s. 6d.

Atlas of Physical Geography, illustrating, in a Series of Original Designs, the Elementary Facts of GEOLOGY, HYDROGRAPHY, METEOROLOGY, and NATURAL HISTORY. A New and Enlarged Edition, containing 4 new Maps and Letterpress. 20 Coloured Maps. Imperial 8vo, half-bound, 12s. 6d.

Atlas of Astronomy. A New and Enlarged Edition, 21 Coloured Plates. With an Elementary Survey of the Heavens, designed as an accompaniment to this Atlas, by **Robert Grant, LL.D.**, &c., Professor of Astronomy and Director of the Observatory in the University of Glasgow. Imperial 8vo, half-bound, 12s. 6d.

Atlas of Classical Geography. A New and Enlarged Edition. Constructed from the best materials, and embodying the results of the most Recent Investigations, accompanied by a complete INDEX OF PLACES, in which the proper quantities are given by **T. Harvey** and **E. Worsley, MM.A.** Oxon. 21 Coloured Maps. Imperial 8vo, half-bound, 12s. 6d.

"This edition is so much enlarged and improved as to be virtually a new work, surpassing everything else of the kind extant, both in utility and beauty." —*Athenæum.*

Elementary Atlas of General and Descriptive Geography, for the Use of Junior Classes; including a MAP OF CANAAN and PALESTINE, with GENERAL INDEX. 8vo, half-bound, 5s.

Keith Johnston's School Atlases—OPINIONS OF THE PRESS.

"They are as superior to all School Atlases within our knowledge, as were the larger works of the same Author in advance of those that preceded them."—*Educational Times.*

"Decidedly the best School Atlases we have ever seen."—*English Journal of Education.*

"... The *Physical Atlas* seems to us particularly well executed.... The last generation had no such help to learning as is afforded in these excellent elementary Maps. The *Classical Atlas* is a great improvement on what has usually gone by that name; not only is it fuller, but in some cases it gives the same country more than once in different periods of time. Thus it approaches the special value of a historical atlas.... The *General Atlas* is wonderfully full and accurate for its scale.... Finally, the *Astronomical Atlas*, in which Mr Hind is responsible for the scientific accuracy of the maps, supplies an admitted educational want. No better companion to an elementary astronomical treatise could be found than this cheap and convenient collection of maps."—*Saturday Review.*

"The plan of these Atlases is admirable, and the excellence of the plan is rivalled by the beauty of the execution.... The best security for the accuracy and substantial value of a School Atlas is to have it from the hands of a man like our Author, who has perfected his skill by the execution of much larger works, and gained a character which he will be careful not to jeopardise by attaching his name to anything that is crude, slovenly, or superficial."—*Scotsman.*

Keith Johnston's Hand Atlases.

Being the Maps of the School Atlases on Large and Thick Paper, bound in half-morocco. Imperial quarto, 25s. each,—viz.,

General and Descriptive Geography
Physical Geography.
Astronomy.
Classical Geography.

Keith Johnston's Tourists' Maps.

(From the Royal Atlas), each with Index, in cloth case for the pocket:—

	£	s.	d.
Scotland, two sheets,	0	7	6
Italy, two sheets,	0	8	0
Switzerland, one sheet,	0	4	6
The Shores of the Mediterranean, one sheet,	0	4	6
The Canadas, two sheets,	0	8	0
Austria, two sheets,	0	8	0
Prussia, one sheet,	0	4	6
America (U.S.), two sheets,	0	8	0
America (South), two sheets,	0	8	0
Australia, one sheet,	0	4	6
Belgium and the Netherlands, one sheet,	0	4	6
China and Japan, one sheet,	0	4	6
England, two sheets,	0	8	0
India, two sheets,	0	8	0
Ireland, one sheet,	0	4	6
Palestine, one sheet,	0	4	6
Spain and Portugal, one sheet,	0	4	6
Sweden and Norway, one sheet,	0	4	6

Map of Europe.

By **A. Keith Johnston**, F.R.S.E., F.R.G.S., Geographer to the Queen. The Map is fully coloured, and measures 4 feet 2 inches by 3 feet 5 inches. Price, mounted on Cloth and Mahogany Roller, varnished, 25s., or Folded in Quarto in a handsome Cloth Case, 21s.

Index Geographicus:

Being a List, Alphabetically arranged, of the Principal Places on the Globe, with the Countries and Subdivisions of the Countries in which they are situated, and their Latitudes and Longitudes. Compiled specially with reference to Keith Johnston's Royal Atlas, but applicable to all Modern Atlases and Maps. In 1 vol. Imperial 8vo, pp. 676, 21s.

Notes on North America:

Agricultural, Economical, and Social. By **Professor J. F. W. Johnston.** 2 vols. post 8vo, 21s.

"Professor Johnston's admirable Notes. . . . The very best manual for intelligent emigrants, whilst to the British agriculturist and general reader it conveys a more complete conception of the condition of these prosperous regions than all that has hitherto been written."—*Economist.*

The Chemistry of Common Life.

By **Professor J. F. W. Johnston.** With 113 Illustrations on Wood, and a Copious Index. 2 vols. crown 8vo, 11s. 6d.

"It is just one of those books which will best serve to show men how minute is the provision which has been made for human support, and that if the laws prescribed by Nature are duly observed, she, on her part, will see to it that her functions are performed with fidelity and success."—*Durham Chronicle.*

Professor Johnston's Elements of Agricultural

Chemistry and Geology. A New Edition, revised and brought down to the Present Time. By **G. T. Atkinson, B.A., F.C.S.** Fcap., 6s. 6d.

Professor Johnston's Catechism of Agricultural

Chemistry. A New Edition. Edited by **Professor Voelcker.** With Engravings. 1s.

Ex Eremo:

Poems chiefly written in India. By **H. G. Keene.** Crown 8vo, 6s.

The Invasion of the Crimea:

Its Origin, and an Account of its Progress down to the Death of Lord Raglan. By **Alexander William Kinglake.** Vols. I. and II., 32s., and Vols. III. and IV., 34s.

John Knox's Liturgy:

THE BOOK OF COMMON ORDER, AND THE DIRECTORY FOR PUBLIC WORSHIP OF THE CHURCH OF SCOTLAND. With Historical Introductions and Illustrative Notes by the **Rev. George W. Sprott, B.A.**, and the **Rev. Thomas Leishman, D.D.** Handsomely printed, in imitation of the large editions of Andro Hart, on toned paper, bound in cloth, red edges, 8s. 6d.

"We heartily recommend Mr Sprott's Introduction to the 'Book of Common Order' to every one who wishes honestly to get the truth, and the whole truth, about the history, so far as Scotland is concerned, concerning a devotional formulary which has had so curious a destiny. This Introduction is full of learning, used with a candour that deserves all honour. In reading it we cannot find whether the author is a supporter or an opponent of a formulary of worship—he has undertaken the history of one book of that kind, and he tells it fairly out."—*Scotsman.*

On Primary Instruction in Relation to Education.

By **Simon S. Laurie, A.M.**; Author of 'Philosophy of Ethics, &c. Crown 8vo, 4s. 6d.

The Rural Economy of England, Scotland, and Ireland.

By **Leonce de Lavergne.** Translated from the French. With Notes by a Scottish Farmer. In 8vo, 12s.

"One of the best works on the philosophy of agriculture and of agricultural political economy that has appeared."—*Spectator.*

Lectures on the History of the Church of Scotland,

FROM THE REFORMATION TO THE REVOLUTION SETTLEMENT. By the late **Very Rev. John Lee, D.D., LL.D.**, Principal of the University of Edinburgh. With Notes and Appendices from the Author's Papers. Edited by the **Rev. William Lee, D.D.** 2 vols. 8vo, 21s.

The Physiology of Common Life.

By **George H. Lewes**, Author of 'Sea-side Studies,' &c. Illustrated with numerous Engravings. 2 vols., 12s.

CONTENTS:—Hunger and Thirst—Food and Drink—Digestion and Indigestion—The Structure and Uses of the Blood—The Circulation—Respiration and Suffocation—Why we are warm, and how we keep so—Feeling and Thinking—The Mind and the Brain—Our Senses and Sensations—Sleep and Dreams—The Qualities we Inherit from our Parents—Life and Death.

Linda Tressel.

By the Author of 'Nina Balatka.' 2 vols. fcap. 8vo, 12s.

Doubles and Quits.

By **Laurence Lockhart**, late Captain 92d Highlanders. With Twelve Illustrations. In 2 vols. post 8vo, 21s.

Fair to See:

A Novel. By **Laurence W. M. Lockhart**, Author of 'Doubles and Quits.' New Edition in 1 vol. post 8vo, 6s.

"But politics are the smallest part of this very readable novel, the interest of which never flags, for the story is as full of 'situations' as a good play."—*Times.*

"'Fair to See' is something better than a clever novel. It shows no little artistic power; and as you read it you feel that there is much more in the book than at first you fancied. . . . The scenes on the moors, in the barracks, and the ball-rooms are all dashed off by an expert. These are minor merits, but they go far towards assuring the success of a story which marks a decided advance on the author's first novel."—*Pall Mall Gazette.*

History of the Rise and Progress of Freemasonry

In Scotland. By **David Murray Lyon**, one of the Grand Stewards of the Grand Lodge of Scotland; Honorary Corresponding Member of the "Verein Deutscher Friemaurer," Leipzig, &c. &c. In small quarto. Illustrated with numerous Portraits of Eminent Members of the Craft, and Facsimiles of Ancient Charters and other curious Documents. £1, 10s.

Kenelm Chillingly.

His Adventures and Opinions. By the Author of 'The Caxtons,' &c.
[*In the press.*

Complete Library Edition of Lord Lytton's Novels.

In Volumes of a convenient and handsome form. Printed from a large and readable type. 43 vols. fcap. 8vo, 5s. each.

"It is of the handiest of sizes; the paper is good; and the type, which seems to be new, is very clear and beautiful. There are no pictures. The whole charm of the presentment of the volume consists in its handiness, and the tempting clearness and beauty of the type, which almost converts into a pleasure the mere act of following the printer's lines, and leaves the author's mind free to exert its unobstructed force upon the reader."—*Examiner.*

"Nothing could be better as to size, type, paper, and general getting-up."—*Athenæum.*

Walpole; or, Every Man has his Price.

A Comedy in Rhyme. By **Lord Lytton**. Fcap. 8vo, 5s.

The Boatman.

By **Pisistratus Caxton**. 8vo, sewed, 1s.

Cattle and Cattle-Breeders.

By **William M'Combie, M.P.**, Tillyfour. A New and Cheaper Edition. 2s. 6d., cloth.

"This charming book, full of the incidents of a Scotch breeder's and dealer's experience, will be read with more interest in its second edition, now that the author has attained to Parliamentary distinction. Much as we enjoy the first part of the book, which is mainly a record of trading incident, the hints on breeding and care of capital are most useful. The student will do well to carefully study this section of the book; every sentence, being the result of practical experience, is thoroughly reliable."—*Field.*

Works of the Rev. Thomas M'Crie, D.D.

Uniform Edition. Four vols. crown 8vo, 24s. Sold separately.

Life of John Knox. Containing Illustrations of the History of the Reformation in Scotland. Crown 8vo, 6s.

Life of Andrew Melville. Containing Illustrations of the Ecclesiastical and Literary History of Scotland in the Sixteenth and Seventeenth Centuries. Crown 8vo, 6s.

History of the Progress and Suppression of the Reformation in Italy in the Sixteenth Century. Crown 8vo, 4s.

History of the Progress and Suppression of the Reformation in Spain in the Sixteenth Century. Crown 8vo, 3s. 6d.

Sermons, and Review of the 'Tales of My Landlord.' In 1 vol. crown 8vo, 6s.

Lectures on the Book of Esther. Fcap. 8vo, 5s.

The Book of the Garden.

By **Charles M'Intosh**, formerly Curator of the Royal Gardens of his Majesty the King of the Belgians, and lately of those of his Grace the Duke of Buccleuch, K.G., at Dalkeith Palace. In two large vols. royal 8vo, embellished with 1350 Engravings.

The work is divided into two great sections, each occupying a volume—the first comprising the formation, arrangement, and laying out of gardens, and the construction of garden buildings; the second treating of the theory and practice of horticulture. Sold separately—viz.:

VOL. I. ON THE FORMATION OF GARDENS AND CONSTRUCTION OF GARDEN EDIFICES. 776 pages, and 1073 Engravings, £2, 10s.

VOL. II. PRACTICAL GARDENING. 868 pages, and 279 Engravings, £1, 17s. 6d.

Studies in Roman Law.

With Comparative Views of the Laws of France, England, and Scotland. By **Lord Mackenzie**, one of the Judges of the Court of Session in Scotland. Second Edition, 8vo, 12s.

"We know not in the English language where else to look for a history of the Roman Law so clear, and at the same time so short. More improving reading, both for the general student and for the lawyer, we cannot well imagine; and there are few, even among learned professional men, who will not gather some novel information from Lord Mackenzie's simple pages."—*London Review.*

"This is, in many respects, one of the most interesting works that the legal press has issued in our time.... The explanation of the Roman Law, historical and expository—the 'Studies'—is admirably given, clear and simple, and yet very learned, and the whole work is conceived in a candid and liberal spirit, being, besides, distinguished by a calmness of tone eminently befitting the judicial pen."—*Law Magazine and Review.*

A Manual of Modern Geography,

Mathematical, Physical, and Political. By the **Rev. Alexander Mackay LL.D., F.R.G.S.** New and greatly Improved Edition. Crown 8vo, pp. 676, 7s. 6d.

This volume—the result of many years' unremitting application—is specially adapted for the use of Teachers, Advanced Classes, Candidates for the Civil Service, and proficients in geography generally.

Gems of German Poetry.

Translated by **Lady John Manners.** Small quarto, 3s. 6d.

Translations by Theodore Martin:

Goethe's Faust. Second Edition, crown 8vo, 6s. Cheap Edition, 3s. 6d.

The Odes of Horace. With Life and Notes. Second Edition, post 8vo, 9s.

Catullus. With Life and Notes. Post 8vo, 6s. 6d.

The Vita Nuova of Dante. With an Introduction and Notes. Second Edition, crown 8vo, 5s.

Alladin: A Dramatic Poem. By *Adam Oehlenschlaeger.* Fcap. 8vo, 5s.

Correggio: A Tragedy. By *Oehlenschlaeger.* With Notes. Fcap. 8vo, 3s.

King Rene's Daughter: A Danish Lyrical Drama. By *Henrik Hertz.* Second Edition, fcap., 2s. 6d.

The System of Field Manœuvres

Best adapted for Enabling our Troops to meet a Continental Army. Being the Wellington Prize Essay. By **Lieutenant F. Maurice,** Royal Artillery, Instructor of Tactics and Organisation, Royal Military College, Sandhurst. Crown 8vo, 5s.

"We are prepared to say that this brilliant and most readable treatise clearly sets forth the momentous issues, and points out the direction in which not only military chiefs but statesmen must go, if our army is to be brought up to that standard which will permit it to enter war on a level, in excellence at least, with contemporary armies."—*Spectator.*

"No work, English or foreign, has treated this subject (infantry tactics) better than the 'Wellington Prize Essay.'"—*Times.*

"Lieutenant Maurice may well claim credit for having built up a work of such living interest as his is, even to the layman, upon such a set of dry bones as the given thesis afforded."—*The Saturday Review.*

Journal of the Waterloo Campaign:

Kept throughout the Campaign of 1815. By **General Cavalie Mercer,** Commanding the 9th Brigade Royal Artillery. 2 vols. post 8vo, 21s.

"No actor in the terrible scene ushered in by the following day has ever painted it in more vivid colours than the officer of artillery who led his troop into the very heart of the carnage, and escaped to write a book more real, more lifelike, more enthralling, than any tale of war it has ever been our lot to read."—*Athenæum.*

C

Maxims of Sir Morgan O'Doherty, Bart.

Originally published in Blackwood's Magazine. Cloth, 1s.

The Life and Labours of the Apostle Paul.

A continuous Narrative for School and Bible Classes. By **Charles Michie, M.A.**, Author of an 'Outline of the Geography of Palestine.' 1s., with a Map.

A Manual of English Prose Literature,

Biographical and Critical: designed mainly to show Characteristics of Style. By **W. Minto, M.A.** Crown 8vo, 10s. 6d.

Biographies of Eminent Soldiers of the last Four

Centuries. By **Major-General John Mitchell**, Author of 'Life of Wallenstein,' 'The Fall of Napoleon,' &c. Edited, with a Memoir of the Author, by Leonhard Schmitz, LL.D. 8vo, 9s.

Poetical Works of D. M. Moir (Delta).

With Memoir by **Thomas Aird**, and Portrait. Second Edition. 2 vols. fcap. 8vo, 12s.

Domestic Verses. By Delta.

New Edition, fcap. 8vo, cloth gilt, 4s. 6d.

Lectures on the Poetical Literature of the Past

Half-Century. By **D. M. Moir.** Third Edition. Fcap. 8vo, 5s.

Memoir of Count De Montalembert.

A Chapter of Recent French History. By **Mrs Oliphant**, Author of the 'Life of Edward Irving,' &c. In 2 vols. crown 8vo, £1, 4s.

"Having a delightful subject, she has handled it in an altogether delightful way. . . . It is as good, full, and truthful a portrait of his life and character as could be desired, and while the skill of the author makes it as interesting as a novel, it may be read as an altogether trustworthy 'chapter of recent French history.'"—*Examiner.*

"It is to Mrs Oliphant that we owe the very beautiful English translation of the 'Monks of the West.' The author has written to her:—'What I must insist upon is—the exact reproduction of all the passages in my book, which, to you, must seem the most offensive to English and Protestant ears' (p. 336). And when it was completed, he bore witness to 'the good faith and straightforward equity of a most literal translation' (p. 337). We are happy to be able to say that Mrs Oliphant has shown equal 'good faith and straightforward equity' in translating the character of Count de Montalembert so as to make him known and appreciated by English readers. . . . Would that all biographies were written in such good taste and in such a generous spirit!"—*Tablet.*

"In its delicacy, in its fine insight and sympathy, no less than in its eloquence, Mrs Oliphant's 'Life of Montalembert,' with all its faults, will take high rank among standard English biographies."—*The Nonconformist.*

The Wedderburns and their Work;

Or, the Sacred Poetry of the Scottish Reformation in its Historical Relation to that of Germany. By **Alexander F. Mitchell, D.D.**, Professor of Hebrew, St Andrews. Small quarto, 2s. 6d.

The Origin of the Seasons,

Considered from a Geological Point of View: showing the remarkable Disparities that exist between the Physical Geography and Natural Phenomena of the North and South Hemispheres. By **Samuel Mossman**. In crown 8vo, with Engravings, 10s. 6d.

A Geological Map of Europe,

Exhibiting the different Systems of Rocks according to the latest Researches, and from Inedited Materials. By **Sir R. I. Murchison, D.C.L., F.R.S.**, &c., Director-General of the Geological Survey of Great Britain and Ireland; and **James Nicol, F.R.S.E., F.G.S.**, Professor of Natural History in the University of Aberdeen. Constructed by Alex. Keith Johnston, F.R.S.E., &c., Geographer to the Queen, Author of the 'Physical Atlas,' &c. Scale $\frac{1}{\text{enxuo}}$ of Nature, 76 miles to an inch. Four Sheets Imperial, beautifully printed in Colours. Size, 4 feet 2 inches by 3 feet 5 inches. In Sheets, £3, 3s.; in a Cloth Case, 4to, £3, 10s.

Manual of the Law of Insolvency and Bankruptcy:

Comprehending a Treatise on the Law of Insolvency, Notour Bankruptcy, Composition Contracts, Trust Deeds, Cessios, and Sequestrations; with Annotations on the various Insolvency and Bankruptcy Statutes; and with Forms of Procedure applicable to these subjects. By **James Murdoch**, Member of the Faculty of Procurators in Glasgow. Third Edition. 8vo, 19s.

Catalogue of the Coleoptera of Scotland.

By **Andrew Murray** of Conland, W.S., Member of the Royal Physical Society of Edinburgh, of the Entymological Society of France, &c. Fcap. 8vo, cloth limp, 2s. 6d.

A Glance at some of the Principles of Comparative Philology.

As illustrated in the Latin and Anglican Forms of Speech. By the **Hon. Lord Neaves**. Crown 8vo, 1s. 6d.

"Lord Neaves's remarks, as well as his very clear and well-ordered display of the principles of the science, characterised by great modesty and simplicity, well deserve attention."—*Pall Mall Gazette.*

The Uses of Leisure:

An Address delivered to the Students of the School of Arts, Edinburgh. By the **Hon. Lord Neaves**, President of the School. Sewed, 6d.

On Fiction as a Means of Popular Teaching.

A Lecture. By the Hon. Lord Neaves. 6d.

The New "Examen;"

Or, An Inquiry into the Evidence of certain Passages in Macaulay's 'History of England' concerning the Duke of Marlborough, the Massacre of Glencoe, the Highlands of Scotland, Viscount Dundee, William Penn. By **John Paget**, Esq., Barrister-at-Law. In crown 8vo, 6s.

A Manual of Zoology,

For the Use of Students. With a General Introduction on the Principles of Zoology. By **Henry Alleyne Nicholson, M.D., F.R.S.E., F.G.S.**, &c., Professor of Natural History in the University of Toronto. Second Edition. Crown 8vo, pp. 674, with 243 Engravings on Wood, 12s. 6d.

"It is the best manual of zoology yet published, not merely in England, but in Europe."—*Pall Mall Gazette, July* 20, 1871.

"The best treatise on Zoology in moderate compass that we possess."—*Lancet, May* 18, 1872.

BY THE SAME AUTHOR.

Elementary Text-Book of Zoology for Schools. Crown 8vo, 3s. 6d.

Advanced Text-Book of Zoology. Crown 8vo, 6s.

Introduction to the Study of Biology.

By **Henry Alleyne Nicholson, M.D.**, &c. Crown 8vo, with numerous Engravings, 5s.

"Admirably written and fairly illustrated, and brings within the compass of 160 pages the record of investigations and discoveries scattered over as many volumes. Seldom indeed do we find such subjects treated in a style at once so popular and yet so minutely accurate in scientific detail."—*Scotsman*.

A Manual of Palæontology,

For the Use of Students. By **Henry Alleyne Nicholson, M.D.**, &c. Crown 8vo, with upwards of 400 Engravings, 15s.

Nina Balatka:

The Story of a Maiden of Prague. In 2 vols. small 8vo, 10s. 6d. cloth.

Piccadilly:

A Fragment of Contemporary Biography. By **Laurence Oliphant**. With Eight Illustrations by Richard Doyle. 4th Edition, 6s.

"The picture of 'Good Society'—meaning thereby the society of men and women of wealth or rank—contained in this book, constitutes its chief merit, and is remarkable for the point and vigour of the author's style."—*Athenæum*.

"The real interest of 'Piccadilly' lies in the clever *morceaux* with which it is literally jewelled. They sparkle in every page. Mr Oliphant is one of the wittiest Jeremiahs of his time."—*Pall Mall Gazette*.

Narrative of Lord Elgin's Mission to China and Japan. By **Laurence Oliphant**, Private Secretary to Lord Elgin. Illustrated with numerous Engravings in Chromo-Lithography, Maps, and Engravings on Wood, from Original Drawings and Photographs. Second Edition. In two vols. 8vo, 21s.

"The volumes in which Mr Oliphant has related these transactions will be read with the strongest interest now, and deserve to retain a permanent place in the literary and historical annals of our time."—*Edinburgh Review.*

Russian Shores of the Black Sea in the Autumn of 1852, with a Voyage down the Volga and a Tour through the Country of the Don Cossacks. By **Laurence Oliphant.** 8vo, with Map and other Illustrations. Fourth Edition, 14s.

The Transcaucasian Campaign of the Turkish Army under Omer Pasha: A Personal Narrative. By **Laurence Oliphant.** With Map and Illustrations. Post 8vo, 10s. 6d.

Patriots and Filibusters; or, Incidents of Political and Exploratory Travel. By **Laurence Oliphant.** Crown 8vo, 5s.

Historical Sketches of the Reign of George Second. By **Mrs Oliphant.** Second Edition, in one vol., 10s. 6d.

"Her aim has simply been, by means of judicious selection and careful and sympathetic painting, to form a portrait-gallery which shall illustrate the characters of a given age. We think that she has been, on the whole, very successful."—*Saturday Review.*

"Mrs Oliphant's Historical Sketches form two attractive volumes whose contents are happily arranged so as to bring out some of the salient points at a period in our social history richly illustrated by epistolary and biographical remains."—*Examiner.*

"The most graphic and vigorous Historical Sketches which have ever been published. It is indeed difficult to exaggerate the interest which attaches to these two volumes, or the high literary merit by which they are marked."—*John Bull.*

John: A Love Story. By **Mrs Oliphant.** 2 vols. post 8vo, 21s.

Brownlows. By **Mrs Oliphant.** 3 vols. post 8vo, 31s. 6d.

The Athelings; Or, The Three Gifts. By **Mrs Oliphant.** 3 vols. post 8vo, 31s. 6d.

Zaidee: A Romance. By **Mrs Oliphant.** 3 vols. post 8vo, 31s. 6d.

Katie Stewart: A True Story.

By **Mrs Oliphant.** Fcap. 8vo, with Frontispiece and Vignette, 4s.

"A singularly characteristic Scottish story, most agreeable to read and pleasant to recollect. The charm lies in the faithful and lifelike pictures it presents of Scottish character and customs, and manners and modes of life."—*Tait's Magazine.*

Chronicles of Carlingford.

By **Mrs Oliphant.**

Salem Chapel. 2s. in boards, or 2s. 6d. cloth.
The Perpetual Curate. 2s. in boards, or 2s. 6d. cloth.
Miss Marjoribanks. 2s. in boards, or 2s. 6d. cloth.
The Rector and the Doctor's Family. 1s. sewed, or 1s. 6d. cloth.

Modern Practical Cookery,

PASTRY, CONFECTIONERY, PICKLING, AND PRESERVING, WITH A GREAT VARIETY OF USEFUL RECEIPTS. By **Mrs Nourse.** Fcap. 8vo, boards, 5s. 6d.

Narratives of Voyage and Adventure.

By **Sherard Osborn, C.B.,** Captain Royal Navy. 3 vols. crown 8vo, 17s. 6d., or separately:—

Stray Leaves from an Arctic Journal;
or, Eighteen Months in the Polar Regions in Search of Sir John Franklin's Expedition in 1850-51. To which is added the Career, Last Voyage, and Fate of Captain Sir John Franklin. New Edition, crown 8vo, 5s.

The Discovery of a North-West Passage by H.M.S. Investigator,
During the years 1850-51-52-53-54. Edited from the Logs and Journals of CAPTAIN ROBERT C. M'CLURE. Fourth Edition, crown 8vo, 5s.

Quedah; a Cruise in Japanese Waters; and, *The Fight on the Peiho.* New Edition, crown 8vo, 7s. 6d.

The Poems of Ossian

In the Original Gaelic. With a Literal Translation into English, and a Dissertation on the Authenticity of the Poems. By the **Rev. Archibald Clerk.** 2 vols. imperial 8vo, £1, 11s. 6d.

"The most thoughtful and able book in connection with Celtic literature that has appeared for a long time."—*Perthshire Journal.*

"We feel assured that the present work, by the well-condensed information it contains, by the honest translation of the Gaelic it gives, by the mere weight of its fair statements of fact, will do more to vindicate the authenticity of Caledonia's Bard from the pompous ignorance of Johnson, the envious spite of Pinkerton, the cold incredulity of Laing, and even the self-asserting vanity of Macpherson, than any champion that has yet appeared."—*Glasgow Mail.*

The Conquest of Scinde.

A Commentary. By **General Sir James Outram, C.B.** 8vo, 18s.

The Metamorphoses of Ovid.

Translated in English Blank Verse. By **Henry King**, M.A., Fellow of Wadham College, Oxford, and of the Inner Temple, Barrister-at-Law. Crown 8vo, 10s. 6d.

"Turning to Mr King's version of the poet's Metamorphoses, we have very much to say in its praise. He has given us by far the most elegant and trustworthy version of the Metamorphoses in the English language. . . . Cordially do we commend this version of Ovid's Metamorphoses to our readers as by far the best and purest in our language."—*Graphic.*

"An excellent translation."—*Athenæum.*

"The execution is admirable. . . . It is but scant and inadequate praise to say of it that it is the best translation of the Metamorphoses which we have."—*Observer.*

Our Domesticated Dogs:

Their Treatment in Reference to Food, Diseases, Habits, Punishment, Accomplishments, &c. By the Author of 'The Handy Horse-Book.' 2s. 6d. bound in gilt cloth.

"How frequently do we hear ladies complain that just when their favourites come to know and love them, 'they are sure to die.' If instead of constantly cramming them with unwholesome food, they would follow the directions given in the pages before us, not only would the mortality be less, but the appearance and even the dispositions of their pets would be marvellously improved."—*Land and Water.*

Highway Law:

A Manual for the Use of Waywardens, Clerks, and Surveyors; to which are added Notes, Forms, Cases, and Statute; Hints as to Road-making, and a Complete System of the Accounts necessary to be kept. By **Hiram A. Owston**, Author of 'The Highway Act, 1862: Its Objects and Uses,' &c. Crown 8vo, 7s. 6d.

Introductory Text-Book of Geology.

By **David Page**, LL.D., Professor of Geology in the Durham University of Physical Science, Newcastle. With Engravings on Wood and Glossarial Index. Ninth Edition. 2s.

Advanced Text-Book of Geology,

Descriptive and Industrial. By **David Page**, LL.D. With Engravings and Glossary of Scientific Terms. Fifth Edition, Revised and Enlarged. 7s. 6d.

"We have carefully read this truly satisfactory book, and do not hesitate to say that it is an excellent compendium of the great facts of Geology, and written in a truthful and philosophic spirit."—*Edinburgh Philosophical Journal.*

"As a school-book nothing can match the 'Advanced Text-Book of Geology' by Professor Page of Newcastle."—*Mechanic's Magazine.*

Handbook of Geological Terms, Geology and

Physical Geography. By **David Page**, LL.D. Second Edition, enlarged, 7s. 6d.

Geology for General Readers.

A Series of Popular Sketches in Geology and Palæontology. By **David Page, LL.D.** Third Edition, enlarged, 6s.

"This is one of the best of Mr Page's many good books. It is written in a flowing popular style. Without illustration or any extraneous aid, the narrative must prove attractive to any intelligent reader."—*Geological Magazine.*

Chips and Chapters.

A Book for Amateurs and Young Geologists. By David Page, LL.D. 5s.

The Past and Present Life of the Globe.

With numerous Illustrations. By **David Page, LL.D.** Crown 8vo, 6s.

The Crust of the Earth:

A Handy Outline of Geology. By **David Page, LL.D.** 1s.

Introductory Text-Book of Physical Geography.

With Sketch-Maps and Illustrations. By **David Page, LL.D.** Fifth Edition, 2s.

Advanced Text-Book of Physical Geography.

By **David Page, LL.D.** With Engravings. 5s.

"A thoroughly good Text-Book of Physical Geography."—*Saturday Review.*

Spindrift.

By **Sir J. Noel Paton.** Fcap., cloth, 5s.

Poems by a Painter.

By **Sir J. Noel Paton.** Fcap., cloth, 5s.

An Essay on the National Character of the Athenians.

By **John Brown Patterson.** Edited from the Author's revision, by **Professor Pillans,** of the University of Edinburgh. With a Sketch of his Life. Crown 8vo, 4s. 6d.

Essays in History and Art.

By **R. H. Patterson.** 8vo, 12s.

"A volume which no discerning reader will open only once. Fine appreciative taste, and original observation, are found united with range of thought and rare command over the powers of the English language."—*Athenæum.*

The Science of Finance.

A Practical Treatise. By **R. H. Patterson,** Member of the Society of Political Economy of Paris, Author of 'The Economy of Capital,' &c.

The Economy of Capital;

or, Gold and Trade. By **R. H. Patterson,** Author of 'The New Revolution,' &c. 12s., cloth.

"It displays throughout a thorough acquaintance with our Monetary System, and is written in the lucid and graceful style which distinguishes Mr Patterson's works."—*Morning Post.*

"A very brilliant chapter of Mr Patterson's volume is devoted to the City, and to the business carried on therein. . . . We feel almost as if we heard the roar of the ceaseless traffic, and joined in the restless activity, as we read Mr Patterson's descriptions."—*The British Quarterly Review.*

Analysis and Critical Interpretation of the Hebrew

Text of the Book of Genesis. Preceded by a Hebrew Grammar, and Dissertations on the Genuineness of the Pentateuch, and on the Structure of the Hebrew Language. By the **Rev. William Paul, A.M.** 8vo, 18s.

Egypt, the Soudan, and Central Africa.

With Explorations from Khartoum on the White Nile to the Regions of the Equator. By **John Petherick, F.R.G.S.**, Her Britannic Majesty's Consul for the Soudan. In 8vo, with a Map, 16s.

The Handy-Book of Bees,

AND THEIR PROFITABLE MANAGEMENT. By **A. Pettigrew,** Rusholme, Manchester. Crown 8vo, 4s. 6d.

"The author of this volume is evidently a practical man, and knows a great deal more about bees and their habits than most of the bee-keepers in England; indeed he may be said to be a very master in the art of bee mysteries."—*Bell's Life in London.*

Poems. By Isa.

Fcap. 8vo, cloth, 4s. 6d.

The Course of Time: A Poem.

By **Robert Pollok, A.M.** Small fcap. 8vo, cloth, gilt, 2s. 6d.
THE COTTAGE EDITION, 32mo, sewed, 1s. The Same, cloth, gilt edges, 1s. 6d. Another Edition, with Illustrations by Birket Foster and others, fcap. gilt cloth, 3s. 6d., or with edges gilt, 4s.

An Illustrated Edition of the Course of Time.

The Illustrations by Birket Foster, Tenniel, and Clayton. In large 8vo. bound in cloth, richly gilt, 21s.

"Of deep and hallowed impress, full of noble thoughts and graphic conceptions—the production of a mind alive to the great relations of being, and the sublime simplicity of our religion."—*Blackwood's Magazine.*

The Port Royal Logic.

Translated from the French: with Introduction, Notes, and Appendix. By **Thomas Spencer Baynes**, LL.B., Professor in the University of St Andrews; Author of 'An Essay on the New Analytic of Logical Forms.' Seventh Edition, 12mo, 4s.

"Through his excellent translation of the Port Royal, his introduction and notes, Professor Baynes has rendered good service to logical studies in this country; for if the student desires to understand something of the *rationale* of the rules laid down in ordinary texts, he could not have recourse to a better work."—*London Quarterly Review.*

On the Priory of Inchmahome:

NOTES, HISTORICAL AND DESCRIPTIVE; with Introductory Verses, and an Appendix of Original Papers. 4to, 31s. 6d.

Collection of Public General Statutes Affecting

Scotland. Containing a Table of all the Public General Statutes, the Statutes affecting Scotland being printed entire, with a GENERAL INDEX, and Tables of all the General, Local, and Private Acts.

The Volumes are supplied at the following prices:—11° & 12° VICTORIÆ, 1848, 8vo., cloth boards, 5s.; 1849, 2s. 6d.; 1850, 5s. 6d.; 1851, 2s. 6d.; 1852, 2s. 6d.; 1853, 7s.; 1854, 4s. 6d.; 1855, 6s.; 1856, 6s. 6d.; 1857, 5s. 6d.; 1858, 5s.; 1859, 3s. 6.; 1860, 10s.; 1861, 6s.; 1862, 9s. 6d.; 1863, 6s.; 1864, 5s.; 1865, 4s.; 1866, 5s.; 1867, 9s.; 1868, 10s. 6d.; 1869, with General Index to all the Public Acts of Parliament relating to Scotland, 1800 to 1868, 9s. 6d; 1870, 8s.; 1871, 8s.; 1872, 8vo., cloth boards, 9s.

The Public Schools:

Winchester—Westminster—Shrewsbury—Harrow—Rugby. Notes of their History and Traditions. By the Author of 'Etoniana.' Crown 8vo, 8s. 6d.

"In continuation of the delightful volume about Eton, we have here, by the same author, a volume of gossip as delightful concerning five other public schools. Neither volume professes to be history, but it is history of the best sort."—*Pall Mall Gazette.*

Two Lectures on the Genius of Handel,

AND THE DISTINCTIVE CHARACTER OF HIS SACRED COMPOSITIONS. Delivered to the Members of the Edinburgh Philosophical Institution. By **the Very Rev. Dean Ramsay**, Author of 'Reminiscences of Scottish Life and Character.' In Crown 8vo, 3s. 6d.

An Historical View of the Law of Maritime

Commerce. By **James Reddie**, Esq., Advocate. 8vo, 14s.

The Life of Carl Ritter.

Late Professor of Geography in the University of Berlin. By **W. L. Gage**. Crown 8vo, 7s. 6d.

Life of the late Rev. James Robertson, D.D.,

F.R.S.E., Professor of Divinity and Ecclesiastical History in the University of Edinburgh. By **Professor Charteris**. With Portrait. 8vo, 10s. 6d.

"This is a beautiful record of the life of a true man. . . . Mr Charteris has discharged the duty of biographer with fidelity and candour, with rare good taste, and an affectionate reverence. The memoir is worthy of its subject, and supplies one of the most interesting biographies which has seen the light for many a day."—*Aberdeen Free Press.*

The Geology of Pennsylvania:

A Government Survey; with a General View of the Geology of the United States, Essays on the Coal Formation and its Fossils, and a Description of the Coal-Fields of North America and Great Britain. By **Professor Henry Darwin Rogers, F.R.S., F.G.S.**, Professor of Natural History in the University of Glasgow. With Seven large Maps, and numerous Illustrations engraved on Copper and on Wood. In Three Volumes, Royal 4to, £8, 8s.

A Visit to the Cities and Camps of the Confederate States.

By **Fitzgerald Ross**, Captain of Hussars in the Imperial Austrian Service. Crown 8vo, 7s. 6d.

The War for the Rhine Frontier, 1870:

Its Political and Military History. By **Col. W. Rustow**, translated from the German, by **John Layland Needham**, Lieutenant R.M. Artillery. 3 vols. 8vo, with Maps and Plans, £1, 11s. 6d.

"Colonel Rustow is already well known as an able military writer, and the present work cannot fail to increase his reputation. . . . He has given to the world a valuable book; and we honour him for his evident desire to be just. The military merits of the book are great; and the reader derives much advantage from the numerous maps interspersed throughout the three volumes. As to the translator, he has performed his task in a thoroughly satisfactory and highly creditable manner.—*Athenæum.*

"The work is faithfully and intelligibly executed; and it is of importance that the work of one who was once himself a Prussian Officer, and who is confessedly one of the first military critics of the day, should be placed ready at hand for the perusal and consultation of that great mass of Englishmen who do not read German works in the original."—*Saturday Review.*

The St Andrews University Calendar.

Published yearly, price 1s. 6d.

Lord St Leonards' Handy Book on Property

Law. Eighth Edition. Revised and Enlarged, 5s.

"Seven large editions indicate the popularity which this admirable manual has obtained, not merely with the profession but with the public. It should be made a text-book in schools. It gives just as much of the law as every man ought to know, conveyed in a manner which every man can understand. This new edition has been considerably enlarged by the venerable author."—*Law Times.*

The Great Governing Families of England.

By **J. Langton Sandford** and **Meredith Townsend**. 2 vols., 8vo, 15s., in extra binding, with richly-gilt cover.

"In the 'Great Governing Families of England' we have a really meritorious compilation. The spirit in which it is conceived, the care expended on the collection and arrangement of the material out of which the various memoirs are fashioned, and the vigorous and sometimes picturesque statement which relieves the drier narrative portions, place it high above the ordinary range of biographical reference books."—*Fortnightly Review.*

"Some of these sketches, of these family pictures, are admirably done, none of them are otherwise than well done. Anecdote and comment serve to relieve or explain the narrative of incidents. The book is, in its kind, a thoroughly satisfactory book, showing research, thought, and decision."—*Westminster Review.*

St Stephens;

Or, Illustrations of Parliamentary Oratory. A Poem. *Comprising*—Pym—Vane—Strafford—Halifax—Shaftesbury—St John—Sir R. Walpole—Chesterfield—Carteret—Chatham—Pitt—Fox—Burke—Sheridan—Wilberforce—Wyndham—Conway—Castlereagh—William Lamb (Lord Melbourne)—Tierney—Lord Gray—O'Connell—Plunkett—Shiel—Follett—Macaulay—Peel. Second Edition. Crown 8vo, 5s.

Lectures on the History of Literature.

Ancient and Modern. By **Frederick Schlegel.** Translated by **J. G. Lockhart.** Fcap., 5s.

Physiology at the Farm.

In Aid of Rearing and Feeding the Live Stock. By **William Seller, M.D., F.R.S.E.**, Fellow of the Royal College of Physicians, Edinburgh, formerly Lecturer on Materia Medica and Dietetics; and **Henry Stephens, F.R.S.E.**, Author of the 'Book of the Farm,' &c. Post 8vo, with Engravings, 16s.

The Passion Play in the Highlands of Bavaria.

By **Alexander Craig Sellar.** Third Edition. Fcap., sewed, 1s.

A Treatise upon Breeding, Rearing, and Feeding, Cheviot and Black-faced Sheep in High Districts. By a **Lammermoor Farmer.** Crown 8vo, cloth, 2s. 6d.

Traverse Tables to Five Places,

FOR EVERY 2' OF ANGLE UP TO 100 OF DISTANCE. By **Robert Shortrede, F.R.A.S.** Edited by Edward Sang, F.R.S.E. 8vo, 21s.

Sketches of French Life and Character.

Originally published in 'Blackwood's Magazine.' [*In the Press.*]

Italian Irrigation:

A Report on the Agricultural Canals of Piedmont and Lombardy, addressed to the Hon. the Directors of the East India Company; WITH AN APPENDIX, containing a Sketch of the Irrigation System of Northern and Central India. By **Lieut.-Col. R. Baird Smith, F.G.S.**, Captain, Bengal Engineers. Second Edition. 2 vols. 8vo, with Atlas in folio, 30s.

Legends, Lyrics, and other Poems.

By **B. Simmons**. Fcap. 8vo, 1s. 6d.

Paris after Waterloo.

A Revised Edition of a "Visit to Flanders and the Field of Waterloo." By **James Simpson**, Advocate. With Two coloured Plans of the Battle. Crown 8vo, 5s.

Poems, Songs, and Ballads.

By **James Smith**. Third Edition. 5s.

"The collection is certainly a rich and remarkable one, containing many specimens of finely pathetic and descriptive verse, imbued with the true spirit of poetry and song."—*Scotsman.*

"A most meritorious and enjoyable volume."—*Courant.*

Thorndale; or, the Conflict of Opinions.

By **William Smith**, Author of "A Discourse on Ethics," &c. Second Edition. Crown 8vo, 10s. 6d.

"Mr Smith has read deeply and accurately into human nature, in all its weaknesses, fancies, hopes, and fears. It is long since we have met with a more remarkable or worthy book. . . . We know few works in which there may be found so many fine thoughts, light-bringing illustrations, and happy turns of expression, to invite the reader's pencil."—*Fraser's Magazine.*

Gravenhurst; or, Thoughts on Good and Evil.

By **William Smith**, Author of 'Thorndale,' &c. Crown 8vo, 7s. 6d.

"One of those rare books which, being filled with noble and beautiful thoughts, deserves an attentive and thoughtful perusal."—*Westminster Review.*

"Our space will only allow us to mention, in passing, the charming volume of subtle thought expressed in a graceful transparent style, which the author of 'Thorndale' has just issued under the title of 'Gravenhurst; or, Thoughts on Good and Evil.' . . . We will simply recommend every reader, fond of thoughtful writing on the moral aspects of life, to carry 'Gravenhurst' with him into some delightful solitude."—*Cornhill Magazine.*

A Discourse on Ethics of the School of Paley.

By **William Smith**, Author of 'Thorndale.' 8vo, 4s.

Dramas by William Smith.

Author of 'Thorndale,' &c. 1. SIR WILLIAM CRICHTON. 2. ATHELWOLD. 3. GUIDONE. 24mo, boards, 3s.

Songs and Verses:

Social and Scientific. By an **Old Contributor to 'Maga.'** A New Edition, with Music of some of the Songs. Fcap. 8vo, 3s. 6d.

"The productions thrown off by this eccentric muse have all the merits of originality and variety. . . . He has written songs, not essays—such a hotch-potch of science and humour, jest and literature, gossip and criticism, as might have been served at the Noctes Ambrosianæ in the blue parlour at Ambrose's."—*Saturday Review.*

Poetical Works of Caroline Bowles Southey.

In 1 vol. fcap. 8vo, 5s.

"In one of those well-bound, neatly printed, toned paper editions, in turning out which our leading publishers so laudably vie with each other, Messrs Blackwood have gathered up the precious remains of Caroline Bowles Southey. We call them *precious* advisedly, because they illustrate a style of authorship which is somewhat out of date, and has been superseded by other styles neither so natural nor so attractive to cultivated tastes. Caroline Bowles was nursed, so to speak, in the school of nature, taught with all the fostering care of home influence, and allowed to ripen in intellect and fancy amidst the varied charms of a country life."—*The Churchman.*

"We do not remember any recent author whose poetry is so unmixedly native; and this English complexion constitutes one of its characteristic charms. No purer model of our genuine home feeling and language."—*Quarterly Review.*

The Birthday, and other Poems.

By **Mrs Southey**. Second Edition. 5s.

Chapters on Churchyards.

By **Mrs Southey**. Second Edition. Fcap. 8vo, 2s. 6d.

Robin Hood: a Fragment.

By the late **Robert Southey** and **Caroline Southey**. With other Fragments and Poems. Post 8vo, 8s.

What led to the Discovery of the Nile Source.

By **John Hanning Speke**, Captain H.M. Indian Army. 8vo, with Maps, &c., 14s.

"Will be read with peculiar interest, as it makes the record of his travels complete, and at the same time heightens, if possible, our admiration of his indomitable perseverance, as well as tact."—*Dispatch.*

Journal of the Discovery of the Source of the Nile.

By **J. H. Speke**, Captain H.M. Indian Army. 8vo, 21s. With a Map of Eastern Equatorial Africa by CAPTAIN SPEKE; numerous illustrations, chiefly from Drawings by CAPTAIN GRANT; and Portraits, engraved on Steel, of CAPTAINS SPEKE and GRANT.

"The volume which Captain Speke has presented to the world possesses more than a geographical interest. It is a monument of perseverance, courage, and temper displayed under difficulties which have perhaps never been equalled." —*Times*.

"Captain Speke has not written a noble book so much as he has done a noble deed. The volume which records his vast achievement is but the minor fact—the history of his discovery, not the discovery itself: yet even as a literary performance it is worthy of very high praise. It is wholly free from the traces of book manufacture. . . . It is, however, a great story that is thus plainly told; a story of which nearly all the interest lies in the strange facts related, and, more than all, in the crowning fact that it frees us in a large degree from a geographical puzzle which had excited the curiosity of mankind—of the most illustrious emperors and communities—from very early times."—*Athenæum*.

Villa Residences and Farm Architecture:

A Series of Designs. By **John Starforth**, Architect. 102 Engravings. Second Edition, medium 4to, £2, 17s. 6d.

The Statistical Account of Scotland.

Complete, with Index, 15 vols. 8vo, £16, 16s. Each County sold separately, with Title, Index, and Map, neatly bound in cloth, at the prices annexed, forming a very valuable Manual to the Landowner, the Tenant, the Manufacturer, the Naturalist, the Tourist, &c.

	s.	d.		s.	d.
Aberdeen	25	0	Kincardine	8	0
Argyll	15	0	Kinross	2	6
Ayr	18	0	Kirkcudbright	8	6
Banff	9	0	Lanark	21	0
Berwick	8	6	Linlithgow	4	6
Bute	3	0	Nairn	1	6
Caithness	4	6	Orkney	5	6
Clackmannan	3	6	Peebles	4	6
Dumbarton	6	0	Perth	27	0
Dumfries	12	6	Renfrew	12	6
Edinburgh	16	6	Ross and Cromarty	10	6
Elgin	6	0	Roxburgh	10	6
Fife	21	0	Selkirk	2	6
Forfar	15	0	Shetland	4	6
Haddington	8	6	Stirling	10	0
Inverness	11	6	Sutherland	5	6

Wigtown..................5s. 6d.

The Book of Farm-Buildings;

THEIR ARRANGEMENT AND CONSTRUCTION. By **Henry Stephens**, **F.R.S.E.**, Author of 'The Book of the Farm;' and **Robert Scott Burn**. Illustrated with 1045 Plates and Engravings. In 1 vol., large 8vo, uniform with 'The Book of the Farm,' &c. £1, 11s. 6d.

The Book of the Farm,

Detailing the Labours of the Farmer, Farm-Steward, Ploughman, Shepherd, Hedger, Farm-Labourer, Field-Worker, and Cattleman. By **Henry Stephens, F.R.S.E.** Illustrated with Portraits of Animals painted from the life; and with 557 Engravings on Wood, representing the principal Field Operations, Implements, and animals treated of in the Work. A New and Revised Edition, the third, in great part Rewritten. 2 vols., large 8vo, £2, 10s.

"The best practical book I have ever met with."—*Professor Johnston.*

"We assure agricultural students that they will derive both pleasure and profit from a diligent perusal of this clear directory to rural labour. . . . We have thoroughly examined these volumes; but to give a full notice of their varied and valuable contents would occupy a larger space than we can conveniently devote to their discussion; we therefore, in general terms, commend them to the careful study of every young man who wishes to become a good practical farmer."—*Times.*

The Book of Farm Implements and Machines.

By **J. Slight** and **R. Scott Burn**, Engineers. Edited by **Henry Stephens, F.R.S.E.**, Author of 'The Book of the Farm,' &c. In 1 vol., large 8vo, uniform with 'The Book of the Farm,' £2, 2s.

Catechism of Practical Agriculture.

By **Henry Stephens, F.R.S.E.**, Author of 'The Book of the Farm.' With Engravings. 1s.

A Concise Hebrew Grammar;

with the Pronunciation, Syllabic Division and Tone of the Words, and Quantity of the Vowels. By the **Rev. Duncan Stewart, B.A.** 8vo, cloth, limp, 3s.

Advice to Purchasers of Horses.

By **John Stewart, V.S.** Author of 'Stable Economy.' 2s. 6d.

To the farmer, the sportsman, and all interested in obtaining a sound and well-conditioned animal, calculated either for work or pleasure, this work will be found to be eminently useful. It is the result of the experience of a first-rate authority on the subject.

Stable Economy.

A Treatise on the Management of Horses in relation to Stabling, Grooming, Feeding, Watering, and Working. By **John Stewart, V.S.** Seventh Edition, fcap. 8vo, 6s. 6d.

The Angler's Companion to the Rivers and

Lochs of Scotland. By **T. T. Stoddart.** With Map of the Fishing Streams and Lakes of Scotland. Second Edition. Crown 8vo, 3s. 6d.

Graffiti D'Italia.

By **W. W. Story**, Author of 'Roba di Roma.' Fcap. 8vo, 7s. 6d.

"As a sculptor's sketches in a kind of poetic neutral tint, they are of great value, quite apart from their intrinsic value as poems."—*Athenæum.*

"In the present volume he has translated the marble for us into poetry. Goethe used to say that sculpture was the most poetical of all the arts. And in a certain high transcendental sense he is perfectly right. Those who are interested in the question should certainly study the Cleopatra of Story in marble, and the Cleopatra as we find her translated in the present volume into verse."—*Westminster Review.*

Etymological and Pronouncing Dictionary of the

English Language. Including a very Copious Selection of Scientific Terms. For Use in Schools and Colleges, and as a Book of General Reference. By the **Rev. James Stormonth**. The Pronunciation carefully Revised by the **Rev. P. H. Phelp, M.A.**, Cantab. Crown 8vo, pp. 755. 7s. 6d.

The School Etymological Dictionary and Word-

Book. Combining the advantages of an ordinary pronouncing School Dictionary and an Etymological Spelling-book. By the **Rev. James Stormonth**. Fcap. 8vo, pp. 254. 2s.

Lives of the Queens of Scotland,

AND ENGLISH PRINCESSES CONNECTED WITH THE REGAL SUCCESSION OF GREAT BRITAIN. By **Agnes Strickland.** With Portraits and Historical Vignettes. 8 vols. post 8vo, £4, 4s.

"Every step in Scotland is historical; the shades of the dead arise on every side; the very rocks breathe. Miss Strickland's talents as a writer, and turn of mind as an individual, in a peculiar manner fit her for painting a historical gallery of the most illustrious or dignified female characters in that land of chivalry and song."—*Blackwood's Magazine.*

Agricultural Labourers,

AS THEY WERE, ARE, AND SHOULD BE, IN THEIR SOCIAL CONDITION. By the **Rev. Harry Stuart, A.M.**, Minister of Oathlaw. 8vo, Second Edition, 1s.

Lake Victoria.

A Narrative of Explorations in Search of the Source of the Nile. Compiled from the Memoirs of Captains Speke and Grant. By **George C. Swayne, M.A.**, Late Fellow of Corpus Christi College, Oxford. Illustrated with Woodcuts and Map. Crown 8vo, 7s. 6d.

"Mr Swayne has admirably discharged his task, and has produced a very excellent and truly readable volume."—*Daily News.*

"The volume before us is a very readable one. We anticipate for it a wide popularity."—*London Review.*

D

Handbook of Hardy Herbaceous and Alpine Flowers,

FOR GENERAL GARDEN DECORATION. Containing Descriptions, in Plain Language, of upwards of 1000 Species of Ornamental Hardy Perennial and Alpine Plants, adapted to all classes of Flower-Gardens, Rockwork, and Waters; along with Concise and Plain Instructions for their Propagation and Culture. By **William Sutherland**, Gardener to the Earl of Minto; formerly Manager of the Herbaceous Department at Kew. Crown 8vo, 7s. 6d.

"This is an unpretending but valuable work, well adapted to furnish information respecting a class of plants certainly rising in popular estimation. . . . We cordially recommend his book to the notice of our readers, as likely to be, from a gardening point of view, the standard work on Herbaceous Plants."—*Gardeners' Chronicle.*

"The best book of its class available for English readers."—*Gardeners' Magazine.*

Lays of the Deer Forest.

With Sketches of Olden and Modern Deer-Hunting, &c. By **John Sobieski** and **Charles Edward Stuart**. 2 vols. post 8vo, 21s.

The Jerusalem Delivered of Torquato Tasso.

Translated by **Col. Alex. Cunningham Robertson**. Crown 8vo, 10s. 6d.

Tara: A Mahratta Tale.

By **Captain Meadows Taylor**. 3 vols. post 8vo, £1, 11s. 6d.

"A picture of Indian life which it is impossible not to admire. We have no hesitation in saying, that a more perfect knowledge of India is to be acquired from an attentive perusal and study of this work, than could be gleaned from a whole library."—*Press.*

The Greek Grammar of Thiersch.

Translated from the German, with brief Remarks. By **Sir Daniel K. Sandford, M.A.**, Professor of Greek in the University of Glasgow. 8vo, 16s.

Hours of Christian Devotion.

Translated from the German of A. Tholuck, D.D., Professor of Theology in the University of Halle, and Councillor of the Supreme Consistory, Prussia. By the **Rev. Robert Menzies, D.D.** With a Preface written for this Translation by the Author. Crown 8vo, 9s.

"To many of these meditations four or five great texts are prefixed, and the reader feels that the gentle pressure of a powerful hand has crushed these sacred fruits, and handed him the fragrant wine of the kingdom in a golden goblet. . . . The abundance and variety of the material furnished in this volume for quiet pondering render farther characterisation difficult. We are thankful for the introduction of this wise, thoughtful, helpful book in this dark, sad season."—*British Quarterly Review.*

Handy-Book of the Flower-Garden:

Being Practical Directions for the Propagation, Culture, and Arrangement of Plants in Flower-Gardens all the year round. Embracing all classes of Gardens, from the largest to the smallest. With Engraved and Coloured Plans, illustrative of the various systems of Grouping in Beds and Borders. By **David Thomson**, Gardener to his Grace the Duke of Buccleuch, K.G., at Drumlanrig. A New and Enlarged Edition, crown 8vo, 7s. 6d.

"Its author is entitled to great praise for the simple and clear manner in which he has explained the cultural directions, which, if carefully complied with, will enable the non-professional floriculturist to grow plants as well as any gardener."—*Gardeners' Chronicle.*

A Practical Treatise on the Culture of the Pine-Apple.
By **David Thomson**. 8vo, 5s.

"The name of the author, one of the very best gardeners in the British Islands, guarantees that this volume contains no directions that are not sound and tested by experience."—*Journal of Horticulture.*
"The best work extant upon this important subject."—*Gardeners' Magazine.*

A Practical Treatise on the Cultivation of the Grape-Vine.
By **William Thomson**, formerly Gardener to his Grace the Duke of Buccleuch, K.G., Dalkeith Park. Seventh Edition, Enlarged, 8vo, 5s.

"We cannot too strongly recommend Mr Thomson's treatise as a thoroughly practical and sure guide to the cultivation of the vine."—*Journal of Horticulture.*
"We urge our readers to procure the work, and they will get so clear an insight into vine-growing that a vinery will become one of the necessaries of existence."—*Field.*

A COMPANION VOLUME TO THE 'HANDY-BOOK OF THE FLOWER-GARDEN.'

The Handy-Book of Fruit Culture under Glass.

Being a series of Elaborate Practical Treatises on the cultivation and forcing of Pines, Vines, Peaches, Figs, Melons, Strawberries, and Cucumbers. With Engravings of hothouses, &c., most suitable for the cultivation of and forcing of these fruits. By **David Thomson**, author of 'Handy-Book of the Flower-Garden,' 'A Practical Treatise on the Culture of the Pine-Apple,' &c., in crown 8vo, with Engravings. [*In the Press.*

Introduction to Meteorology.
By **David P. Thomson**, **M.D.** Octavo, with Engravings, 14s.

Notes on the Pecuniary Interests of Heirs of Entail.

With Calculations regarding such Interests in reference to the Acts of Parliament affecting Entails, and Tables showing the values of Liferent Interests. By **William Thomas Thomson**, Fellow of the Institute of Actuaries, Manager of the Standard Life Assurance Cmpaony. 8vo, **10s**.

County Law, a Practical Treatise on the Functions,

Qualifications and Duties of County Officials, Lords-Lieutenants, and Conveners of Counties, Commissioners of Supply, Clerks of Supply, &c. &c. With special reference to the Acts of Parliament which they administer as members of Road Trusts, Prison Boards, Police Committees, Local Authorities, &c. By **John Comrie Thomson, Esq.**, in 1 vol.

[In the Press.

Ralph Darnell. A Novel.

By **Captain Meadows Taylor.** 3 vols. post 8vo, £1, 11s. 6d.

The Company and the Crown.

By the **Hon. T. J. Hovell-Thurlow.** Second Edition, corrected and revised. 8vo, 7s. 6d.

"Those who wish to understand what our work actually is in India, and how it is being done, will find an abundant store of information, both about persons and things, in Mr Thurlow's interesting pages."—*Times.*

The Elegies of Albius Tibullus.

Translated into English Verse, with Life of the Poet, and Illustrative Notes. By **James Cranstoun, B.A.**, Author of a Translation of 'Catullus.' In crown 8vo, 6s. 6d.

"We may congratulate Mr Cranstoun on having occupied a place for which his poetical skill, no less than his manifest classical training and acquirements, abundantly fits him."—*Saturday Review.*

"He comes nearer the originals than any of his predecessors that we are acquainted with. . . . The notes are scholarly and really illustrative."—*Examiner.*

"By far the best of the few versions we have of this sweet and graceful poet."—*Standard.*

Tom Cringle's Log.

A New Edition, with Illustrations. Crown 8vo, 6s.

"Everybody who has failed to read 'Tom Cringle's Log' should do so at once. The 'Quarterly Review' went so far as to say that the papers composing it, when it first appeared in 'Blackwood,' were the most brilliant series of the time, and that time one unrivalled for the number of famous magazinists existing in it. Coleridge says in his 'Table Talk' that the 'Log' is most excellent: and these verdicts have been ratified by generations of men and boys, and by the manifestation of Continental approval, which is shown by repeated translations. The engravings illustrating the present issue are excellent."—*Standard.*

The Buchanites from First to Last.

By **Joseph Train.** Fcap. 8vo, 4s.

Journal of Agriculture,

AND TRANSACTIONS OF THE HIGHLAND AND AGRICULTURAL SOCIETY OF SCOTLAND. Old Series, 1828 to 1843, 21 vols. bound in cloth, £3, 3s. New Series, 1843 to 1865, 22 vols., £4, 4s.

Rational Theology and Christian Philosophy in
England in the Seventeenth Century. By **Rev. John Tulloch**, D.D., Senior Principal in the University of St Andrews; and one of Her Majesty's Chaplains in Ordinary in Scotland. Author of 'Leaders of the Reformation,' &c. 2 vols. 8vo, 28s.

Leaders of the Reformation:
LUTHER, CALVIN, LATIMER, and KNOX. By the **Rev. John Tulloch, D.D.**, Principal, and Primarius Professor of Theology, St Mary's College, St Andrews. Second Edition, Crown 8vo, 6s. 6d.

English Puritanism and its Leaders:
CROMWELL, MILTON, BAXTER, and BUNYAN. By the **Rev. John Tulloch, D.D.** Uniform with the 'Leaders of the Reformation.' 7s. 6d.

"It is a book which, from its style—firm and interesting, dispassionate and impartial, but yet warm with admiration—will be hailed for fireside reading in the families of the descendants of those Puritan men and their times."—*Eclectic Review.*

Theism.
The Witness of Reason and Nature to an All-Wise and Beneficial Creator. By the **Rev. John Tulloch, D.D.** 8vo, 10s. 6d.

"Dr Tulloch's Essays, in its masterly statement of the real nature and difficulties of the subject, its logical exactness in distinguishing the illustrative from the suggestive, its lucid arrangement of the argument, its simplicity of expression, is quite unequalled by any work we have seen on the subject."—*Christian Remembrancer.*

Transactions of the Highland and Agricultural
Society of Scotland. 1866-1871, 6 Nos., sewed, 4s. each; 1872, cloth, 5s. Continued annually.

A Treatise upon Terrestrial Magnetism.
With numerous Charts, 8vo, 10s. 6d.

Tweed Salmon Reports, 1866.
Reports on the Natural History and Habits of Salmonoids in the Tweed and its Tributaries. Published by authority of the Tweed Fishery Commissioners. Demy 8vo, 3s. 6d.

Narrative of a Journey through Syria and
Palestine. By **Lieut. Van de Velde.** 2 vols. 8vo, with Maps, &c., £1, 10s.

"He has contributed much to knowledge of the country, and the unction with which he speaks of the holy places which he has visited, will commend the book to the notice of all religious readers. His illustrations of Scripture are numerous and admirable."—*Daily News.*

The Æneid of Virgil.

Translated in English Blank Verse by **G. K. Rickards, M.A.**, and **Lord Ravensworth**. 2 vols. fcap. 8vo, 10s.

"Mr Rickards has done good service to the non-classical public by the faithful and beautiful version of Virgil's Æneid now before us, and he has enhanced the boon by a preface of special value, as setting forth fairly and conclusively the respective merits of previous translations, and the special qualities of Virgil as a poet."—*Standard.*

"Lord Ravensworth's success and strength are to be found, not so much in his verbal force as in the Virgilian spirit which breathes throughout his lines. No English reader can well miss their poetical grace and vigour; no scholar will deem unfaithful the clean cut, decisive lines of this masterly version."—*Evening Standard.*

The Wonder Seeker,

Or the History of Charles Douglas. By **M. Fraser Tytler**, Author of 'Tales of the Great and Brave,' &c. A New Edition. Fcap., 3s. 6d.

Memoirs of the Confederate War for Independence.

By **Heros Von Borcke**, lately Chief of Staff to General J. E. B. Stuart. 2 vols. post 8vo, with Map, 21s.

Works of Samuel Warren, D.C.L.

Library Edition.

The Diary of a late Physician. In 2 vols. fcap., 12s. Also an Illustrated Edition, in crown 8vo, handsomely printed, 7s. 6d.

Ten Thousand A-Year. Three vols. fcap., 18s.

Now and Then. Fcap., 6s.

Miscellanies. 2 vols. crown 8vo, 24s.

The Lily and the Bee. Fcap. 8vo, 5s.

Samuel Warren's Works.

People's Edition, 4 vols. crown 8vo, cloth, 18s. Or separately:—

Diary of a late Physician. 3s. 6d.

Ten Thousand A-Year. 5s.

Now and Then. Lily and Bee. Intellectual and Moral Development of the Present Age. 1 vol., 4s. 6d.

Essays, Critical, Imaginative, and Juridical. 1 vol., 5s.

The Moral, Social, and Professional Duties of

Attornies and Solicitors. By **Samuel Warren, Esq., F.R.S.**, of the Inner Temple, Barrister-at-Law. Fcap. 8vo, 9s.

Essays Written for the Wellington Prize.

Selected for Publication, by His Grace's desire, from those specially mentioned by the Arbiter. 8vo, 12s. 6d.

List of Authors.

I. By Lieut. J. T. HILDYARD, 71st Highland Light Infantry.
II. By Lieutenant STANIER WALLER, Royal Engineers.
III. By Captain J. C. RUSSELL, 10th Royal Hussars.
IV. By Colonel Sir GARNET J. WOLSELEY, C.B., K.C.M.G.
V. By General J. R. CRAUFURD.
VI. By Lieutenant C. COOPER KING, Royal Marine Artillery.

The Eighteen Christian Centuries.

By the **Rev. James White**, Author of 'The History of France.' Seventh Edition, post 8vo, with Index, 6s.

"He has seized the salient points—indeed, the governing incidents—in each century, and shown their received bearing as well on their own age as on the progress of the world. Vigorously and briefly, often by a single touch, has he marked the traits of leading men; when needful, he touches slightly their biographical career. The state of the country and of society, of arts and learning, and, more than all, of the modes of living, are graphically sketched, and, upon the whole, with more fulness than any other division."—*Spectator.*

History of France,

FROM THE EARLIEST TIMES. By the **Rev. James White**, Author of 'The Eighteen Christian Centuries.' Fifth Edition, post 8vo, with Index, 6s.

Archæological Sketches in Scotland—Kintyre.

By **Captain T. P. White, R.E.**, &c., of the Ordnance Survey. With 138 Illustrations. Folio, £2, 2s.

Through Burmah to Western China:

Being Notes of a Journey in 1863, to Establish the Practicability of a Trade-Route between the Irawaddi and the Yang-tse-Kiang. By **Clement Williams**, formerly Assistant-Surgeon in the 68th Light Infantry, and First Political Agent at Mandalay to the Chief-Commissioner of British Burmah. Crown 8vo, with Two Maps and Numerous Engravings, 6s.

The "Ever-Victorious Army."

A History of the Chinese Campaign under Lieut.-Col. C. G. Gordon, and of the Suppression of the Tai-ping Rebellion. By **Andrew Wilson, F.A.S.L.**, Author of 'England's Policy in China;' and formerly Editor of the 'China Mail.' In 8vo, with Maps, 15s.

"In addition to a good deal of information respecting China and its recent history, this volume contains an interesting account of a brilliant passage in the military career of an English officer of remarkable promise, and of the important results of his skill and heroism. . . . It brings out clearly the eminent qualities of Colonel Gordon, his intrepidity and resources as a military leader, his rare aptitude for a difficult command, his dauntless courage, calmness, and prudence, his lofty character and unsullied honour."—*Times.*

Works of Professor Wilson.

Edited by his Son-in-Law, **Professor Ferrier**. In Twelve Vols. Crown 8vo, £2, 8s.

The Noctes Ambrosianæ.

By **Professor Wilson**. With Notes and a Glossary. In Four Vols. Crown 8vo, 16s.

Recreations of Christopher North.

By **Professor Wilson**. In Two Vols. New Edition, with Portrait, 8s.

"Welcome, right welcome, Christopher North; we cordially greet thee in thy new dress, thou genial and hearty old man, whose 'Ambrosian nights' have so often in imagination transported us from solitude to the social circle, and whose vivid pictures of flood and fell, of loch and glen, have carried us in thought from the smoke, din, and pent-up opulence of London, to the rushing stream or tranquil tarn of those mountain-ranges," &c.—*Times.*

Essays, Critical and Imaginative.

By **Professor Wilson**. Four Vols. Crown 8vo, 16s.

Tales.

By **Professor Wilson**. Comprising 'The Lights and Shadows of Scottish Life;' 'The Trials of Margaret Lyndsay;' and 'The Foresters.' In One Vol. Crown 8vo, 4s., cloth. Cheap Edition. Fcap. 8vo, 2s. 6d.

Professor Wilson's Poems.

Containing the 'Isle of Palms,' the 'City of the Plague,' 'Unimore,' and other Poems. Complete Edition. Crown 8vo, 4s.

Homer and his Translators, and the Greek Drama.

By **Professor Wilson**. Crown 8vo, 4s.

Poems and Songs.

By **David Wingate**. In fcap. 8vo, 5s.

"It contains genuine poetic ore, poems which win for their author a place among Scotland's true sons of song, and such as any man in any country might rejoice to have written."—*London Review.*

"We are delighted to welcome into the brotherhood of real poets a countryman of Burns, and whose verse will go far to render the rougher Border Scottish a classic dialect in our literature."—*John Bull.*

Annie Weir, and other Poems.

By **David Wingate**. Fcap. 8vo, 5s.

Fortification:

For the Use of Officers in the Army, and Readers of Military History. By **Lieut. H. Yule**, Bengal Engineers. 8vo, with numerous Illustrations, 10s. 6d.

"An excellent manual: one of the best works of its class."—*British Army Despatch.*

NOW PUBLISHING.

ANCIENT CLASSICS
FOR
ENGLISH READERS
BY VARIOUS AUTHORS.

EDITED BY

REV. W. LUCAS COLLINS, M.A.

Author of 'Etoniana,' 'The Public Schools,' &c.

OPINIONS OF THE PRESS.

"We gladly avail ourselves of this opportunity to recommend the other volumes of this useful series, most of which are executed with discrimination and ability."—*Quarterly Review.*

"These Ancient Classics have, without an exception, a twofold value. They are rich in literary interest, and they are rich in social and historical interest. We not only have a faithful presentation of the stamp and quality of the literature which the master-minds of the classical world have bequeathed to the modern world, but we have a series of admirably vivid and graphic pictures of what life at Athens and Rome was. We are not merely taken back over a space of twenty centuries, and placed immediately under the shadow of the Acropolis, or in the very heart of the Forum, but we are at once brought behind the scenes of the old Roman and Athenian existence. As we see how the heroes of this 'new world which is the old' plotted, intrigued, and planned; how private ambition and political partisanship were dominant and active motives then as they are now; how the passions and the prejudices which reign supreme now reigned supreme then; above all, as we discover how completely many of what we may have been accustomed to consider our most essentially modern thoughts and sayings have been anticipated by the poets and orators, the philosophers and historians, who drank their inspiration by the banks of Ilissus or on the plains of Tiber, we are prompted to ask whether the advance of some twenty centuries has worked any great change in humanity, and whether, substituting the coat for the toga, the park for the Campus Martius, the Houses of Parliament for the Forum, Cicero might not have been a public man in London as well as an orator in Rome?"—*Morning Advertiser.*

"A series which has done, and is doing, so much towards spreading among Englishmen intelligent and appreciative views of the chief classical authors."—*Standard.*

"To sum up in a phrase our sincere and hearty commendation of one of the best serial publications we have ever examined, we may just say that to the student and the scholar, and to him who is neither scholar nor student, they are simply priceless as a means of acquiring and extending a familiar acquaintance with the great classic writers of Greece and Rome."—*Belfast Northern Whig.*

List of the Volumes published.

I.—HOMER: THE ILIAD.
By THE EDITOR.

" We can confidently recommend this first volume of 'Ancient Classics for English Readers' to all who have forgotten their Greek and desire to refresh their knowledge of Homer. As to those to whom the series is chiefly addressed, who have never learnt Greek at all, this little book gives them an opportunity which they had not before—an opportunity not only of remedying a want they must often have felt, but of remedying it by no patient and irksome toil, but by a few hours of pleasant reading."—*Times.*

II.—HOMER: THE ODYSSEY.
By THE EDITOR.

" Mr Collins has gone over the 'Odyssey' with loving hands, and he tells its eternally fresh story so admirably, and picks out the best passages so skilfully, that he gives us a charming volume. In the 'Odyssey,' as treated by Mr Collins, we have a story-book that might charm a child or amuse and instruct the wisest man."—*Scotsman.*

III.—HERODOTUS.
By GEORGE C. SWAYNE, M.A.

" This volume altogether confirms the highest anticipations that were formed as to the workmanship and the value of the series."—*Daily Telegraph.*

IV.—THE COMMENTARIES OF CÆSAR.
By ANTHONY TROLLOPE.

" We can only say that all admirers of Mr Trollope will find his 'Cæsar' almost, if not quite, as attractive as his most popular novel, while they will also find that the exigencies of faithful translation have not been able to subdue the charm of his peculiar style. The original part of his little book—the introduction and conclusion—are admirably written, and the whole work is quite up to the standard of its predecessors, than saying which, we can give no higher praise."—*Vanity Fair.*

V.—VIRGIL.
By THE EDITOR.

" Such a volume cannot fail to enhance the reputation of this promising series, and deserves the perusal of the most devoted Latinists, not less than of the English readers for whom it is designed."—*Contemporary Review.*

" It would be difficult to describe the 'Æneid' better than it is done here, and still more difficult to find three more delightful works than the 'Iliad,' the 'Odyssey,' and the 'Virgil' of Mr Collins."—*Standard.*

VI.—HORACE.

By Theodore Martin.

"Though we have neither quoted it, nor made use of it, we have no hesitation in saying that the reader who is wholly or for the most part unable to appreciate Horace untranslated, may, with the insight he gains from the lively, bright, and, for its size, exhaustive little volume to which we refer, account himself hereafter familiar with the many-sided charms of the Venusian, and able to enjoy allusions to his life and works which would otherwise have been a sealed book to him."—*Quarterly Review.*

"We wish, after closing his book, to be able to read it again for the first time; it is suited to every occasion; a pleasant travelling companion; welcome in the library where Horace himself may be consulted; welcome also in the intervals of business, or when leisure is abundant."—*Edinburgh Review.*

"In our judgment, no volume (of the series) hitherto has come up to the singular excellence of that now under consideration. The secret of this is, that its author so completely puts himself in Horace's place, scans the phases of his life with such an insight into the poet's character and motives, and leaves on the reader's mind so little of an impression that he is following the attempts of a mere modern to realise the feelings and expressions of an ancient. Real genius is a freemasonry, by which the touch of one hand transmits its secret to another; and a capital proof of this is to be found in the skill, tact, and fellow-feeling with which Mr Martin has executed a task, the merit and value of which is quite out of proportion to the size and pretensions of his volume."—*Saturday Review.*

VII.—ÆSCHYLUS.

By Reginald S. Copleston, B.A.

"A really delightful little volume."—*The Examiner.*

"The author with whom Mr Copleston has here to deal exemplifies the advantage of the method which has been used in this series. . . . Mr Copleston has apprehended this main principle, as we take it to be, of his work: has worked it out with skill and care, and has given to the public a volume which fulfils its intention as perfectly as any of the series."—*Spectator.*

VIII.—XENOPHON.

By Sir Alexander Grant, Bart.,
Principal of the University of Edinburgh.

"Sir Alexander Grant tells the story of Xenophon's life with much eloquence and power. It has evidently been with him a labour of love; while his wide reading and accurate scholarship are manifest on nearly every page."—*The Examiner.*

IX.—CICERO.
By THE EDITOR.

"No charm of style, no facility and eloquence of illustration, is wanting to enable us to see the great Roman advocate, statesman, and orator, in the days of Rome's grandeur, in the time of her first fatal hastening to her decadence, with whom fell her liberty two thousand years ago. The first lines of introduction to this fascinating book are full of help and light to the student of the classical times who has not mastered the classical literature, and in whose interests this book is done, simply to perfection."—*Saunders' News-Letter.*

X.—SOPHOCLES.
By CLIFTON W. COLLINS, M.A.

"Sophocles has now been added to the acceptable and singularly equal series of 'Ancient Classics for English Readers.' Mr Collins shows great skill and judgment in analysing and discriminating the plays of the sweet singer of Colonus."—*Guardian.*

XI.—PLINY'S LETTERS.
By the Rev. ALFRED CHURCH, M.A., and
The Rev. W. J. BRODRIBB, M.A.

"This is one of the best volumes of the series called 'Ancient Classics for English Readers.' . . . This graceful little volume will introduce Pliny to many who have hitherto known nothing of the Silver Age."—*Athenæum.*

"Mr Lucas Collins's very useful and popular series has afforded a fit opportunity for a sketch of the life and writings of the younger Pliny; and the writers of the volume before us have contrived, out of their intimate and complete familiarity with their subject, to place the man, his traits of character, his friends, and his surroundings so vividly before us, that a hitherto shadowy acquaintance becomes a distinct and real personage."—*Saturday Review.*

XII.—EURIPIDES.
By W. B. DONNE.

"This is the twelfth instalment of this admirably conducted series, and one of the very best that has yet appeared."—*Bell's Weekly Messenger.*

XIII.—JUVENAL.
By EDWARD WALFORD, M.A.

"This is one of the best executed volumes of the whole series of 'Ancient Classics,' and exhibits Mr Walford's critical powers in a very favourable light."—*Pall Mall Gazette.*

XIV.—ARISTOPHANES.
By the EDITOR.

Other Authors, by various contributors, are in preparation.
A Volume is published Quarterly, price 2s. 6d.

45 GEORGE STREET, EDINBURGH; 37 PATERNOSTER ROW, LONDON.

BLACKWOOD'S CLASS-BOOKS.

Strongly Bound in Cloth, unless otherwise stated.

GEOLOGY.

Introductory Text-Book of Geology. By David Page, LL.D., &c.,	2s. 0d.
Advanced Text-Book of Geology. By the same,	7s. 6d.
The Crust of the Earth: A Handy Outline of Geology. By the Same,	1s. 0d.
The Geological Examiner. By the same. Sewed,	9d.
Handbook of Terms in Geology and Physical Geography. By the same,	7s. 6d.

ZOOLOGY.

Text-Book of Zoology. By H. Alleyne Nicholson, M.D., &c.,	6s. 0d.
Introductory Text-Book of Zoology. By the same,	3s. 6d.
Manual of Zoology. By the same,	12s. 6d.
Examinations in Natural History: Being a Progressive Series of Questions adapted to the Author's Introductory and Advanced Text-Books and the Students' Manual of Zoology. By the same,	1s.

METEOROLOGY.

Introductory Text-Book of Meteorology. By Alexander Buchan, M.A., &c.	4s. 6d.

PHYSICAL GEOGRAPHY.

Introductory Text-Book of Physical Geography. By David Page, LL.D., &c.,	2s. 0d.
Advanced Text-Book of Physical Geography. By the same,	5s. 0d.
Examinations in Physical Geography. By the same. Sewed,	9d.
Ritter's Comparative Geography. Translated by W. L. Gage,	3s. 6d.
Atlas of Physical Geography. By A. Keith Johnston, LL.D., &c. Half-bound,	12s. 6d.

PHYSICS.

Elementary Handbook of Physics. With 210 Diagrams. By William Rossiter, F.R.A.S., &c.	5s. 0d.

ENGLISH LANGUAGE.

Etymological Dictionary of the English Language. Crown 8vo,	7s. 6d.
The School Etymological Dictionary and Wordbook. Fcap. 8vo, pp. 254,	2s. 0d.
English Prose Composition. By Rev. J. Currie, M.A.,	1s. 6d.
A Manual of English Prose Literature. Designed mainly for the Assistance of Students in English Composition. By W. Minto, M.A.,	10s. 6d.
Progressive and Classified Spelling-Book. By Miss Lockwood,	1s. 6d.

BLACKWOOD'S CLASS-BOOKS—*Continued.*

PALÆONTOLOGY.

A MANUAL OF PALÆONTOLOGY, for the Use of Students. With a General Introduction on the Principles of Palæontology. With upwards of 400 Engravings. By H. Alleyne Nicholson, M.D., &c. One volume, crown 8vo. [*In the press.*

BOTANY.

ADVANCED TEXT-BOOK OF BOTANY. For the Use of Students. By Robert Brown, M.A., Ph.D., Göt., F.R.G.S., Lecturer on Botany under the Science and Art Department of the Committee of the Privy Council on Education. [*In the press.*

GEOGRAPHY.

MANUAL OF GEOGRAPHY. By Rev. Alex. Mackay, LL.D., &c. New edition, revised and enlarged, . . 7s. 6d.
ELEMENTS OF GEOGRAPHY. By the same, . . 3s. 0d.
OUTLINES OF GEOGRAPHY. By the same, . . 1s. 0d.
FIRST STEPS IN GEOGRAPHY. By the same. Sewed, 4d.
Or in cloth, ... 6d.
GEOGRAPHY OF THE BRITISH EMPIRE. By the same. Sewed, ... 3d.
ATLAS OF GENERAL GEOGRAPHY. By A. Keith Johnston, LL.D., &c. Half-bound, . . 12s. 6d.
ELEMENTARY ATLAS OF GEOGRAPHY. By A. Keith Johnston, LL.D., &c. Half-bound, . . . 5s. 0d.

HISTORY.

THE EIGHTEEN CHRISTIAN CENTURIES. By Rev. J. White, ... 6s. 0d.
HISTORY OF FRANCE. By Rev. J. White, . . 6s. 0d.
EPITOME OF ALISON'S HISTORY OF EUROPE, . . 7s. 6d.

CLASSICS.

ANCIENT CLASSICS FOR ENGLISH READERS. Edited by the Rev. W. Lucas Collins. 14 Volumes are published, ... 2s. 6d. each.

The above series is well adapted for Ladies' Schools.

ATLAS OF CLASSICAL GEOGRAPHY. By A. Keith Johnston, LL.D., &c. Half-bound, . . 12s. 6d.

AGRICULTURE.

ELEMENTS OF AGRICULTURAL CHEMISTRY. By J. F. W. Johnston, ... 6s. 6d.
CATECHISM OF AGRICULTURAL CHEMISTRY. By J. F. W. Johnston, ... 1s. 0d.
CATECHISM OF AGRICULTURE. By Henry Stephens, 1s. 0d.

ARITHMETIC.

THE THEORY OF ARITHMETIC. By David Munn, F.R.S.E., ... 5s. 0d.

www.ingramcontent.com/pod-product-compliance
Lightning Source LLC
Chambersburg PA
CBHW020322240426
43673CB00039B/886